Comprehending Drug Use

Comprehending Drug Use

Ethnographic Research
at the Social Margins

J. BRYAN PAGE

AND

MERRILL SINGER

RUTGERS UNIVERSITY PRESS

NEW BRUNSWICK, NEW JERSEY, AND LONDON

LIBRARY OF CONGRESS CATALOGING-IN-PUBLICATION DATA

Page, J. Bryan, 1947–
    Comprehending drug use : ethnographic research at the social margins /
J. Bryan Page and Merrill Singer.
        p. cm. — (Studies in medical anthropology)
    Includes bibliographical references and index.
    ISBN 978-0-8135-4803-6 (hardcover : alk. paper) — ISBN 978-0-8135-4804-3
(pbk : alk. paper)
    1. Drug abuse.   2. Ethnology.   I. Singer, Merrill.   II. Title.
    HSV5801.P27   2010
    362.29089—dc22   2009048295

A British Cataloging-in-Publication record for this book is available
from the British Library.

Visit our Web site: http://rutgerspress.rutgers.edu

Manufactured in the United States of America

For Eleanor Carroll,
whose vision of ethnography's importance got us started

CONTENTS

Preface   ix

1   Through Ethnographic Eyes   1

2   The Emergence of Drug Ethnography   25

3   Systematic Modernist Ethnography and
     Ethnopharmacology   50

4   Drug Ethnography since the Emergence of AIDS   70

5   Drugs and Globalization: From the Ground Up and
     the Sky Down   86

6   The Conduct of Drug Ethnography: Risks, Rewards, and
     Ethical Quandaries in Drug Research Careers   113

7   Career Paths in Drug-related Ethnography:
     From Falling to Calling   133

8   Gender and Drug Use: Drug Ethnography by Women
     about Women   149

9   The Future of Drug Ethnography as Reflected in Recent
     Developments   162

Appendix: Nuts and Bolts of Ethnographic Methods   185
Notes   191
References   193
Index   223

PREFACE

We had been talking at breakfast (June 2007, while participating in a workshop for young scholars on the scientific study of drug use) about the literature's lack of any books on the ethnography of drug use. There was a book by a nonresearcher that had gone out of print three years prior, but no bona fide drug researcher had ever attempted a book treatment of the field of ethnographic drug research, even though the field had burgeoned during the last three decades. As we listened to our colleagues' presentations, we put together an outline of what such a book would look like and agreed to flesh it out into a book proposal. We knew that the book should emphasize several points: (1) ethnographic approaches contribute important formative information about personal behavior; (2) ethnographic approaches provide key content for use by efforts (e.g., surveys) to obtain quantitative data on the personal behaviors of a population; (3) ethnographic approaches enhance the findings of surveys through delineation of cultural process; (4) the narratives produced by ethnographic interviews underscore the humanity of drug users; and (5) the ethnographic perspective points out key flaws in the larger society's policies to "control" drug use, suggesting strategies for reforming a system that fails to accomplish its objectives.

Our personal need for a textbook that accomplished these objectives directed much of our early conversation about this project. Nevertheless, we also see the book as a resource for those who think about and form policy on drug use and for those who try to treat impaired drug users.

The book that we have written devotes most of its space to consideration of how people go about using drugs that are disapproved by the larger society, acknowledging that ethnographies of alcohol and tobacco use could have occupied a more prominent place in our presentation. We made this choice in order to focus on the implications for society of imposing prohibition on some drugs and not others (see aim 5 above), although we recognize that the solution to the total problem of drug use must include legal drugs. Indeed, as time goes by, tobacco incurs increasing public outrage over its toll in human lives, rendering it every day more analogous to the illegal drugs that we study ethnographically. Our presentation tilts in the direction of illegal drugs also because of the opportunities afforded by the NIH to engage in this kind of research. The National Institute on Drug Abuse (NIDA) currently enjoys a research budget that is double that of the National Institute on Alcohol Abuse and Alcoholism (NIAAA), and this discrepancy has translated into far more profuse opportunities for studying illegal drugs than for studying alcohol. The National Cancer Institute (NCI) traditionally limited its research on tobacco using behaviors to surveys, affording few opportunities for ethnographers to ply their trade in this important area of human behavior. We have noted that since the early 1970s, NIDA has demonstrated a unique vision of the value of ethnographic research in the study of drug use, and for this, the program officers of that institute deserve credit for nurturing many ethnographers' careers.

We thank the people who helped us to get to this point, including mentors Bill Carter, Paul Doughty, and Will Coggins, and research assistants Zulema Villalta, James "Sweetness" Griffin, and Maureen Vicaria. We can only name the deceased cultural guides, Fito (Costa Rica), Baltimore (Miami), and Boshack (Miami), because the ones who are still alive are still vulnerable to police scrutiny. They especially make this kind of work possible through their transcendent sociologic imagination. As mentors, they are at least as important as the academic ones, because without their endorsement, we would not have crossed into the realm of accepted observer and interviewer.

In the preparation of this manuscript, we thank Adi Hovav of Rutgers University Press for her patience and attentiveness to detail. Mac Marshall, who has taken on the task of editing the series of books on medical anthropology for Rutgers Press, has lent us his formidable expertise in assembling this kind of a book, with detailed suggestions and unfailing encouragement. Gretel Rodriguez deserves special credit for yanking our messy manuscript into line with the Rutgers specifications and for her assistance in the procurement and handling of references.

Miami and Storrs, February 27, 2009

Comprehending Drug Use

1

Through Ethnographic Eyes

Fernando and Javier lead me through Barrio Cuba, past the Sodita Estrella del Sur and along streets filled with people walking around the neighborhood on a sunny Sunday morning. The people are variously dressed: some with immaculate dresses or shirt-and-slack ensembles (en route to Mass?), and others with jeans and T-shirts. We walk past the bakery where I met Arnoldo two days before and through the muddy street under construction to the west of the Barrio proper. We walk about three blocks farther west to the edge of a cafetal[1] and cross a saggy barbed wire fence into a weedy area in which stands a small shed with a corrugated iron roof. One side of the shed is up against the fence. A slight (maybe 110 pounds), copper-skinned man with a wispy tracing of beard along his chin line is standing in the shed's doorway. He seems to flinch at first sight, as if to flee, but then recognizes Fernando and Javier and relaxes. Fernando says, "There's a gringo I want you to meet." The man in the doorway welcomes us, waving us inside, and Fernando presents me to Ronulfo, who seems to dwell in the shed, or as they call it, the shanty. Ronulfo urges us to sit down on some stools and crates he has arranged in a circle around a crate covered by a cloth. He offers to make us tea, and we thank him. He sets a plate of white packets and a cup of what looks like milk on the cloth-topped crate, using it as a low table. The interior of the shanty is unadorned, with a makeshift pallet in one corner covered in a swirling mix of sheets, blankets, and articles of clothing. Other than the cabinet from which he gets the packets and milk, the crates, and the stools, the shed has no furnishings. Ronulfo leaves and goes down the street to fill his teapot with water, as Fernando explains, "This is one of our shanties where we can go to smoke tranquilly. Some other boys will be here soon." We wait and talk about the morning sunshine and the

women walking to mass, and Ronulfo soon returns with the teapot full of
water which he places on top of a charcoal fire outside the front door of
the shanty. Two more young men arrive in the shanty, one sporting
nearly shoulder-length frizzy hair that he has parted down the middle
while the other is dressed in what appears to be parochial school
clothes—white shirt and dark trousers. Fernando introduces them as
Bogus Hippy and Guito. They sit on two of the three remaining stools as
Ronulfo attends to the teapot. Fernando pulls a yellow paper package out
of his jacket pocket and opens it to reveal small, rolled cylinders of the
same paper as the package. Each paper object is about 5 or 6 cm in length
and 5 mm or less in thickness. He distributes one of these to each of the
group, including me, and the others set about opening the paper, pick-
ing out objects in the small pile of material in the middle of the unrolled
papers. They tear about a third of the paper away and lick the remaining
paper along the edges before rerolling the cylinder. I imitate what they do
as best I can and fashion my own cylinder. Fernando hands a cylinder to
Ronulfo and brings a stick with a coal at one end from the fire outside
to light our paper cylinders. The participants light up one by one from
the coal-tipped stick, inhaling deeply and holding the smoke. I follow
suit. (JBP; October, 1973; Barrio Cuba, San José, Costa Rica)

This passage represents the kinds of raw data on drug use that are collected by
drug ethnographers, complete with errors and unrefined prose. I (Bryan Page)
was in Costa Rica in 1973 working on a study of the effects of long-term marihuana[2] use among working-class Costa Rican males when I recorded these field
notes. We present them here to reflect the most basic aspect of ethnography's
process—that it takes the ethnographer to places where he or she may never
have been before and demands utmost attention to detail of both behavioral
and contextual content and sequence of events.

This method has been applied to any number of other topics in the study of
the human condition, but we are convinced that its application to the study of drug
use had a transformative effect on both the science of human drug use and on the
practice of the method itself. Our initial motivation for writing this book emerged
from our fruitless search for suitable texts from which to teach about drug use from
an ethnographic perspective. We concluded that the interaction between ethnographic methods and the subject of drug use had significance for both the method
and the content. In the sections of this chapter that follow, we shall delineate that
unique interaction, leading to discussion of how ethnography applied to drug use
produced both new areas of knowledge and new modes of inquiry.

Several components comprise this interaction between ethnography and
drug use. Some involve ways that the broader science of drug use has benefited

from the use of ethnographic methods, and some reflect how the wider anthropological practice of ethnography has benefited from drug ethnography.

Perhaps the most important product of applying ethnographic methods to the scientific study of drug use involved the development and use of methods that facilitated locating, delineating, and studying "hidden populations." This term refers to populations that live somewhat outside the boundaries of mainstream society. Consequently, they are less known and, if in need of services, less hooked into available health care and social programs. During its development, the ethnography of drug use focused on the scientific need to find and characterize patterns of drug consumption that operated outside of the public view in complex society. Its focus, in short, was on concealed behaviors among poorly understood populations.

The process of characterizing drug use through ethnography led to the development of specific techniques (e.g., network-based sampling, targeted sampling) that other ethnographers could borrow for studies of other kinds of covert behavior such as "down-low" homosexuality, fencing stolen goods, or the growing phenomenon of suburban street gangs. These techniques enabled ethnographers to gain an understanding of populations with a limited, fleeting, and shifting "community" but with shared behaviors. The ethnography that brought these ways of life to light offered new views of the complexities of urban life as it is lived in alleyways, "abandoned" buildings, rooftops, and forested patches in the city. In other words, it contributed to the study of the secluded, the unnoticed, and those who disguise their presence by staying in the shadows of urban life.

The study of illegal drug use behaviors presented special ethical challenges, such as potential police interference or witnessing behavior that was not only against the law but potentially destructive to those who engaged in it. The whole domain of illegality and its impact on what drug ethnographers do and how they do it provided lessons for the ethnography of other kinds of illegal behavior.

Ethnographic characterization of addiction has been a major focus of drug ethnography. Biochemistry, in part, drives addictive behavior, and study participants sometimes die from overdoses, vehicular accidents, or street violence during the research. The ethnography of these phenomena gave scientists needed perspective on the health impacts of drug use, sometimes contradicting exaggerations and sometimes confirming health risks.

Uses of ethnography in drug-related global health crises (e.g., HIV, HCV) helped to meet pressing demands for findings that had practical applications to public health intervention. This process entailed focused observational ethnography to understand behaviors, contexts, and contingencies that could not be elicited through interviews but had specific relevance to public health interventions. This use of ethnography as a public health sentinel and risk identifier predates AIDS and at least goes back to James Spradley's work in Seattle with "urban nomads" engaged in public inebriation (1970).

Transdisciplinary team research in pursuit of complex information on drug use (e.g., Carter, Coggins, and Doughty 1980; Rubin and Comitas 1975) employed ethnography long before ethnographers in other subfields began to form (or join) these kinds of teams. The value of transdisciplinary research carried out in more than one site in a globalizing world (e.g., Booth et al. 1991) continues to be endorsed by drug ethnographers in recent studies (e.g., Clair et al. 2009; Koester et al. 2003).

By the late 1980s, drug ethnography became sufficiently differentiated from the practice of ethnography in general that ethnographers from other subfields—with no prior experience in drug ethnography—had to be trained (sometimes quite rapidly, as described in chapter 4) as drug ethnographers. The need for applied ethnographic research in the midst of the growing AIDS pandemic necessitated a "pressing into service" of available ethnographers to characterize fully the health risks associated with injecting and other drug use. Finally, immediate relevance to policy development has become a hallmark of drug ethnography, as drug ethnographers have provided essential information regarding addiction treatment, syringe exchange, prevention strategies, and drug users' unhealthy mistreatment in the criminal justice system. This kind of work has proven to have local, state, and sometimes national or international implications.

The remaining sections of this chapter—and the chapters that follow—describe the background, development, important contributors, and key issues involved with combining ethnographic methods with the study of human drug use. By the time the reader has finished, we would expect him or her to understand the process, challenges, and rewards of studying drug use ethnographically, beginning with its earliest glimmers in the works of Herodotus, Bernardino de Sahagún, and Richard Burton to its first clear manifestations in the studies of Richard Evans Schultes, Weston La Barre, and Robert Lowie and, ultimately, to its contemporary expression in the writings of Claire Sterk, Philippe Bourgois, Michael Agar, Dwight Heath, Mark and Mimi Nichter, Robert Carlson, Stephen Koester, J. Bryan Page, and Merrill Singer, among many others.

Two Definitions

The starting point for engaging the ethnography of drug use lies in clearly defining two essential concepts: *ethnography* and *drugs*. We define *ethnography* as the practice of systematically studying the cultural contexts in which behaviors of interest occur, using the field-based techniques of participant observation, open-ended interviewing, and other strategies for collecting and analyzing qualitative and quantitative information at the ground level. Ethnography requires some degree of immersion in the field so as to understand behaviors in the social contexts in which they unfold. Central to the ethnographic approach (but not limited by it) is a focus on emic—insider—perspectives on the behaviors of interest, on experience gained through the performance of these behaviors in interaction with others, and on the unfolding of everyday activities, both routine and novel. From this definitional base, we can build an understanding of the kinds of drug research that ethnographers have produced and how this research contrasts with other approaches to the study of widespread, diverse drug use in human societies.

Our focus on drug using behavior also requires a definition of the word *drug*. As we use the term in this book, a drug is any chemical compound that, when brought into contact with the human body, produces a change in that body's functional condition, especially the mental and emotional states. This definition is sufficiently broad to include topical ointments, pills, teas, and powders, as well as smokable, chewable, or inhalable plant products, and injectable and drinkable liquids. Throughout, we shall avoid the unfortunate gloss *substance*, which was apparently invented to reinforce bureaucratic distinctions between legal and illegal drugs (Page 2009). In our view, the notion of substance (e.g., substance use and abuse) is not a very useful analytic separation for much that we want to understand about drugs. The standard definitions of *substance* subsume all matter except gas, including water, phlegm, polyvinyl chloride, and laundry starch. In our experience, most substances are not drugs, but all drugs are substances. Therefore, the term *substance* is not sufficiently specific to be used when writing about drugs. Our purview includes the sometimes legally "exempt" drugs—alcohol and tobacco—with the "nonexempt" drugs—cocaine, heroin, marihuana, and many other banned drugs—because they all have a background of long-term psychotropic use among humans and are consumed for the same reasons: their bodily effects (Hunt and Barker 2001; Singer 2008). We also include pharmaceuticals that are diverted for use outside of medical/ treatment contexts, such as opiate analgesics, diet pills, and steroids. As suggested above, the issue of legality (as this changes over time and place) is not critical to the definition of drugs, although it can be critical to the behaviors involved in drug use (and, hence, of great interest ethnographically).

About Culture

While we are engaged in presenting initial definitions, we should also offer one for the central anthropological paradigm—culture: the behaviors, and the system of ideas and values that underlie those behaviors, occurring within a given social context. Although not as elaborately worded as the one originally offered by E. B. Tylor in 1863,[3] this definition gives a sense of the cultural paradigm's inclusiveness and breadth. Any manifestation of learned human behavior, including buttons and zippers, love songs, the work performed in a transnational corporation, and the criteria used by drug users to evaluate the quality of drugs sold by various local dealers, is considered an item of cultural content. In the past, anthropologists tended to see culture as a somewhat fixed set of intertwined elements. More recently, they have come to understand culture in processual terms. As research by Dwight Heath, for example, has shown, heavy drinking among the Camba of Bolivia has a long history, but the behavior has changed significantly over times as a consequence of changing relations between the Camba and the wider world (Heath 1991).

The cultural paradigm distinguishes anthropologists' studies of the human condition from those of other social/behavioral scientists. Sociologists tend to focus on people behaving in groups (therein lies the haziness of the boundary between sociology and anthropology—the distinction between social organization and cultural context), and psychologists focus on the intrapsychic dimensions of behavior. Each of these somewhat different (if overlapping) points of view lead their proponents to well-defined approaches to studying human behavior. In sociology, the dominant approach (a substantial minority of sociologist ethnographers notwithstanding) to understanding and predicting human behavior involves brief inquiries about self-reported actions and attitudes based on responses to inventories of short-answer questions. In psychology, investigators query and probe to discover the thought processes (or neurologic functions) of the people being studied. In cultural anthropology, the researcher attempts to discover and characterize a set of ideas and values—but also social structures, meanings, emotions, and lived experiences—that reflects patterns of behavior that occur in a given social context (e.g., behavior in a London bar; at an illicit drug shooting site in Chennai, India; at a gathering of the peyote-using Native American Church). These ideas, values, and other patterned elements of life are shared to varying degrees (and in understandable ways, including patterns of nonsharing) by the participants in a cultural context. An ethnographic study attempts to link process with content. Proponents of all three disciplines have engaged in ethnography, but they almost always use the parameters of their dominant paradigms.

While we are both committed anthropologists and active researchers, we have spent most of our scholarly careers working on multimethod research projects in multidisciplinary settings. During this time, we have both come to value the advantages of collaborative work across disciplinary boundaries and appreciate its challenges. We have regularly witnessed the significant contributions of a cultural perspective, yet we also recognize the folly of assigning some behaviors to culture (e.g., assertions that have been made over the years that the poor live in a culture of poverty that perpetuates material insufficiency) as if oppressive and unequal social structures were not critical determinants of human social life. We would also like to add that we both have carried out broad ethnographic research that has incorporated data collection on illicit drug use, drinking, and tobacco consumption, as well as specific studies focused more narrowly on each of these drug use behaviors. In emphasizing the concept of culture, we underscore two overarching attributes common to the anthropological perspective on this domain of human life: culture is holistic, and it is relativistic.

Culture's Holistic Attribute

The holistic attribute drives the all-encompassing approach used by anthropologists in studying the human condition. The anthropologist's sense of culture includes all aspects of the human condition, from food recipes to rocket schematics. It also includes emotions and values and the kinds of technologies and knowledge employed by drug users to acquire, prepare, and consume drugs (as well as, among producers and dealers, to manufacture and distribute drugs). Anthropological practitioners of ethnography may focus on a specific set of behaviors, but they consistently seek to understand relationships between the behaviors of central interest and other aspects of the human condition that may affect them. This approach is especially advantageous in the study of complex behaviors such as drug use, because so many aspects of the human condition affect and/or are affected by drug use—many more, in fact, than are commonly realized without reflection. Family relations, religious practice, economics, labor, diet, arts, warfare, healing, and leisure time activities are just a few aspects of the human experience that exemplify the relatedness of drug use to other human behaviors.

Culture's Relativistic Attribute

Because anthropologists view the process of becoming a functional adult as equally demanding in any cultural setting, we tend to view all cultural traditions as equal (which is not to say equally beneficial or just). Some cultural traditions may have highly developed technological devices, while others may have elaborate spiritual beliefs and practices, but in each case, it takes many years to produce a fully functional adult (especially relative to other species). Our appreciation, as anthropologists, for the complexity of learning processes involved in the formation of adult human beings within specific cultural contexts comes in part from our own experiences as adults trying to learn the behavioral patterns necessary to survive in cultural settings different from our own. Anthropologists are not "accidental tourists," but rather, as Agar so aptly put it, "professional strangers" (1996). We put ourselves into different cultural contexts, on purpose, to learn what we can about them. In so doing, we also discover how difficult it is to enact the behaviors required to meet basic needs as someone who grew up using a different set of behaviors. Language alone presents a formidable barrier to the novice. The complex processes involved in living in a given cultural context far outweigh the relatively minor trappings of haute cuisine, symphony orchestras, or advanced communication technology, all of which are components of Western culture that some might feel are signs of superior cultural development. Therefore, we take the approach that cultural complexes are equally difficult to learn, thus producing a relativistic view of different cultural systems.

One principle is fundamental to all considerations of culture as a concept in social and behavioral science: cultures are not entities of themselves. Rather, people behaving together in pursuit of their basic and not-so-basic needs operate in cultural contexts, enacting ideas and values that may be ancient or new, or that may reflect broad consensus or narrow opinion, but these ideas and values, and the emotions we attach to them, comprise the performance of the human condition in that particular cultural context. Cultures do not do anything; people do things within cultural contexts. With this in mind, the practice of ethnography can be seen as an attempt to characterize the relationship between specific behavior patterns and the values and ideas held among the people who practice those behaviors.

Further, although there may have been a time in the distant past when small human communities existed in relative isolation—as intact social wholes somewhat independent of other human communities for periods of time—this has not been the case for tens of thousands of years. Specific drug user cultures (e.g., injection drug users in Madrid, beer drinkers in a New Zealand pub, or smokers sharing a smoking lounge at Denver's airport), for example, do not exist independent of overarching cultural traditions and broader hierarchies of social relationships. Understanding how drug use ideas, values, and practices fit into and are affected by these wider social and cultural patterns, including those that cross-cut and weave together localities, regions, and nations, is also part of the work of drug ethnographers. To our minds, the contributions that we enumerated in the beginning of this chapter emanate from efforts by anthropologists to apply cultural learning to the ethnographic study of drug use.

Ethnicity, Nationality, and Class

The view of cultural process described above, as it relates to drug use, has particular relevance to the concept of ethnicity. As part of our examination, we describe the work of ethnographic practitioners who have focused on specific ethnicities (e.g., Bourgois 2003b—Puerto Ricans; Cepeda and Valdez 2003—Mexican Americans; Dunlap and Johnson 1996—African Americans; Garcia 2007—Mexican migrant farm workers) in broad narratives about the emergence of drug ethnography in part because we have come to perceive that drug use behavior incorporates markers of various cultural contexts. For example, we have seen white non-Hispanics, Hispanics, and African Americans pump mixed drugs and blood to and from their veins via syringes, and we have heard them all call this practice "booting." In this instance, ethnicity is secondary to affiliation in the subcultural complex of injection. This complex has an international reach, as Spanish drug injectors speak of *chutaderos*—places where they go to shoot drugs—using a word that clearly comes from English. While we support the notion that the field of drug research needs more ethnic minority researchers (and we have both worked for many years to expand the number and skills of minority researchers), and that minority researchers sometimes bring to their investigations heightened sensitivity to cultural issues and singular opportunities for contact, we incorporate their work and findings into the broad narrative of drug ethnography rather than discuss it separately as a distinct body of work. Drug ethnographies by researchers from around the world (e.g., Gamella 1994; Maher 1996b; Maher 2004; Page and Salazar 1999; Ripoll, Page, and Salazar 2003, Taylor 1993, Clair et al. 2009) are also cited as part of this broad narrative. Regular, national, and transnational exchange of ideas, approaches, and thoughts about directions for the field have helped to create an ethnography of drug use that transcends national or subgroup boundaries.

Regarding socioeconomic status and drug use, the vast majority of drug ethnographies have focused on the working class and the poor. Suburban drug use among the middle class (e.g., Boeri, Gibson, and Harby 2009; Maher 2002) has attracted some ethnographic attention. Nevertheless, the absence of research on upper-middle-class and upper-class study participants in ethnographic investigation of drug use represents a major lacuna in the state of knowledge about drug use patterns in the United States and around the world. Notable exceptions include Patricia Adler's study of upper-level marihuana dealing (1993) and Brian Kelly's study of bong and blunt use in suburbia (2006). Entry into the social echelons where the rich and well-to-do operate remains difficult and dependent on relatively deep ties between the researcher and the social context of interest. To "study up"—transcending class boundaries in order to characterize the drug use of people whose wealth buffers them from access by social/behavioral science—is one of the most difficult assignments an ethnographic researcher can undertake.

Strongly related to the concept of class in framing ethnography of drug use is the notion of the "recreational" drug. When some pharmaceutical preparations or other drugs are consumed in contexts where the intention of the consumers is to "party," "get high," or "get wasted," this consumption is sometimes termed "recreational." This term is usually invoked when the consumers are not perceived to be impaired by or addicted to the drugs in question; rather, they are in the process of pursuing a temporary but potent altered state of consciousness. The subtext of this term is that, because of their socioeconomic status and their status as occasional users of their drugs of choice, "recreational" users are somehow exempt from the risk that their drug use may lead to regular, impaired, or addictive use (i.e., misuse). They are not. More importantly, not all lower-class users of illegal, socially disapproved drugs such as heroin and cocaine inevitably slip into conditions of impairment and dependence. It is more accurate and less confusing to call all drug use by a common name and sort out the consequences as they emerge from the study of specific drug using populations. We therefore reject the "recreational" modifier as unproductive for scientific investigation. Additionally, we recognize that some drug use occurs in a religious or spiritual context, as part of the ritual complex of a particular tradition (e.g., peyote use among members of the Native American Church). Again, our focus is on drug use in context, regardless of the users' motivations, the effects those users experience, or the views that society has of the users' behavior (although all of these are important issues to investigate to understand specific drug use patterns and contexts).

The Ethnography of Tobacco Use

While the ethnography of drug use cross-cuts all categories of drugs, it is important to recognize differences brought to light by ethnography of behaviors, users, contexts, and consequences of tobacco, alcohol, and illicit drugs (including diverted pharmaceutical drugs). There are also differences in the quantity of ethnographic research on these different kinds of drugs. The topic of tobacco use, for example, is relatively limited in anthropological texts, with only passing mentions in most ethnographic accounts of day-to-day social life in various communities. Black maintains that tobacco use has been understudied by anthropologists because of its place in the Western cultures in which most anthropologists traditionally have been socialized (1984). As a commonly individualized act with limited ritual elaboration and symbolic content in the West (although, as Mark Nichter stresses, these certainly are not absent [2003]), cigarette smoking, in particular, is more expressive of internal mood states (e.g., a time-out from a daily routine) than shared cultural content. As such, the behavior did not attract extensive ethnographic attention as anthropologists examined the social worlds of diverse societies, although, in recent years, with growing awareness of the health risks of tobacco use, this has been changing (Nichter et al. 2002; Tessler 2000). At the same time, there has been increased attention to the heretofore understudied Western cultural content of smoking. One ritualization of smoking that has been described ethnographically involves tobacco use as an anticipatory rite of passage for subordinated social groups, including youth, women, and ethnic minorities (Robb 1986). Smoking can also sometimes serve as a badge of group membership (Eckert 1983). Ironically, the antismoking movement may have contributed to heightened sharing of "resistance themes" among smokers (Rhodes et al. 2008). In her ethnographic study of smoking among Puerto Rican adolescents Susan

McGraw (1989) emphasizes as well the ways in which this behavior is used to establish or affirm social connections.

One of the earliest ethnographic descriptions of tobacco use is Alfred Louis Kroeber's account of the roles of tobacco, salt, and dogs among several western U.S. Native American groups (1941). He observed that tobacco was an important ritual offering in religious rites among tobacco cultivators. Among groups that gathered wild tobacco but did not grow the crop, he found that tobacco did not serve this religious function. He also noted that the use of tobacco in shamanic healing only occurred in groups that smoked tobacco and not in those that chewed the drug. It is in Oceania that the most extensive ethnographic studies of tobacco use have been conducted (Haddon 1947; Hays 1991). In this context, Peter Black (1984) carried out his ethnographic study on tobacco use in the Tobian Islands, tracing the ethnohistorical development of tobacco consumption after its introduction by European explorers and traders. Ultimately, tobacco came to be highly valued among the people of the Tobian Islands as a marker of social status. In a related study, Mac Marshall (1979, 1990) assessed the social role of tobacco on Truk, noting that by age nineteen all young men in the village he studied had begun smoking, while girls were less likely to smoke. Marshall analyzed both tobacco and alcohol consumption on Truk as key cultural symbols of masculinity, a pattern also seen elsewhere in Micronesia. As contrasted with the gender patterning noted by Marshall, pipe smoking in Melanesia has been found to be a common practice among women (Douglas 1955; Keesing 1983). Among the Trobriand Islanders, tobacco was seen as a tool used by sorcerers to attack their victims (Weiner 1988). In contrast, some Caribbean spiritist religions such as *espiritismo* believe that tobacco smoke passed over the body has a cleansing effect, and it is thus used in the ethnomedical treatment of alcoholism and other personal problems (Singer and Borrero 1984). Gilbert Herdt's ethnographic work among the Sambia of New Guinea led to observations of tobacco's role in relaxation and multigenerational socializing (1987).

In recent years, a number of anthropologists have taken up studies of tobacco use in light of globalization and the worldwide marketing of tobacco products as commodities sold for profit. Part and parcel of this trend is the transition to studying the health consequences of tobacco consumption in relation to the mass marketing of tobacco products. As Ken Stebbins stresses, many traditional smoking behaviors around the world, including limitations on the frequency and quantity of consumption, have generally been overwhelmed "by aggressive marketing by transnational tobacco companies" (2001, 148). In his own studies of smoking, Stebbins has shown how the tobacco industry has turned to markets in the developing world to make up for a loss in sales first in the United States and subsequently in parts of the European market. Governments in developing nations often do not have the ability to limit tobacco marketing and, usually in need of financial help, they are open to introducing taxable commodities to their citizens. As a result of extensive advertising in developing nations, Stebbins notes that worldwide tobacco consumption has increased at the rate of 1 percent a year, and countries such as Brazil, India, and Kenya exhibit the greatest increases (1990). Results include rising rates of cancer and other adverse health outcomes of tobacco consumption. As Stebbins puts it, the tobacco companies "have been making a killing (in more ways than one)" (2001, 164). Related research by Mark and Mimi Nichter and colleagues (Nichter and Cartwright 1991; Nichter and Nichter 1994) describe the complicity of the U.S. government in promoting cigarette use in developing countries. They argue that the U.S. public focus on improving child health in the world diverts attention from the health consequences of expanded tobacco production and consumption in developing nations and ponder if health promotion efforts are saving children from infections only to allow them to fall prey to the multinational tobacco industry (Nichter and Cartwright 1991).

In other research, they examined the perceptions of tobacco use among male college students in India (Nichter, Nichter, and Sickle 2004). They found that these students believe that smoking a cigarette enhances one's manliness, relieves boredom, and eases tension. Moreover, their informants indicated that the more expensive a cigarette was, the less dangerous it was to one's health. Recognizing that physicians can be important in role modeling smoking cessation, researchers subsequently examined tobacco use among doctors in Kerala, India (Mohan et al. 2006). They found that a substantial proportion of physicians and medical students continue to be smokers despite the global promotion of smoking cessation. This work indicates the growing involvement of ethnographers who use their findings in the analysis of tobacco-related health risks (e.g., Page and Evans 2003; Singer et al. 2007; Singer et al. 2010) and the development of ethnographically informed, culturally targeted, and socially appropriate tobacco intervention efforts (Nichter 2006) and policy change initiatives (Ernster et al. 2000; Skeer et al. 2004). Overall, from a public health standpoint, as Nichter points out, the contemporary ethnography of tobacco consumption allows closer examination of "the role that cultural institutions, values, and processes play in: (1) protecting against smoking . . . , (2) fostering smoking as a normative behavior within particular gender and age cohorts, and (3) affecting the distribution of particular smoking trajectories" in society (2003, 140).

The cascading revelations of tobacco consumption's health risks essentially have buried consideration of tobacco use as anything other than a bane of human existence. The ethnographic handling of tobacco use has therefore been forced to begin with assumptions of addiction and damage. Such an approach to tobacco studies is likely to extend into the foreseeable future.

The Ethnography of Alcohol Use

A unique and somewhat insulated research tradition also has developed in the ethnography of alcohol use. Despite the fact that alcohol is the only drug in the pharmacopoeia that has a dedicated institute among the National Institutes of Health focused on the study and control of its use and health consequences, it has received much less attention in ethnographic research than illegal drug use, both in terms of overall expenditures on scientific study and in terms of grant-supported ethnographic efforts. Unlike the case of tobacco, many ethnographers who have written about alcohol consumption have done so based on ethnographic research that set out to focus on patterns of alcohol use, especially in attempts to characterize problematic patterns of consumption (e.g., Bezdek and Spicer 2006; Butler 2006; Garrity 2000; Kunitz 2006; Marshall 1990; Spicer 1997). Heath's work in Latin America (1958; 1991) represents a notable exception to this tendency in the literature. Whether they focused on negative effects of alcohol use (e.g., Marshall 1990; Spradley 1970), ambivalent attitudes toward alcohol use (e.g., Butler 2006; Eber 1994; Lang 1979; Quintero 2002; Spicer 1997), or cycles of recovery from alcohol impairment (e.g., Bezdek and Spicer 2006; Garrity 2000; Kunitz 2006), these works share assumptions about the likelihood of finding a certain rate of impairment in the populations under study, and that intoxication or drunkenness brings about erratic, often embarrassing, and sometimes dangerous behavior that affects those who are not drunk. Furthermore, these alcohol studies only infrequently address the fact that most drug use occurs in a context where people use various drugs. In the United States, for example, the most frequently found patterns of polydrug consumption involve at least three or four of the "big five" drugs (Page 1999), which have extensive histories of use and wide distribution in this country.

Considerably less frequent than studies addressing problematic alcohol use are studies of routine drinking in establishments where people congregate to drink, such as Sherri Cavan's *Liquor License: An Ethnography of Bar Behavior* (1966). Ethnographies like this (e.g., Hunt and Satterlee 1986a, 1986b; Spradley and Mann 2008) have demonstrated the importance of drinking places in the making of social lives, social relations, and personal identities that extend far beyond their immediate settings. They also succeed in avoiding assumptions about the nature and impact of drinking. Still, until recently, studies of this kind were somewhat rare in the literature on alcohol. Fortunately, this pattern has begun to change and ethnographers have in recent years produced a spate of new book-length ethnographies about the place of alcohol consumption in diverse societies (e.g., Brandes 2002; Butler 2006; Eber 1994; Gamburd 2008; Pine 2008). These newer works, which affirm the value of drug ethnography, seek to understand drinking within the intertwined arena of local cultural traditions and fast-paced globalizing changes.

Emphasis on Discovery

Our purpose in this book is to delineate the emergence of ethnographic studies of drug use as exercises in the discovery of lesser-known patterns of behavior. Despite its massive dimensions, the literature on tobacco and alcohol use has met our criterion only when novel information questions conventional views of the drugs under study. Heath's work among the Camba during the 1950s met this criterion for alcohol, as did Johannes Wilbert's work among the Warao and Lowie's work among the Crow for tobacco. In each case, the ethnographer described patterns of drug use that contradicted commonly held assumptions about how humans use these drugs. Heath found the Camba consuming high concentrations of alcohol in ritually circumscribed settings, apparently experiencing no negative consequences worse than a hangover. This finding led him to develop a theory of functional alcohol use that to this day disturbs the biomedical alcohol "experts." Geoffrey Hunt, Karen Joe-Laidler, and Kathleen MacKenzie accomplished a similar exploration of new territory in characterizing the drinking patterns of gang-affiliated girls (2000). In that vein of discovery and exploration, Wilbert and Lowie—in very different cultural contexts— described ritually circumscribed patterns of tobacco use that had no attendant health problems. Although the study of other drugs is not without its underlying assumptions of problematic use, the ethnographic approach to these studies was historically less burdened with these assumptions than the studies of tobacco and alcohol use. Furthermore, studies of drugs other than alcohol and tobacco have tended to acknowledge that consumption often takes place in cultural contexts in which multiple drugs are used serially or in a mixture (e.g., "speedball": a term widely used to refer to mixing heroin and cocaine). For example, if Cannabis was the study topic, alcohol and tobacco also received coverage (Carter, Coggins, and Doughty 1980); if heroin and other street drugs were the focus of the study, intertwined alcohol use required the attention of the investigators because, in fact, illicit drug users also tend to be heavy consumers of alcohol (Singer et al. 2008).

Another distinction between ethnographic studies of illegal drugs and studies of alcohol and tobacco involves the support received for these studies. The NIH has invested far less in ethnographies of alcohol or tobacco use than in ethnographies of illegal drug use. Among the newer alcohol ethnographies cited above, Adrienne Pine received some support from an NIAAA program to write up her findings, although not for the research itself. Nevertheless, NIAAA was not a funding source for the other researchers mentioned. This fact is not especially rational, as it certainly fails to recognize that alcohol and tobacco use has a far more massive impact on public health in the United States than illegal drug use does. Still, Congress routinely allocates three times as much money for illicit drug studies than for tobacco and alcohol studies. Fortunately for drug ethnographers, the National Institute on Drug Abuse (NIDA) has a history of supporting studies that include ethnographic components, in no small part a product of having had a historic cadre of insiders who recognized the value of ensuring that NIDA had funding for drug ethnographies.

Taking the Role of the Ethnographer

Ethnography requires training, skill, and patience. It also demands large amounts of time to cultivate a rapport with crucial people and to gain social acceptance, at least within certain sectors, in the community. Ethnographers studying drug use succeed or fail based on the degree to which they gain access to networks of informal social relations among drug users and/or dealers/distributors, and each ethnographer defines his or her observational role according to different personal skills and situational factors. Regular basketball games with inmates at the Lexington National Institute of Mental Health, Clinical Research Center, for example, provided a suitable neutral setting in which Agar could begin conversations with patients about "getting off" (1973). Page used his repertoire of Mexican songs to begin conversations about marihuana use in barrios known for use of that drug. In fact, he met Fernando the night before the morning described in this chapter's initial field note passage. After Page finished singing and playing, Fernando emerged from the small crowd that had gathered to listen. The brief concert provided the proper opportunity for Fernando, who had been following Page's visits to the barrio for three or four weeks. Singer, in turn, worked for several decades in a community-based organization that provides health and social services to impoverished populations. This setting provided a foundation for him to meet and get to know many drug users and to launch studies about drug-related health risks (beginning with alcohol use and extending over the years to other drug and polydrug use) and necessary interventions. These studies stemmed from initial relations with what became key informants (Singer 2006). In explaining the value of participating in research to drug users, Singer was able to point to existing programs, including drug treatment and HIV prevention initiatives, that had been developed based on the research carried out by the community-based organization.

In another example of initial rapport building, Sterk carried both cigarettes and condoms into the Atlanta neighborhoods where she intended to establish contact with drug users (1999). Most street drug users also consume tobacco, so the availability of spare cigarettes to share made her, as we shall see later, a popular figure with people in the neighborhood of interest. Furthermore, the conversational leap between talking about different addictive habits was small.

Sometimes sheer (naïve) boldness can pay off. Unable to make direct contact with the St. Louis crack dealers he witnessed from his car and that he hoped to study, Bruce Jacobs finally decided simply to walk up to them and explain his research objectives (1999). Predictably, they scoffed at him and warned him to leave the neighborhood or face the consequences. Undeterred, he tried again two days later, showing his prospective informants his university ID card, but he quickly added that they would be paid for their time. This worked, at least in allowing him some preliminary access. The real turning point, Jacobs believes, was the way he was treated by the police. He was stopped repeatedly, his vehicle and his person searched, and he was subjected to somewhat rough treatment (if only to a limited degree compared to the way the inner city youth he was studying were handled by the police). Observing this pattern, a number of crack dealers began to trust that he was indeed a researcher and not an undercover police officer.

Serendipity can also play a role in initiating a drug ethnography. Lee Hoffer, for example, described how he happened to run into an individual he had known from a prior research project who subsequently introduced him to various individuals involved in small-scale heroin dealing, his new area of interest (2006). Similarly, Patricia Adler and her husband Peter found that they were living in a neighborhood that was the residence of a network of middle-class drug dealers (1993). The development of friendly neighborhood relationships, and a realization about the income-generating activities of some of their neighbors, led to a decision to focus research attention on these social connections and the drug-related social world they opened up. The result is one of the few detailed ethnographic accounts of a drug smuggling and dealing group other than a street gang. Along somewhat similar lines, Bourgois commented that he was "forced" into the study of crack dealers in East Harlem by unplanned circumstance: "I was looking for an inexpensive New York City apartment from which I could write a book on the experience of poverty and ethnic segregation. . . . I had never heard of crack when I first arrived in the neighborhood. . . . By the end of the year, however, most of my [local] friends, neighbors, and acquaintances had been swept into the multibillion-dollar crack cyclone" (2003, 1). Awestruck by its enormous impact on the local community, Bourgois began interviewing his neighbors, which led to a full ethnography of the underground world of crack sales and use.

In some cases, such as studies of drinking behavior, ethnographers have initiated their work by regularly going to public drinking locations such as pubs or taverns and weaving their way into social interactions with participants. In Spradley's case, his study of so-called street alcoholics (or "urban nomads," as he preferred to call them) began with participant observation in a criminal court and in an alcoholism treatment center (1970). Contacts made in these settings provided a foundation for ethnographic work on Seattle's Skid Road. In studies of drinking *places* (the physical settings where social drinking regularly occurs) and drinking *spaces* (which can emerge instantaneously anywhere alcohol is present), Geoffrey Hunt and Saundra Satterlee (1986a, 1986b) used ethnography to demonstrate ways in which drinking behavior builds group solidarity while it simultaneously creates social divisions and distinctions (also see Gamburd 2008). Such research entailed spending many hours in pubs and other drinking locations, gaining acceptance among patrons, and engaging them in conversations about their lives inside and outside of the pub.

What Ethnography Contributes to Drug Studies

The prime directive in the ethnographic study of drug use is to achieve an understanding of how and why the behaviors of interest take place in a given natural habitat and what forms these behaviors take. This knowledge contributes to our understanding of the overall epidemiology of drug use by giving all researchers in the field an opportunity to ask the most effective questions possible when inquiring about personal patterns of use in the survey interview or clinic. Perhaps more importantly, ever deepening understanding of the complex relationship between specific sets of drug use and/or trafficking behaviors and the surrounding cultural environment emerges from ethnographic study. Opportunities to gain this kind of knowledge arise from the practice of several techniques described below (and in further detail in the appendix).

Ethnographic Building of Rapport

It takes time to find people who are willing to talk to an ethnographic researcher about their behavior, especially if it is covert or socially disapproved. If the researcher is entering the community without any prior contacts, this process can take weeks, even months. During that time, the ethnographer makes his or her presence known in a neighborhood, ward, or other location where the drug behaviors of interest are reputed to take place. This process often yields spurious contacts with people who are unqualified to serve as key informants. Eventually, however, an individual with sufficient sociologic imagination to understand the role of the researcher and the purpose of research comes forward to guide the alert ethnographer in his or her quest for information about how people in that vicinity use drugs. Once found, this person (or these persons) provides information on the local drug culture and its complexities, translation of alternative drug lexicons, locations of potential interest, and most importantly, contact with additional drug users. Often, relations with a key informant are highly instructive and personal, as exemplified by Singer's friendship and professional collaboration with the daughter of the man described in his article "Why Juan Garcia Has a Drinking Problem" (Singer et al. 1992). Other times, they can prove to be disastrous and put the researcher at risk, as happened to Jacobs when one of his informants, angry that he had moved on to interview other crack dealers, put a gun to the researcher's head and made ominous threats (1998). When the drug use behaviors of interest—such as drinking and other social activities in a tavern—are legal and public, the challenges of rapport building may still be time consuming but emotionally less onerous. Regularly hanging out in a Wisconsin working-class tavern, for example, E. E. LeMasters came to realize that among the farmers-turned-urban laborers, "taverns . . . do more than simply provide settings for leisure activities. They provide—at least for those who are their 'regulars'—havens of personal relationships in an impersonal world. Here is a place, beyond the protection of the immediate family, where the individual can still feel that he belongs, that people know who he is, that someone cares about him" (1973, 50).

Observing Behavior in Context

A principal reward for developing rapport with respondents in an ethnographic study of drug use is access to contexts in which the ethnographer can observe, in their natural setting, the behaviors of most interest. Thick description of how, when, where, and with whom drug users consume their drugs of choice, for example, provides key insights that potentially can guide the framing of grounded interventions to mitigate danger of infection, prevent relapse into addiction, and otherwise inform efforts to reduce the public health impact of that drug use.

There is no substitute, for example, for the kind of observations that Page and colleagues (Page, Chitwood, et al. 1990; Page, Smith, and Kane 1990; Page and Smith 1990; Page and Salazar 1999), Koester (1994a, 1994b), Bourgois (1998, 2003b), Carlson (1996), H. Ann Finlinson and colleagues (1999), Hoffer (2006), Singer (2006, 2007), Singer and colleagues (1995), Sterk (1999), Danielle German and Claire Sterk (2002), and others have conducted in their quest to understand injecting drug use. Important nuances of the behavioral complex surrounding drug use become evident quickly. Because these observations constitute one kind of qualitative data, their analysis reveals the relationships between drug consumption and many components of its cultural context. The passages that follow illustrate some of the cultural contexts observed by drug ethnographers.

> The three men who were already in the room have decided to make speedball, because they have both "boy" (heroin) and "girl" (cocaine). Using separate twist-off bottle caps with the plastic liners removed, two of them mix drugs with water drawn from the baby food jar, the heroin cap being brought to a boil with a lit half-book of matches. The drugs are then drawn into separate syringes. One of the speedball-sharing group removes the needle from his syringe and allows the contents of the other syringe to be squirted into his syringe from the other one. He then replaces his needle and squirts a portion of the mixture into the other two men's syringes. (Page, Smith, and Kane 1990, 78)

This passage describes a mode of drug sharing ("front-loading") not previously seen in the literature. It appeared in a paper that represented the first published report on observed self-injection behavior in the era of disposable syringes and needles, and it pointed out the importance of the cultural context of drug use in determining the risks incurred by its practitioners. The paper suggests that the extent of risk depends heavily on the initiative taken by the proprietor of the "get-off" (a term used in Miami to denote a place where people go to "shoot up") to obtain cleansing materials for the pooled needles/syringes in his or her establishment. If the proprietor recently received these materials from an outreach/intervention program, then he or she makes them available to the clientele. When the supplies run out, there may be no further effort to obtain more.

Findings of this study led to several other investigations, producing a report on the contamination found in needles/syringes collected from get-off houses in Miami (Chitwood et al. 1990), an analysis of the effect of laundry bleach on HIV (Shapshak et al. 1994), a study of an intervention that taught effective rinsing techniques to injection drug users (IDUs) (McCoy et al. 1997), a study of viral load in injection paraphernalia (Shapshak et al. 2000), and a study of the effect of distributing cleansing materials to get-off houses (Page et al. 2006). The findings established HIV prevention by injection behavior modification as a feasible and viable strategy for helping IDUs avoid infection.

In Search of Respect gives readers a glimpse of the social dynamics of crack dealing in East Harlem.

> It was just after midnight, and Ray was visiting his most profitable sales point to make sure the manager of the late-night shift had opened punctually. Business was booming and the heavyset, thirty-two-year-old Puerto Rican crack entrepreneur was surrounded by his coterie of employees, friends, and wanna-be acquaintances—all eager for his attention. We were on the corner of 110th Street by the entrance to the Lexington Avenue subway station right in front of the abandoned four-story tenement building occupied by Ray's dealers. He had camouflaged the ground floor as an after-hours bootleg social club and pool hall. (Bourgois 2003b, 19)

This relatively brief passage offers a helpful orientation to the setting in which the ethnographer worked. People, physical surroundings, daily activities, types of drug-related activities, location in the city, and social standing of the participants all receive attention.

In this setting, Bourgois described his single biggest blunder in five years of fieldwork: he showed Ray a picture of himself in the *New York Post* and asked him to read the caption, putting Ray into a position where he had to admit that he could not read. Actually, this is two blunders: (1) disrespect for a street dealer, and (2) getting your picture taken and published as a scholar who focuses on street drugs while your fieldwork is still in progress. Fortunately, the discomfort caused by this episode helped Bourgois to cement key informant relationships with other actors in that particular scene, and in a later encounter, Ray issued a stern warning about inadvertently bringing attention to his operation.

> Felipe, let me tell you something, people who get other people busted—even if it's by mistake—sometimes get found in the garbage with their heart ripped out and their bodies chopped up into little pieces . . . or else maybe they just get their fingers stuck in electrical sockets. You understand what I'm saying? (Bourgois 2003b, 22)

Apparently, Ray recognized blunder number two as the appropriate one to use in his rebuke.

In the course of presenting the results of five years' ethnographic fieldwork, this book effectively portrays the process of obtaining and trafficking in crack cocaine in East Harlem. Its attention to the cultural context in which Bourgois's key informants pursued their daily lives gives readers a sense of the multiple factors—systematic marginalization, racism, lack of alternatives, and a highly active drug market—that led to the choices made by the young men he studied. Given their considerable intelligence and their unwillingness to accept dead-end marginalization and poverty, the drug market seemed a rational choice at the time they began their participation in trafficking.

Bourgois later applied his searingly intense approach to field observation in studies of homeless IDUs in California, winning NIH funding to learn about the risks incurred by this highly vulnerable population (Bourgois and Schonberg 2009). For a time, his Web page featured a photograph of him peering out of a sleeping bag positioned in a San Francisco encampment of homeless people.

In some of the most finely textured reporting on syringe procurement, investigators in Puerto Rico pointed out how IDUs adapted to the policies of syringe exchange programs, pharmacies, and street dealers to maintain access to the implements of injection (Finlinson et al. 1999). Despite Puerto Rico's policy of access to legally obtained needles/syringes in pharmacies and an active needle exchange program, lacunae in the coverage of demand for needles emerged in this impressive example of observational study. The following passage describes an informal source of needles and syringes.

> Don Carlos sells syringes every day from about 10:00 A.M. to 10:00 P.M. and charges the same price as Don Miguel. Unlike Don Miguel, Don Carlos prefers to conduct business from inside his home. He lowers a small container to users who wait below to buy a syringe. They deposit money in the container, Don Carlos raises it, removes the money, then lowers the container containing the new syringe.

The observed IDUs had to adapt to circumstances in which their personal schedules for using drugs and the management strategies of the pharmacies and needle exchange programs did not match, leading to the use of alternative sources of informally obtained and sold needles/syringes.

> Don Miguel and Don Carlos are characterized by a number of factors that make them popular with IDUs in San Mateo for several reasons. First, both are located very close to where users buy and use drugs. Users who do not have a syringe at the time they buy drugs are often unable to make a 15–20 minute roundtrip to either the pharmacy or the NEP office. Whether users are severely drug dependent or not, they frequently prefer to buy syringes from these private vendors to avoid carrying syringes because they fear harassment by police or negative reactions by people, including family members, who might see their syringes.

These alternative sources offered the desired service of making syringes available according to the consumers' timetables, but they did so at the expense of some hygienic conditions. Work continued in Puerto Rico on harm reduction among IDUs through studies of syringe use (and other paraphernalia) through 2008.

Women who use illegal drugs have received far less attention than men in the drug literature in general (e.g., Romero-Daza, Weeks, and Singer 1998; Singer and Snipes 1992; Weeks, Himmelgreen, et al. 1998). This disparity is true in the ethnographic drug literature as well, but books by Marsha Rosenbaum (1981), Sheigla Murphy and Rosenbaum (1999), and Sterk (1999) on drug using careers pursued by women have helped to narrow the gap. Sterk spent considerable time in neighborhoods where crack-using women lived and obtained their drug of choice. In order to gain access to the venues that were most important to her study, she had to establish sufficient rapport and trust with actors in those venues. She described her own approach to establishing this rapport:

> Especially the condoms made me popular. I began carrying some all the time. I also seem to have become a major supplier of cigarettes, rides, and meals. The one thing I refuse to give people was money. Linda thought it was good for me to listen to their bullshit. Her main message to me is to be myself, and I'll be treated like everyone else. When I asked her what that meant, she responded "They'll love you and they'll use you." (Sterk 1999, 10)

Establishing rapport by these means allowed her to recruit 149 women who contributed in-depth interviews to her study of careers in crack use. Because she established rapport in this manner, she was able to observe and interview women whose activities involved several different variants among crack-using careers, including "Hustlers," "Hookers," "Older Struggling Rookies," and "Queens of the Scene" (Sterk 1999).

The research described above shared strong observational components in authentic contextual settings that reinforced findings on the nature of drug use risks. These studies gave readers a perspective on the human process of HIV risk and risk of problematic drug use that would not have been possible in surveys of the same behaviors. Social relations among actors, adaptations to institutional policies, desire to control others' behavior, the quest for peer respect, and women's status in street drug use settings all came under scrutiny as the researchers conducted their observations. In many cases, observation produced emergent findings that the researchers had not anticipated prior to beginning the study. Page, Smith, and Kane for example, did not expect to see proprietors of "get-offs" directing the cleansing of syringes among their clientele (1990). Sterk expected to see people willing to perform sex in exchange for crack, but she did not expect the wide variety of different roles assumed by women involved in crack use and trafficking (1999). She was especially surprised by the "Older Struggling Rookies" category of user who had no prior history of drug use or sex work. This finding reinforced the seductive character of crack use for certain adult women. In practically every ethnography of drug use, the investigators encountered behaviors that they did not anticipate. Examples of this particular advantage of ethnographic methods will abound in the succeeding chapters.

Conclusion

Mike Agar's book, *The Professional Stranger* (1996), presented the key issues of ethnography in terms of its location and role in the pursuit of social science. Because Agar had been something of a pioneer in the ethnography of drug use (e.g., Agar 1973), much of the characterization in *The Professional Stranger* can be applied to that endeavor. Agar described circumstances of field research that delineated the kinds of observations that may be necessary in the effort to bring the ethnographer close to the behavioral reality of the cultural complex under study, although he did not advocate the use of holistic field notes as we do. He acutely understood the ethnographer's occasionally precarious and liminal position in the field, complete with nuances of establishing a role, developing a strategy for dealing with language problems, and uses of data after the study is complete. He even took a stab at giving advice on how to write a research proposal to do ethnography. In the end, however, Agar made the act of ethnography a somewhat personal and idiosyncratic event, not a procedure that could be replicated by others, as exemplified by his autobiographical account of time as a drug ethnographer (Agar 2007). Our own approach to the process of gathering and analyzing ethnographic data structures activities and content in such a way as to make the "doing of drug ethnography" as accessible and replicable as possible. The ethnographer may gather an infinite number of different kinds of information (e.g., participant diaries, free listing, card sorts), but the staples are observation (as reflected in field notes); informal interviewing in context; formal, in-depth interviewing; and focus groups in the style that Agar himself suggested (Agar and MacDonald 1995). As stressed by Bourgois (2003b), Singer (2007), Gamburd (2008), Alisse Waterston (1993), and other ethnographers, findings from these methods must be located and interpreted within broad social fields and structures of social relationships that extend far beyond the on-the-ground observations and interviews conducted by individual ethnographers.

The approach taken by ethnographers, and the insights it provides that challenge dominant perspectives, is captured in a comment made by the French-speaking Haitian owner of the *pension* that Singer and several of his colleagues stayed in while doing research in the southern Haitian town of Jacmel some years ago. The proprietor was quite pleased to have several Americans and a Haitian with advanced academic degrees rooming with her. Their choice of her *pension* affirmed their good sense and her social status. Further, although she was not aware of the specific nature of their research project, she was certain that upper-class people like herself could explain all there was that was worth knowing about cultural issues in Haiti. Hence, she introduced the researchers to the local military head and several other important town personages. Instead, like fools, in her opinion, the researchers spent much of their time each day with the Creole-speaking people who lived in the low-income neighborhood they were studying. These informants would, some mornings, come to the *pension* to find the researchers, although they were not allowed inside because they were not of the right social class. After observing the behavior of the researchers for some time, the owner of the *pension* finally shook her head and sternly told them, "The problem with you people is that you just don't know who to walk with."

In the study of hidden behaviors like illicit drug consumption, "walking" with drug users (into shooting galleries, crack houses, abandoned buildings, homeless shelters, soup kitchens, drug copping sites, treatment centers, and similar locations where drug users live out their daily lives) has proved to be a productive approach to generating knowledge. Similarly, spending time in bars or other places people routinely drink or hanging out with people while they are smoking has allowed insights into drug use behaviors that are less likely to be discovered by other data collection strategies. Like other research methods, ethnography is a useful strategy for approaching "truth" rather than a guaranteed system for achieving it. As many focus groups conducted with drug users have found, for example, even insiders can sharply disagree about street drug use realities. What ethnography most importantly offers to the study of drug use

2

The Emergence of Drug Ethnography

Bernardino de Sahagún is known to history as a man who passionately devoted himself to interviewing Aztecs—in the Nahuatl language—about their history and culture. A Spanish Franciscan friar assigned by his church to travel to the New World (just eight years after Hernando Cortés's soldiers and Indian allies had conquered the Aztec Empire in 1521), Sahagún served as a teacher and evangelist at the Imperial School of the Holy Cross in Tlatelolco, Mexico. He learned and wrote about the traditional use of various drugs in pre-Columbian Mexico as a result of his research. With reference to use of the spineless, napiform cactus, peyote (*Lophophora williamsii*), for example, he recorded:

> There is another herb ... called peiotl ... it is found in the north country. Those who eat or drink it see visions either frightful or laughable; this inebriation last [sic] two to three days and then ceases. It is a sort of delicacy . . . , it sustains them and gives them courage to fight and not feel fear, nor hunger, and they say it protects them from any danger. (Sahagún 1956, 292)

In this and other passages about indigenous drug use in his massive twelve-volume *General History of the Things of New Spain* (1956), the assiduous Sahagún, called by some the father of modern ethnography, made important contributions both to the careful documentation of pre-Columbian drug use patterns (among many other topics) and to the use of qualitative methods in the study of drug use. His interviews and those of his assistants carried out in several Mexican cities, based on a recognition of the need to query multiple native informants to understand a culture from the insider's point of view, led to the production of a body of work that today would be called a form of salvage ethnography (intended to record a way of life as it passed out of existence; in Sahagún's case, it was in light of the destruction of indigenous records by the Spanish conquistadores and the

25

Catholic Church). This work suggests some important questions about the ethnography of drug use: What are the actual origins of drug use ethnography? How has the field developed and changed over time? What factors have influenced its evolution? Who were the founders and contributors to this line of research, and what motivated and influenced their work?

Answering these questions about the history of drug use ethnography and the influences that shaped its development is the purpose this chapter. Our intention is to locate ethnographic work on drug use within the worldwide historical contexts that have played a role in pushing the field in particular directions, focusing its attention on specific issues and putting it to work in the application of ethnographic knowledge to solve drug-related health and social problems. Before addressing these issues, we must first consider why it is important to know about the history of drug ethnography, including the key players who have contributed to the field and the routes taken in ethnography's evolution as an intellectual pursuit. Our answer to this question stems from our concern that this book contribute to the training of the next generation of ethnographic drug researchers. As the emergence of AIDS or the even newer syringe-related leishmania epidemic teach us, drug-related health problems remain significant and vexing public health issues. Even in the midst of the global AIDS pandemic, drug-related HIV risk behaviors have continued to spread to new populations, as have other forms of drug consumption. Because ethnography has proven to be a valuable approach to understand drug use and drug users in social contexts, and to develop reality- and evidence-based, contextual interventions, improving the skill set of drug ethnographers warrants disciplinary attention. Notably, in this regard, research has shown that the best teachers in any field of study are those who "have an unusually keen sense of the histories of their disciplines," a capacity that enables them "to reflect deeply on the nature of thinking within their fields" and to convey a more integrated understanding to their students (Bain 2004, 25). It is for this reason that we devote three chapters in this book to carefully tracing the historical development of drug ethnography and charting in some detail the unfolding of this arena of research.

This chapter introduces a developmental framework that begins with the earliest recorded observations of drug use behavior and traces the emergence of an ever more systematic, scientific approach to understanding drug use based on direct observation and interaction in the natural settings of drug users around the world (Singer 1999). This framework consists of five primary stages in the development of drug ethnography that stretch unevenly over approximately 2,500 years from the fifth century B.C. to the present. These are: (1) premodern quasi-ethnography, (2) early modernist ethnography, (3) interim modernist ethnography and autobiography, (4) systematic modernist ethnography and ethnopharmacology, and (5) developed public health ethnography since the discovery of AIDS. The first three of these historical stages are discussed in this chapter. The fourth stage—the period of consolidation of modern ethnographic methods in drug research—is addressed in chapter 4, while the fifth stage—which has been characterized by an explosion in the quantity of work done and number of researchers working on drug ethnography—is presented separately in chapter 5. We trace this developmental chronology for each stage of productivity in drug ethnography using four processes. First, we identify and discuss the work of key players in the development of drug ethnography based on analyses of the literature and contemporary interviews. Second, we review key single and multisited ethnographic studies that have contributed to the development of this field of anthropological and related work. Third, we explore the thematic threads that distinguish each historical stage, including the views of key players (to the degree possible) about the stage in which they worked. Finally, we address the challenging "problem inflation / problem minimization" dilemma that has been widely discussed in the field.

Premodern Quasi-Ethnography

The passage from Sahagún previously quoted is an example of the first and longest stage in the development of drug ethnography that we term *Premodern Quasi-Ethnography*. This precursor stage consists primarily of work carried out by a diverse array of interested amateur observers of drug use in the social setting around them. Some were motivated by their own piqued interest, and some were required to record their discoveries by employers. Often, as was the case with Sahagún, they were far from their original home and witnessed practices that were not only foreign but bizarre to them; other times their observations were carried out in neighborhoods closer to home but nonetheless in places where they encountered drug-related behaviors that were new and strange to them. Their understanding of what they witnessed often was hampered by limited botanical and pharmacological knowledge, as well as by prejudice against non-Western peoples (Page 2004). In varying degrees of detail, and guided by differing levels of objectivity, they recorded what they saw and what people told them about their use of drugs. At times, these quasi-ethnographic records included personal accounts of drug consumption and its effects on the chronicler. In the basic sense of viewing ethnography as a form of "writing down observations about people," these very first accounts of drug use qualify as a kind of ethnographic work because they were based on witnessed behaviors and insider accounts of involved individuals. The records these observers made usually were not based on detailed investigations of the behaviors of interest in the manner of contemporary ethnography, but they rather consisted of descriptions of curious exotica from a "foreign" cultural tradition. Taken together, these accounts generally are limited and unsystematic because they were not guided by scientific principles of focus, systematic rigor, and the control of bias. Nonetheless, they can be highly informative and insightful and serve as valuable documentation of drug use behaviors at a particular time and place that would otherwise be lost to contemporary understanding, thereby leaving a far more limited awareness of the depth and diversity of human involvement in drug consumption and its significant place in human societies through time.

Earliest Recorded Observations of Drug Use

In a cross-cultural study of altered states of consciousness (ASC) based on an ethnographic compendium of accounts for diverse peoples, Bourguignon argued that in preindustrial societies, some form of ASC is routinely built into religious beliefs and practices (1968, 1973). Of the 488 societies in her sample, 90 percent had institutionalized ASCs. Nonspiritual integration of ASCs in normal social activity is also quite common. Various mechanisms have been used across time and place to achieve altered consciousness, including sensory deprivation, fasting, and, of interest here, the use of various drugs, usually of a plant derivation. The use of drugs to alter states of consciousness or mood is apparently ancient and very widespread. As Fort confirms, it is found on every continent, although the most common drugs and methods of consumption vary by region (1969). The earliest known use of opium, for example, dates back 6,000–7,000 years to the ancient Sumerians of the Fertile Crescent (Lindesmith 1968). Hesiod's eighth century B.C. description of the ancient Mediterranean city of Mekone ("Poppy Town") near Corinth provides an early glimpse, indeed perhaps the earliest written record of drug plants, of the cultivation of opium poppy (Kritikos and Papadaki 1967a, 1967b).

The Histories of Herodotus

Another early written account of possible drug use is found in the work of the ancient Greek historian Herodotus. The first historian to engage in a high degree of systematic record collection, Herodotus described the practice of sweat bathing in what was probably marihuana fumes among the Scythians, a fifth-century horse-riding nomadic people of Central Asia. In the fourth book of his *Histories*, he wrote:

> Now they have hemp growing in their land, which is very like flax except in thickness and in height, in these respects the hemp is much superior. This grows both of itself and with cultivation. . . . The Scythians . . . take the seed of this hemp and creep under the felt coverings [of their sweat lodges], and then they throw the seed upon the stones which have been heated red-hot: and it burns like incense and produces a vapour so thick that no vapour-bath in Hellas would surpass it: and the Scythians being delighted with the vapour-bath howl like wolves. (2007, 75)

Much of Herodotus's reporting has been questioned in recent academic debates among historians. Some have argued that Herodotus exaggerated the extent of his journeys and invented some his sources, although recent archaeological evidence has provided some support of his observations. His description of the use of an intoxicant among the Scythians, while not based on his own direct observation, represents the first time that a Western scholar took quill in hand to describe drug use behavior among a people of a very distinctive cultural background. The drug in question, marihuana, continues to have an impact on the human condition, as it has become the third most widely consumed drug on the planet.

The New World Observations of Friar Ramon Pané

According to Harvey Feldman and Michael Aldrich (1990), whose historic account is one of the best available reviews of the premodern era of observational drug use studies, the first undisputed direct observation-based account of drug use was penned by Christopher Columbus and Friar Ramon Pané, the man assigned by Columbus to record native customs. Based on conversations with Taíno Indians on the Caribbean island of Hispaniola in 1496, Pané described their experience of taking a drug they called *cohoba*, which was eventually determined to be a hallucinogenic extract (containing dimethyltryptamine, bufotenine, and other alkaloids derived from the indolic amino acid tryptophan) from the bean of the *Anadenanthera peregrina* tree (Altschul 1972; Schultes 1977). Pané wrote that the Taíno shaman "takes a certain powder called cohoba snuffing it up his nose, which intoxicates them so they do not know what they do . . ." (Ott 1993, 164). In his records from the second voyage to the New World (1493–1496), Columbus also commented on a "powder" which the Taíno "snuff up" that causes them to "lose consciousness and become like drunken men" (Ott 1993, 164).

Pané's account of indigenous use of a hallucinogenic snuff—one of at least 100 different snuffs that have been identified among New World peoples (Schultes 1977)—dates the beginning of eyewitness observational drug studies to over 500 years ago. He also provided a description of tobacco use among the Taíno, a drug they smoked in huge cigars to comfort the limbs, induce sleep, and lessen weariness. Not surprisingly, like other accounts of the premodern era, Pané's description was not based on the systematic assembly, comparison, and verification of fine-grained data that characterize ethnography as a social scientific research method. Pané, nonetheless, did base his description on first-hand, on-the-ground observation and informal interviews of participants—hallmarks of the ethnographic approach to socially contextualized research. These European proto-ethnographers clearly did not present the Taínos' powder as desirable for general consumption. On the other hand, tobacco, a plant product also insufflated in powder form, began to be promoted soon after the first expeditions to the "New World" precisely because it did not cause its users to "lose consciousness" or "behave like drunken men" but did tickle their pleasure centers. The spread of tobacco throughout the known world over the next two centuries was the speediest diffusion rate of a drug using behavior ever seen. Its success was due in part to the innocuousness of its acute effects on human behavior and, of course, to its addictive properties.

The Codex of Sahagún

In the period after Columbus, other explorers, European invaders, and their fellow travelers provided additional accounts of New World drug use. Amerigo Vespucci, for example, first described *coca* chewing in South America at the turn of the sixteenth century (Aldrich and Barker 1976). In Latin America, however, it was Sahagún's exploration of life among the Aztecs and the richly illustrated and detailed Codex he produced that provided the most detailed account of drug use in the lives of New World peoples prior to the arrival of the Europeans.

It is evident from Sahagún's records that the Aztecs possessed an extensive pharmacopeia of drugs reflecting the long accumulation of knowledge about the mind-altering properties of many different drug plants. Included in Sahagun's interviews, in addition to peyote, were descriptions of the use of psilocybin mushrooms (*Psilocybe mexicana*), morning glory seeds (*Ipomoea tricolor*), Salvia (*Salvia divinorum*), and jimson weed (*Datura stramonium*). This is not to say, however, that the Aztecs had a drug problem, as that term is now used. Rather, drug use was a socially controlled and culturally meaningful behavior that was integrated with the broad themes of the Aztec way of life and ritual calendar. Drug use was seen by the Aztecs as a sacred behavior linked to the god Xochipilli, the Prince of Flowers and divine shepherd of the hallucinatory experience of sacred communion that they called "the flowery dream." A fifteenth-century Aztec statue of Xochipilli (now housed at the National Museum of Anthropology in Mexico City) is covered with depictions of hallucinogenic plants of various species and portrays a seated, human-like figure with eyes turned toward the sky.

Exemplary of the Aztec ritual use of drugs, Sahagún described the ceremony known as the Feast of Teonanacatl. This feast began at daybreak around a communal fire with the consumption of psilocybin mushrooms mixed with syrup made from the juice of the maguey plant. While Sahagún never witnessed the feast, as such practices were firmly banned by the colonial government of Mexico, he was shown the mushrooms used in the ritual. He reported that during the feast, some participants sang sacred songs while others danced. A number of those who consumed the mixture openly wept or became engaged in deep meditation. Once the effects of the mushroom wore off, participants discussed the visions they received, ensuring their appropriate cultural interpretation. In the case of jimson weed, Sahagún reported that its consumption had both religious and medicinal purposes. Healers consumed jimson weed mixed with peyote to determine appropriate treatments for their patients. Patients also were given the drug for some ailments. Additionally, the plant was one of the ingredients in a salve made of venomous insects, ash, and tobacco that was rubbed on the Aztec priests who performed human sacrifices (Gayton 1928).

In assessing Sahagún's notable contribution to early drug ethnography, it is important to consider why he recorded information about such behavior and the factors that influenced his perspective on drug use. Fortunately, in Sahagún's case, we have his answer to this question in his own words.

> It is inappropriate for the ministers . . . to state that, among this people, there are no other sins but drunkenness, theft, and carnality. For there are many other much graver sins in need of remedy. . . . In order to preach against these things or even to be aware of their existence, we must be familiar with how they were practiced in pagan times, through our ignorance, they do many idolatrous things without our understanding it. (quoted in León-Portilla 2002, 134)

His motivation, in short, was to understand fully so as to change indigenous practices that were in conflict with complete conversion to Catholicism. Beyond this, however, there is ample evidence that Sahagún came to be truly fascinated and even, to a degree, sympathetic with the cultural traditions of his informants.

Sir Richard Burton

A highly adventurous explorer, prolific writer (he published forty-three volumes about his travels and thirty volumes of translations, including the *Kama Sutra*), soldier, diplomat, noted lover of languages, and steadfast supporter of British imperialism, the often-irascible Sir Richard Burton journeyed extensively through what could be called Cannabis country and recorded what he saw there. For example, in one footnote to his highly annotated sixteen-volume translation of *Arabian Nights*, Burton drew on his extensive travels in the Middle East to describe "barsh"—sweet bars—made of the young leaves, buds, and florets of Cannabis, as well as poppy seeds, datura flowers, milk, sugar, nutmeg, cloves, mace, and saffron that have been boiled and left to cool and harden (1885, vol. 4, n. 28). In this footnote, he also described how gum was collected from Cannabis plants by hand or by passing a blanket over the plant during the early morning. Another use of Cannabis, he noted, was a drink called *sabzi*, made of dried Cannabis leaves, poppyseed, cucumber seed, black pepper, and cardamoms ground in a mortar and made drinkable by adding milk or ice cream. Another of the drug recipes that he detailed was a drink made of well-washed Cannabis leaves, black pepper, cloves, nutmeg, and mace (which he notes enhances the level of intoxication). These ingredients are mixed in water, watermelon juice, or cucumber juice and then strained. In another footnote (1885, vol. 2, n. 220),

Burton drew on his less extensive New World travels to describe Cannabis use that he witnessed among African Americans in the southern United States and among the poor in Brazil. He emphasized that, while the drug is well known among subordinated populations, the dominant sectors of society have often never heard of it.

Unfortunately, many of the detailed descriptions Burton recorded of life-ways in various parts of the world, collected during forty years of travels, were lost in a fire set by his wife after his death, but the remnants clearly identify him as an early producer of quasi-ethnography of drug use. Unlike many of his con-temporaries, Burton was not horrified by drug use. He paid attention to drug preparation and use, and he admitted that he certainly tried many of the drugs he described. While his writings contain a wealth of detail about drug use in far-flung regions, there is little in the way of contextualized description, exploration of the meaning of drugs to their users, or discussion of the wider impact of drug use on society, issues of keen ethnographic interest.

The Appetites of Thomas de Quincey

Feldman and Aldrich credit the British writer Thomas de Quincey with being the first individual to produce a book-length work that could fairly be called a premodern drug ethnography (1990). Although he was an adventurer, like other chroniclers of drug use of his era, and not a trained social scientist, de Quincey was born to a family of Manchester textile merchants and spent a number of years (after dropping out of school) living among the urban poor of London. He was a keen observer of the significant upsurge in opium and alcohol use in London's working-class districts during the Industrial Revolution, and he also was interested in drug use among socially prominent individuals, such as the poet Samuel Taylor Coleridge. His book, *Confessions of an English Opium-Eater* (1822), records his personal experiences with and observations of opium use across social classes. Unlike the East, where people smoked it, the opium users de Quincy observed drank it in liquid form, a practice that continued until the introduction of the hypodermic needle. Based on the recommendation of an old college friend, de Quincey's first use of the drug occurred in 1804 as treatment for a prolonged head cold that he could not shake. About this experience, he wrote:

> I was necessarily ignorant of the whole art and mystery of opium-taking; and what I took, I took under every disadvantage. But I took it; and in an hour,—oh heavens! what a revulsion! what an upheaving, from its lowest depths, of the inner spirit! what an apocalypse of the world within me! That my pains had vanished, was now a trifle in my eyes; this negative effect was swallowed up in the immensity of those positive effects which had opened before me, in the abyss of divine enjoyment thus suddenly

revealed. Here was a panacea . . . for all human woes; here was the secret of happiness, about which philosophers had disputed for so many ages, at once discovered; happiness might now be bought for a penny, and carried in the waistcoat pocket; portable ecstasies might be had corked up in a pint bottle; and peace of mind could be sent down in gallons by the mail-coach. But, if I talk in this way, the reader will think I am laughing; and I can assure him, that nobody will laugh long who deals much with opium . . . (de Quincey 1822, 3)

In this account, de Quincey reflects a common experience of first-time opiate users, an experience so powerful that it propels many to continue (unsuccessfully) to try to re-create their initial encounter. As such, de Quincey's work contributes a detailed emic, or insider, description of the drug experience in a social context. In this, it has all the strengths (e.g., extensive contextual detail, reporting not just of behavior but of motivation and experience) and weaknesses (e.g., lack of a theoretical perspective, narrowness of focus on one individual's experience) of much autobiographical writing about drug use that was to be produced in subsequent years.

Frederick Engels: A Foot in Manchester

Another astute observer of street drug use in England during this era was Frederick Engels, who recorded his firsthand observations of Manchester in 1844 in his book *The Conditions of the Working Class*. Engels, who was led through the polluted and heavily crowded backstreets and alleyways of Manchester by his working-class Irish girlfriend Mary Burns, was repulsed by the harsh and degraded living conditions of the urban poor and of the social practices, supported by dominant institutions, that sustained inner-city life during the take-off years of the Industrial Revolution. For example, in a discussion of popularly used and easily accessible patent medicines, Engels observed:

> One of the most injurious of these patent medicines is a drink prepared with opiates, chiefly laudanum, under the name Godfrey's Cordial. Women who work at home, and have their own and other people's children to take care of, give them this drink to keep them quiet, and, as many believe, to strengthen them. They often begin to give this medicine to newly born children, and continue, without knowing the effects of this 'heart's-ease,' until the children die. (1969, 135)

Engels saw in the drug and alcohol use among the urban working class, a population which, given their situation, he believed to be understandably in need of "forgetting for an hour or two the wretchedness and burden of life," a means of coping with oppression (1969, 133). Their living and working conditions were an example of what he pointedly termed "social murder," a term intended to convey a meaning similar to the contemporary use of "structural violence" in the health social sciences. As Farmer explained, structural violence refers to "a host of offenses against human dignity [including]: extreme and relative poverty, social inequalities ranging from racism to gender inequality, and the more spectacular forms of violence that are uncontested human rights abuses . . ." (2003, 1)

In providing a structural (class-based) analysis of drug use, Engels stood apart from most other quasi-ethnographers of drug use. While his actual description of observed drug use behavior is typically uneven, unsystematic, and often buried between long passages of commentary, his use of direct observation in the field was guided by a theoretical orientation and an explanatory purpose. As such, he has been called a father of critical medical anthropology, one of the pivotal perspectives brought to bear by contemporary drug ethnographers.

Lessons from the Quasi-Ethnography of Drug Use

As this review of premodern drug studies suggests, a scattered array of non-scientific descriptive accounts of drug use has accumulated over the centuries. For the most part, these texts are products of the curiosity of the writer (or his or her employer) about unfamiliar and often (from the observer's perspective) exotic behaviors—some among newly encountered peoples, others among hidden populations closer to the author's home. In a few cases, such as in the work of Engels, the observations were directed by a theoretical perspective (which continues to be of value), but usually they were not. Further, like much descriptive ethnography, they serve primarily to document the considerable diversity of drug-involved life patterns found across place and time, affirming that drug use is an ancient, varied, widespread, and often socially integrated practice. Inherent in such description is the insight that drug use should not be narrowly conceived as an example (or, as is often the case, as the epitome) of social deviance (Waterston 1993); rather, modern drug ethnography emphasizes that it must be understood in social context in light of social conditions, beliefs, practices, and structural relationships.

Early Modernist Ethnography

The era of modern ethnographic drug research, consisting of systematic field observations and careful description of actual behaviors in social context, began in the 1930s with four seminal studies. Anthropologists often consider Weston La Barre's field examination of ritual peyote use among Native Americans (1975) to be the first full-fledged drug study by a professional ethnographer. Sociologists, by contrast, point to Bingham Dai's study of opium addicts in Chicago (1937) as the grandfather of modern drug ethnographies.

Together, these two studies constitute the starting points of modern field research on drug use. Also of early importance was work begun during the 1930s, and stretching for many years thereafter, by Richard Evans Schultes. Schultes applied his considerable acumen in botany to the emergent field of ethnopharmacology, characterizing not just the properties of the myriad plants used by indigenous peoples for psychotropic purposes, but achieving at least a limited understanding of what these preparations meant to their users. Finally, the early work of anthropologist Robert Lowie focused on the Crow Indians, a tribal group that had an elaborate cultural complex surrounding the use and veneration of tobacco. Together, these researchers, all of whom were trained professional social or biological scientists, laid the foundation for modern drug ethnography.

Weston La Barre: Research and Application

In 1935, La Barre began research on peyote use among the Kiowa for his doctoral dissertation. Over the next year, he conducted field observations of ritual peyote consumption with 15 different Native American tribes. "The Peyote Cult," La Barre's doctoral dissertation, was presented at Yale University in 1937. The first edition of the book based on this work, also called *The Peyote Cult* (1975), came out during a period of growing anthropological interest in Native American incorporation of the small hallucinogenic cactus into revitalization rituals (Opler 1938; Schultes 1938). One primary concern driving La Barre's research was to reconstruct the historic diffusion of various ritual elements across Native American groups that comprised the "peyote cult." Focus on this issue was fueled by a broader disciplinary concentration on the diffusion of cultural elements, their incorporation into and integration with the existing cultural pattern, and the reconstruction of cultural histories. Based on a careful consideration of the social origin of various peyote cult paraphernalia, beliefs, and practices, La Barre was able to trace the pathway of diffusion and development of the peyote ritual as it moved across tribal groups, beginning in the middle of the nineteenth century.

Given ongoing American ambivalence toward drug use, including a strong moral attitude that condemns all drug use as sinful, Native American peyote users have suffered a long history of persecution, including arrest, trial, and denial of other rights and protections (Calabrese 2001). Anthropologists who have studied peyote use, especially within the context of the Native American Church, have supported the right to use the drug sacramentally on First Amendment grounds of religious freedom. In 1937, for example, when New Mexico state Senator Denis Chavez introduced a bill into the state legislature to prohibit interstate transportation of peyote, La Barre and a number of other anthropologists and ethnobotanists, including Franz Boas, submitted letters opposing the bill, which ultimately was defeated (Stewart 1987). In addition, La

Barre, David McAllester, J. S. Slotkin, Sol Tax, and Omar Stewart signed a "state-ment on peyote," defending this position which was published in the journal *Science* in the early 1950s (La Barre et al. 1951). These activities helped to lay the foundation for an applied focus in the ethnography of drug use—one that was to achieve full construction with the emergence of the HIV/AIDS epidemic.

True to his anthropological orientation to drug use, La Barre's work on peyote emphasized the cultural context of consumption. In the case of Native American peyote use, this was not a difficult task, given the highly ritualized and richly symbolic treatment of peyote by Native Americans. La Barre adopted a similar cultural perspective in his account of Native American alcohol pro-duction and consumption (1975). In this lesser known publication, he identified many of the beers and wines produced by native peoples of North and South America prior to the arrival of Europeans. Less ritualized and socially marginal drug use, such as that found among the urban poor, tended not to attract anthropological attention during this era. Thus, Linda Bennett and Paul Cook could conclude that "as of the early 1970s, anthropology had not yet developed an explicit drug research tradition, especially with respect to abuse of drugs" (1996, 231).

In 1975, La Barre deposited all of his personal and professional papers and related materials in the National Anthropological Archives at the Smithsonian Institution. This collection contains his field notes, photographs, and other products of his study of Native American peyote use. However, it also includes various materials, including reprints, pamphlets, and newspaper and magazine clippings, about the use of drugs in contemporary society (1960s)—hallucinogenic drugs in general, and mescal and peyote in particular—reflecting La Barre's lifelong interest in drug use behavior that was focused on but not limited to the ritual consumption of peyote.

Bingham Dai: The Urban Ethnographic Tradition

Unlike anthropology, sociology developed an explicit drug research tradition relatively early, and its origin is found in the work of Bingham Dai, who was concerned with understanding addicts "as a group and the world they live in" (1937, 645). This is the tradition of "drug use as social deviance." This tradition began with the approach to community-based social research that has come to be called the Chicago School—an orientation developed by Robert E. Park, a student of the German sociologist Georg Simmel. Park believed that modern urban dwelling brought into existence a new way of life that was best under-stood through the direct field observation of numerous small social settings (such as particular work sites or neighborhoods) and subgroups (e.g., street gangs, petty thieves, musicians) that comprise the urban whole. Methodologically, the Chicago School used a mixed approach that included "seeking out the [target

group] member's perspective . . . , observing human group life naturalisti-
cally . . . , and being in situ" (Adler 1990, 96), strategies that form important
components of the ethnographic method. Indeed, as Joan Moore stressed, the
Chicago fieldwork tradition "virtually mandated that major consideration be
given to the point of view of the communities and the people under study," a
sentiment that it shared with the Malinowskian ethnographic research tradition in anthropology (1978, 8). In addition, Park, like his mentor, saw the city as
a stressful environment that produces a breakdown of social bonds, disorgani-
zation, individual isolation, depersonalization, and deviant behavior. In short,
life in cities is pathological and the behavior of urban dwellers, especially inner-
city populations, reflects the urban social crisis. Drug abuse, consequently, is
understood as the direct expression of the deeply damaging effects of urban life.

In his book *Opium Addiction in Chicago* (1937), Dai reported findings from his
fieldwork and life-history interviews with two populations: individuals with an
iatrogenic addiction to morphine as a result of medical treatment, and those
who acquired their addiction on the street through their involvement with
other drug users. This division is important because of the prevailing view
of addiction during the period that Dai conducted his research. In the late
nineteenth century, in the aftermath of the Civil War and the widespread use
of morphine during battlefield surgeries,

> the drug addict was viewed as a helpless victim, an unfortunate sick
> person in need of medical attention. . . . But by the 1920s the public image
> of the addict had become that of a criminal, a willful degenerate, a hedo-
> nistic thrill-seeker in need of imprisonment and stiff punishment.
> (Goode 1984, 217–218)

Congressional passage of the Harrison Act in 1914—prohibiting over-the-
counter sale of narcotics—was one of the factors shaping the public (and
researcher) reconstruction of the drug addict image. By 1925, there were more
than 10,000 arrests on federal drug charges (Lindesmith 1968). Through the
media and other reports of these arrests, the "link between addiction and
crime—the view that the addict was by definition a criminal—was forged"
(Goode 1984, 221).

Nevertheless, another factor also shaped the public image of the drug
addict during this era. By the 1930s, drug addiction among African Americans
was becoming increasingly common. Dai claimed that, in Chicago during the
years 1928–1934, African Americans comprised 6.9 percent of the population but
accounted for 17.3 percent of individuals addicted to drugs (and 22 percent of
those who were unemployed) (1937). The accuracy of these numbers, however,
is thrown open to question by his lack of a systematic sampling methodology.
What is clear, though, is that drug use was adopted by African American

migrants to Chicago and other northern, midwestern, and western U.S. urban centers. Several factors contributed to rising rates of drug use and addiction in this population. For the most part, African Americans were relatively recent arrivals to the city, having migrated northward beginning in the early 1900s in one of the largest population transitions in U.S. history. In cities such as Chicago—which has been called the most segregated city in America—African Americans encountered racism, social isolation, family disruption, broad-based discrimination, and urban poverty (which experientially was considerably more oppressive than the rural poverty most had previously known in the South). During Prohibition, African American neighborhoods "became the place where whites practiced their vices" (James and Johnson 1996, 16). During this period, black-owned jazz clubs, after-hours clubs, houses of prostitution, gambling halls, and dance clubs emerged as important social centers for the growing African American urban population. Whites, anxious for excitement and an escape from the depressive economic situation, flocked into the inner city "to hear African American music, to party, to patronize houses of prostitution, and to gamble" (James and Johnson 1996, 17). Among those who patronized the urban clubs were African American soldiers who had been exposed to drug use in Europe or North Africa during World War I, as well as individuals with a more pecuniary interest in drug use. As St. Clair Drake and Horace Cayton colorfully pointed out, these centers of congregation often became

> points of contact between the purveyors of pleasure "on the illegit" and their clientele—casual prostitutes, bootleggers, reefer peddlers, "pimps," and "freaks." Some of these places [were] merely "fronts" and "blinds" for the organized underworld. . . . The primary institutions of the underworld [were] the tougher taverns, the reefer pads, the gambling dens, the liquor joints, and the call houses and buffet-flats where professional prostitutes cater to the trade in an organized fashion. (1970, 610)

These associations, and the racist sentiments that helped to fuel them, contributed to the demonization of the drug addict as the ultimate deviant—the very embodiment of things strange and threatening to the dominant society.

In this context, Dai launched his field study of opium addiction, bringing to the task a psychoanalytic approach to individual behavior. Though an ethnographic methodology, which by design is geared to the study of social process and performance in context, may seem ill-suited to a highly individualized perspective like psychoanalysis, the combination (known, somewhat tongue-in-cheek, as the "couch in the field" approach) has guided a number of researchers (see Levine 1986, 203–214). As Feldman and Aldrich noted, given Dai's orientation, it is not surprising to find that his observations were "cast in terms like 'infantile' personalities, excessive dependence on other, and a tendency to withdraw or escape from social responsibility" (1990, 18). Use of these constructs was further reinforced by the recruitment of many study participants through the Psychopathic Hospital in Chicago.

Dai helped to usher in the social deviance approach to drug studies. This understanding, suggested although never fully developed in Dai's work, depicts the drug user as caught up in "an all-consuming life-style" (Waterston 1993, 13) or a total way of life (Bell 1971; Inciardi 1986). Some researchers have referred to the existence of a "deviance syndrome" among impoverished inner-city drug users (McGee and Newcomb 1992). For example, Gilles Bibeau asserted that regular intravenous drug use "quickly leads to a lifestyle often associated with social marginality, a lifestyle where risk-taking and danger play central roles" (1989). Thus, Dai, in discussing the link between drug use and prostitution, wrote: "That the pimp in his attempt to entice a girl to his service not seldom 'dopes' her and makes her an addict so that she will have to depend on him for her drug and thereby becomes his woman is a matter of common knowledge" (1937, 136). Once addicted, from the perspective of the deviance model, drug users come to view "themselves as culturally and socially detached from the life style and everyday preoccupations of members of the conventional world" (Rettig, Torres and Garrett 1977, 244). The deviance model presents the issue not just in terms of drugs and their pharmacological effects. Rather, the model asserts that "addicts become addicted not only to drugs but to a way of life" (Lindesmith, Strauss and Denzin 1975, 571).

Stuart Hills observed:

> The use of illicit mood-altering substances is assumed to play a *radically* different role in the lives of drug users than is the case for legal drug users. All aspects of the lives of [illicit] drug users may be seen as centering around the use of this demoniac, forbidden substance. . . . Similarly, the label 'addict' in the United States typically conjures up a picture of a strung-out, dirty, furtive, lower-class street junkie—but does not readily bring to mind the millions of middle-class alcohol- and barbiturate-addicted housewives. Nor does it convey a mental picture of the thousands of clean-shaven, affluent, hardworking physicians, stethoscopes dangling from their necks, who are currently addicted to narcotics. (1980, 12–13)

Consequently, later writers questioned the deviance model, arguing that it "leads to an exaggerated picture of [drug] users' lives, as well as an overstatement of differences between users and nonusers. . . . [Indeed] the deviant subculture seems to insert itself in the middle of the metropolis, and we have no sense of it being part of anything larger than its own demi-world" (Waterston 1993, 14–15.).

Richard Evans Schultes: The Birth of Ethnopharmacology

In the book he edited with Siri Von Reis, *Ethnobotany: The Evolution of a Discipline*, Richard Evans Schultes defined ethnobotany, a field he helped to bring into existence, as "the uses, symbolism, ritualistic, [and] other aspects of the practical, everyday interrelationship between people and plants" (1995, 19). During his remarkably productive career as a researcher, adventurer, teacher, and rainforest conservationist, Schultes collected more than 30,000 plant specimens, coming mostly from the Americas (particularly from Colombia's Amazon region) and including at least 300 species that were new to scientific awareness (120 of which, such as *Pourouma schultesii*—a bark whose ashes are used to treat ulcers, bear his name). He held a strong interest in ethnopharmacological plants—those used for healing in indigenous societies, especially those with psychotropic properties. In his obituary in *The New York Times*, Schultes was described as "a swashbuckling scientist and influential Harvard educator who was widely considered the preeminent authority on hallucinogenic and medicinal plants" (Kandell 2001). His fieldwork style, which was no doubt a model for the Indiana Jones movies, is suggested by the meager material assemblage that supported his efforts.

> He carried very few supplies and food while in the Amazon, relying on the jungle to provide him with much of what he needed. Along with a fifty-three-pound canoe, his pack contained one change of clothing, notebooks and pencils, a camera and film, a first-aid kit, a hammock, a thin blanket, clippers, plant collecting paraphernalia, and a few cans of B & M baked beans. (Harvard University Herbaria 2002)

Schultes's research on plants that produce hallucinogenic effects, such as peyote and ayahuasca, resulted in several books, such as his richly illustrated *Hallucinogenic Plants* (1976), which became cult favorites among the wave of Western drug experimenters during the 1960s. He was drawn to this area of research as a child. Confined to his room for many months because of sickness, he passed his time listening to excerpts read to him by his parents from *Notes of a Botanist on the Amazon and the Andes*, a travel diary written by the nineteenth-century British naturalist Richard Spruce. Schultes was powerfully influenced by Spruce's writing, and he decided to model his life after Spruce. In 1936, Schultes wrote an undergraduate term paper on the psychotropic properties of peyote, based on research he had carried out with the Kiowa in Oklahoma. His doctoral thesis, "Economic Aspects of the Flora of Northeastern Oaxaca," completed in 1941, focused on plants used by the native residents of Oaxaca, Mexico.

A prolific writer over many decades, Schultes published 10 books and more than 450 professional articles on ethnobotanical topics. His opus includes very detailed field accounts of drug-related behaviors, such as the following description of hallucinogenic snuff preparation among the Waiká people of Colombia.

Several different methods characterize the Waiká preparation of epená. . . . Sometimes, the softer inner layer of the bark is scraped and the dried shavings are gently roasted over a slow fire. They are then stored until needed for preparation of a new batch of snuff, when they are crushed and pulverized, triturated in a mortar and pestle of a fruit of the Brazil nut tree *Bertholletia excelsa*. The powder is then sifted to a very fine, homogeneous chocolate-brown, highly pungent dust. Next, a powder of dried leaves of an aromatic weedy plant, *Justicia pectoralis* . . . is prepared and added to the brown dust of *Virola* resin in approximately equal amounts. A third ingredient is the ash of the bark of a rare leguminous tree, *Elizabetha princeps*. (Schultes and Hoffman 1991, 126)

Perhaps Schultes's greatest contribution (from the perspective of this book), beyond his incredible compendium of knowledge concerning the interaction of humans and psychotropic plants, was that it ensured drug ethnography would become a biocultural field—one that synthesized the nature and effects of the biochemistry of drugs with the diverse cultural patterns and meanings associated with their use in varied social settings around the globe.

Robert Lowie: Stumbling into Drug Ethnography

Unlike Schultes, but like many ethnographers who would follow him, Robert Lowie did not set out to become a drug researcher (and probably never thought of himself as such). Rather, he encountered drug use in the field and could not escape investigation because of its importance to the people he was studying. As a result, he provided a very early—yet fully modern—ethnographic account of drug use, namely the ritual and medicinal use of tobacco among the Crow people in Montana. Beginning in 1907 and continuing for almost twenty-five years, Lowie lived for long stretches of time among the Crow, observing their ways, listening to elders tell tales of the past, and learning the intricacies of their religious and ceremonial life, tribal organization, and values. His book, *The Crow Indians* (1983), is considered a classic work of ethnographic literature.

The place of tobacco among the Crow drew Lowie's attention because, as he noted, it "was one of the three holiest objects of worship, hence all children wore a small packet of it as an amulet necklace" (1983, xiv). The place of tobacco in Crow traditional religious life is reflected in the many religious songs they sang about their "sacred weed." Lowie documented the lyrics of some of these songs, including: "I, the Tobacco, am a person, look at me. I, I am the Tobacco, I am the medicine-rock, look at it" (1983, 214).

Lowie noted, "Smoking was an inveterate Crow custom, but the tobacco they smoked (*Nicotiana quadrivalvis* or Tall Tobacco) was not the species they grew" for use in ceremonies (*Nicotiana multivalvis* or Short Tobacco) (1983, xvii–xviii). Only the latter was believed to be holy, and it was mystically identified with the stars.

According to the creation story told by one of Lowie's informants, the Creator (known as the Transformer) and other spiritual beings walked across the newly formed earth and saw a person who quickly changed himself into a tobacco plant, the first plant on the planet. At which point, "The Transformer decrees that the Crow shall plant [tobacco] in the spring and dance with it; it shall be their 'means of living,' their mainstay" (Lowie 1983, xvii–xviii). Responsibility for the sacred tobacco fell to the Tobacco Society, an important association and ritual group within Crow society. The enduring importance of Lowie's account was his recognition of the integration of tobacco with most other cultural components of Crow society and its ceremonial contribution to sustaining their way of life. In this, his work presaged the later ethnographic work of Dwight Heath and other anthropologists who struggled to counter the War on Drugs depiction of psychotropics as inevitably disruptive and destructive.

Along with a number of other ethnographers of his era, Lowie recognized the importance of drugs in the day-to-day lives of people in various societies. While some (such as Dai) brought a "drugs as a social problem" perspective to their ethnographic work, others (such as Lowie) developed a different, more integrative understanding and delineated the lines of disagreement in the problem inflation / problem deflation debate that would arise many years later.

Lessons from the Initial Modernist Phase of Drug Ethnography

During this phase in the development of drug ethnography, qualitative researchers in both anthropology and sociology established drug research as a topic of interest. At the same time, as reflected in concerns Lowie expressed in his work on the Crow, there was also a degree of uncertainty—even defensiveness—in laying claim to this domain as a legitimate field of disciplinary study. This was especially true in anthropology, a field that, unlike sociology, did not begin with an emphasis on analyzing the social problems of industrial nations but was instead intent on describing preindustrial lifeways as coherent and legitimate social systems in light of European global domination and prejudicial attitudes toward colonized societies. In an early article he wrote on peyote use among Native Americans, for example, Schultes emphasized the nonharmful effects of the drug when used in socially controlled cultural contexts: "Many investigators agree that peyote is not a habit-forming narcotic. Its use is productive of little social and moral degradation or physical harm, notwithstanding statements to the contrary" (1938, 699).

As a result of these differences in focus, a conceptual divide quickly developed between anthropologists who were focused on the integration of drug use with the broader cultural systems of smaller scale societies in nonurban settings and sociologists who maintained a deviance and social-disruption perspective on the effects of urban life. While this tension would be revisited, and to a degree resolved, during subsequent phases, it succeeded in temporarily limiting communication about drug use and its effects across social science disciplines.

Interim Modernist Ethnography

The advances in understanding achieved through the ethnographic study of drugs that took place during the first phase of modernist ethnography did not continue in a natural developmental course. Rather, world events, namely World War II, intervened and disturbed both the global flow of drugs and the demands placed on the lives of most ethnographers (even the ethnobotanical work of Schultes was influenced by the war, a period during which he focused on identifying disease-resistant rubber species, given the importance of this substance for the war effort). As a result, the years immediately surrounding World War II largely constitute a lull in the ethnography of drugs. While the work of a number of researchers from this period, such as Alfred Lindesmith, is noteworthy, some of the greatest ethnographic insights on drug use during the war years were penned by individual drug users in their autobiographical texts.

Lindesmith and the Definition of Addiction

Alfred Lindesmith, who helped Bingham Dai select and recruit his sample, went on to make his own contribution to ethnographic drug research and to the broader drug use and addiction fields. As Feldman and Aldrich pointed out, Lindesmith "used qualitative interviewing techniques to develop definitions of addiction—probably the first in the world derived from ethnographic research" (1990, 18). During the post–World War II years, his work helped move professional thinking about addiction toward a medical model. Lindesmith proposed a social theory of addiction (1947, 1968). In doing so, he rejected explanations of addiction that were based solely on the alleged pharmacological and dependence-producing characteristics of drugs, arguing instead that when drug users seek to stop using drugs,

> they find themselves drawn back to their old haunts and associates. They also find it difficult to adjust themselves to the normal routines and values of the ordinary world and to escape the stigma of their past. The failure of addicts to "kick the habit" permanently is doubtless tied up with their reluctance to abandon old associates and a familiar environment. The use of drugs thus is much more than a biological matter or a mere question of pharmacology. (Lindesmith, Strauss and Denzin 1975, 571)

Employing an emic approach to the problem of addiction, Lindesmith argued that a definition of this phenomenon "must come from those 'addicted' rather than those who have never used opiates, and that definition should reflect common experiences of this population" (Knipe 1995, 91).

In his interviews with heroin users, Lindesmith found a range of experiences associated with heroin injection; some users reported pleasurable responses and others indicated that the pleasure was minimal. All respondents, however, affirmed that continued use protected them from the painful discomfort of withdrawal. Thus, Lindesmith wrote:

> The addict's craving for opiates is born in his experience of relief of withdrawal which follows with(in) a matter of five to ten minutes after an injection ... the craving develops in this situation only when the individuals understand the withdrawal symptoms and attribute them to the proper cause. (1968, 100)

Addiction, in Lindesmith's view, is not simply a physical need for a particular drug but also a body of shared cultural knowledge about the drug and its effects. In seeking to understand the nature of addiction, Lindesmith's work reflects the primary question driving the work of drug researchers of this era: Why do people use drugs? Lindesmith's answer is that they become ensnared in a set of social relationships and life patterns, which, along with the chemical properties of the drug, drive the drug use process. Additionally, Lindesmith sought to counter various popular ideas about drug use that he believed were not based on known facts. Thus, he emphasized that, for most drug users, the initial euphoria and pleasure of drug use

> vanishes and is replaced by the negative effect of relieving withdrawal distress achieving approximate normality between shots. . . . The long-continued use of such drugs as morphine and heroin, contrary to popular belief, does not lead to major tissue destruction or to insanity. Tooth decay, constipation, and sexual impotence, which are relatively frequent among drug addicts, are not invariable or necessary consequences of addiction, and some addicts, especially those who are well-to-do, do not experience them. The principal deleterious effects are psychological in nature and are connected with the tabooed and secret nature of the habit, with the extreme cost of obtaining a supply of drugs at black-market prices, and resulting changes in self-conception, occupation, and social relationships. (Lindesmith, Strauss and Denzin 1975, 226–227)

Because of his refusal to demonize drug users, and his belief that existing drug laws were too harsh, Lindesmith drew the ire of the U.S. Department of the Treasury, which had drug enforcement responsibilities. According to Howard Becker:

> After [Lindesmith] had done his dissertation and published an article or two, and he was at Indiana teaching, one day an agent from the Treasury Department showed up and told him he had to stop publishing this stuff.

And Lindy was a kind of bull-headed Midwest farmer, a no-nonsense kind of guy. The guy from the Treasury told him that if he didn't stop publishing, they would plant drugs in his office or his house and arrest him.

Although this did not occur, it was chilling for many drug researchers to realize that failure to embrace the dominant perspective on drug use could draw a backlash from sectors of the government (Campbell 2005a, 3)

With some of the key questions about the nature of addiction settled—at least for the time being—the focus of ethnographic drug research shifted in the years after Lindesmith began to publish his research. As noted, however, the line of ethnographic research on drug use that was beginning to develop during the 1930s stalled during the war and did not begin to regather momentum until the late 1950s and early 1960s.

Emic Research Contributions of Drug Users' Autobiographies

In the immediate post–World War II years, a period during which heroin began to flow back into the United States in increasing quantities and the number of inner-city drug users began to rise quickly, one must turn to a number of excellent autobiographies of drug users to gain socially contextualized and true-to-life accounts of drug use during this period. Several books, including *The Autobiography of Malcolm X* (1965), Claude Brown's *Manchild in the Promised Land* (1965), Piri Thomas's *Down These Mean Streets* (1967), and Richard Rettig, Manuel Torres, and Gerald Garrett's *Manny: A Criminal-Addict's Story* (1977) are particularly important resources in this regard.

Prior to his conversion to Islam and subsequent emergence as a charismatic and militant African American leader, Malcolm X spent a number of years (beginning during World War II) as a drug dealer. His specialty was marihuana, which he rolled into cigarettes ("reefers") and sold to musicians in Harlem. For a while, he even went on the road carrying a jar filled with marihuana "sticks" for sale to musicians in various East Coast cities. This association between the arts and drug use helped to create a street image of the drug user as a glamorous role worthy of emulation.

> In every band, a least half of the musicians smoked reefers. . . . I kept turning over my profit, increasing my supplies, and I sold reefers like a wild man. I scarcely slept; I was everywhere musicians congregated. A roll of money was in my pocket. Every day, I cleared at least fifty or sixty dollars. In those days . . . this was a fortune to a seventeen-year-old Negro. I felt, for the first time in my life, that great feeling of free! Suddenly, now, I was the peer of the other young hustlers I had admired. (Malcolm X 1965, 99)

Before long, Malcolm X caught the attention of the police. Under increasingly intense police pressure, he gave up selling marihuana and turned to other hustles. However, he continued to smoke marihuana and developed a dependence on cocaine that lasted until his arrest and imprisonment on burglary charges. In prison, he underwent a radical personal transformation that entailed both his conversion to Islam and his rejection of drug use.

As a result of his conversion to Islam, Malcolm X was never swallowed up by New York City's postwar heroin boom. By the time Claude Brown, a few years younger than Malcolm X, was 13, heroin was such a powerful attractant that he could hardly contain his desire to try it. Like Malcolm X, Brown was introduced to drug use by his friends, especially a group of older boys whom he greatly admired. They first taught him to use marihuana. When they moved on to heroin, which, among other names, was called "horse," he intensely wanted to join them. For several months in 1950, all he could think about was his desire for heroin.

> Horse was a new thing, not only in our neighborhood but in Brooklyn, the Bronx, and everyplace I went, uptown and downtown. It was like horse had just taken over. Everybody was talking about it. All the hip people were using it and snorting it and getting this new high. . . . I had been smoking reefers and had gotten high a lot of times, but I had the feeling that this horse was out of this world. (Brown 1965, 110–111)

Ultimately, Brown got his chance to try heroin.

> I couldn't believe it was really happening. I almost wanted to break out and laugh for joy, but I held back, and I snorted. . . . Something hit me right in the top of the head. It felt like a little spray of pepper on my brain. . . . Everything was getting rosy, beautiful. The sun got brighter in the sky and the whole day lit up and was twice as bright as it was before. . . . Everything was so slo-o-ow. (1965, 110–111)

Some heroin users report that their first exposure to the drug is extremely pleasurable—like love at first sight—and this leads to a long-term chase intended to relive that initial experience. Brown, however, had a different reaction. After a few moments of euphoria,

> my head seemed to stretch, and I thought my brain was going to burst. It was like a headache taking place all over the head at once and trying to break its way out. And then it seemed to get hot and hot and hot. And I was so slow . . . I got scared. I'd never felt this way before in my life. . . . My guts felt like they were going to come out. Everything was bursting out all at once, and there was nothing I could do. . . . And I said, "O Lawd, if you'll just give me one more chance, one more chance, I'll never get high again." (1965, 111)

During these years, in nearby Spanish Harlem, Piri Thomas, a boy of mixed Puerto Rican and African American heritage, was a member of the younger post-war generation that was coming of age and coming into contact with drugs. He recalled one of his earliest encounters with marihuana at age thirteen. Drinking whiskey with several friends, one of them produced a "stick" of marihuana and asked if he would like some.

> I felt its size. It was king-sized, a bomber. I put it to my lips and began to hiss my reserve away. It was going, going, going. I was gonna get a gone high. I inhaled. I held my nose, stopped up my mouth. I was gonna get a gone high . . . a gone high . . . a gone high . . . and then the stick was gone, burnt to a little bit of a roach. (Thomas 1967, 58)

Like Malcolm X and Claude Brown, Thomas was using and selling marihuana within a few years, and he was soon addicted to heroin. He also, like Malcolm X, wound up in prison, where his habit switched to benzedrine, phenobarbital, alcohol, strained shellac, and whatever else the inmates could get their hands on that would take them away from the stone-cold reality of prison life. Ultimately, he too overcame his addiction, although without religious conversion. He became an author and was active in drug rehabilitation.

A final autobiographical work of note focuses on the life history of Manuel Torres. In many ways, Torres's life story is the same as those that have been presented. A gang member from his early teens during the 1950s, he tried heroin under circumstances not very different from those of Claude Brown. Like Brown, his first experience with heroin was very unpleasant, but his uncle—his addict role model—encouraged Torres to try heroin a second time.

> So I snort again and hey, it's like the shit really hit the fan . . . you can't describe it. All the colors of Times Square tumble right over your forehead and explode in your eyeballs like a million, jillion shooting stars. . . . Everything's beautiful, and it's like nothing's happening baby but clear, crisp light. (Rettig, Torres and Garrett 1977, 33–34)

Torres was soon snorting heroin every day, and then his uncle showed him how to "skinpop" (subcutaneous drug injection). Before long, Torres was injecting heroin four times a day, not to achieve a rush but "just to maintain" (Rettig, Torres and Garrett 1977, 33). He began to "boost" (shoplift) to support his drug habit and then turned to armed robbery, which led to arrest and imprisonment. Many years later, reflecting on his life, Torres emphasized the political and economic origins of drug involvement among inner-city youth. Responding to a statement about Emile Durkheim's theory that the social role of criminals is to set the boundaries of acceptable behavior for the rest of society, Torres stated:

> That's fine if you're on the right side of the tracks. But what if you are locked into the streets and locked out of the jobs because of your

background or your dope habit? Hell, man, its simple for me to see, because I've been there. The social order created the drug problem and anything that comes of heroin addiction is their fault. Personal break-downs are an aspect of social breakdowns. (Rettig, Torres and Garrett 1977, 175)

These four autobiographical accounts and related material (e.g., Burroughs 1977; Courtwright, Joseph and Des Jarlais 1989; Pepper and Pepper 1994) clearly reveal the development of the postwar urban drug scene. Building on the image of the "cool" marihuana user of the depression and war years, the end of the World War II ushered in a period of significant increase in heroin use and addiction. The street addict, a social role in modern urban life (Stephens 1991), became a common sight on inner-city streets, as each new generation of youth—boys and girls alike—sought to prove themselves to their peers by adopting the valued image of a fearless drug adventurer. Alternative options and role models were few, and none seemed to offer as much opportunity to impoverished youth who felt the need to prove their worth to their peers or face rejection in the one arena—the streets—that offered any potential life validation. In the wake of the heroin "plague," however, Harlem and other U.S. inner cities changed. The sense of community that somehow had managed to survive the migration of African Americans from the South and Puerto Ricans from the island, the grinding poverty they encountered in their new northern and midwestern homes, and the fierce racial discrimination that undercut self-esteem and self-worth, now fell victim to widespread drug addiction among impoverished individuals who had nowhere to turn for drug money except robbery, burglary, prostitution, and other crimes against themselves, their families, and their neighbors.

Interestingly, rampant inner-city drug use after World War II did not attract much attention or real concern from the dominant society or from social scientists, except to the degree that drug users were mentioned as either psychologically damaged individuals or as criminal deviants in need of harsh punishment. In the social and behavioral science literature, drug addicts were portrayed as "either psychotic or neurotic casualties" (Inciardi 1992, 30). Among policy makers, drug users were of interest because of their involvement in crime and because they were assumed to come from ethnic minority communities. Strengthening the criminal justice approach to drug addiction, the Estes Kefauver Committee on Crime held a series of televised hearings that drew public attention to the role of drug use in criminal behavior. Meanwhile, a number of widely read popular magazines published alarmist articles about the rising peril of drug use. In light of the reigning, McCarthyite beliefs of this era, drug use was soon linked not only with property crimes but also with communism. In many ways, the re-emergence of drug ethnography in the 1960s was a direct response to the harsh view of drugs touted by the Drug Warriors of the postwar years.

Lessons from the Second Phase of Modernist Drug Ethnography

An issue of growing concern during this phase, characterized by very limited work on indigenous drug use, was the comprehension of urban addiction as a response to users' internal psychological factors or, conversely, to the pressures of social discrimination and marginalization among inner-city poor and people of color. To the degree that the lifeways of drug users were defined solely as responses to psychological or social conditions, the actual content of drug user culture remained of minimal concern, except as affirmation of the exotic and/or deviant nature of this social phenomenon.

Conclusion

The three stages in the development of drug ethnography examined in this chapter constitute the prehistory of the field—the period before a truly distinctive and named domain of professional research existed. Nonetheless, a lot was learned during this period about drug users and drug use through observation and participation. During the long stretch of time in which these three stages occurred, drug use slowly unfolded as an issue of health and social concern, with the result that drug users sometimes became the objects of social opprobrium or even outright brutality (e.g., during the period of Mexico's Inquisition). Those who employed descriptive methods that approximated ethnography differed in whether or not they saw drug use as a problem that warranted outside intervention. Thus, during the second stage, ethnographers' views of drug use depended upon which drug users they were viewing. The observed users varied in terms of both social location and motivation for taking psychotropic drugs, and ethnographers often differed in their appraisals of drug use and users. In and of itself, drug use is not inherently socially beneficial (e.g., contributing to recovery from social collapse as occurred among Native American peyote users) or socially damaging (e.g., expressing and magnifying social disruption as occurred among the street drug users studied by Dai). This point highlights the importance of the ethnographic approach, which is designed to study behavior in its natural social context without influence of prior prejudice.

3

Systematic Modernist Ethnography and Ethnopharmacology

In the late 1950s, an alternative to what had become the reigning view of drug users as social deviants began to appear. Its source was the qualitative, interactive study of drug users, and its focus came to be guided by what would come to be called the "drug use as subculture" paradigm. This transition marked the emergence of systematic drug ethnography and psychotropic ethnopharmacology. We refer to this period as modernist in the sense that it was characterized by the modern scientific understanding that if we are systematic and objective in data collection, we can understand foreign ways of life and develop accurate descriptions of the world's cultural patterns.

The Drug Use as Subculture Paradigm

One of the first qualitative studies to mark this turning point was conducted by sociologist Harold Finestone among African Americans in Chicago (1957). Though not based on ethnographic research *per se*, Finestone's office-based qualitative interviews with approximately fifty African American heroin addicts helped to focus social scientific attention on the existence of a worldview and subculture among drug addicts. In this work, Finestone sought to describe the ideal African American drug user role (the "cat") on the street, the often illegal income-generating activities needed to sustain a life organized around drug use (the "hustle"), and the behaviors and experiences involved in the actual consumption of drugs (the "kick"). As Feldman and Aldrich noted, Finestone's work began to shift the emphasis of qualitative drug studies away "from asking why people used drugs [and toward] asking how they went about getting involved in drug use and how they remained involved. . . . Ethnographers began to find their search for etiological influences in the social world rather than the internal [psychological] world of experimenters" (1990, 19). In other words, open-ended qualitative interviewing of drug users resulted in a movement away from psychoanalytic and psychiatric thinking, as seen in the work of researchers such as Dai, and began toward a more sociocultural and meaning-centered approach to drug use.

Interestingly, even the title of Finestone's most important paper, "Cats, Kicks, and Color" (1957a), reflects this shift toward a concern with drug user experience of "the life," the details of insider speech, and the contours of the subculture(s) of drug users. The change is further evidenced in two other seminal papers that ushered in the new orientation: Alan Sutter's "The World of the Righteous Dope Fiend" (1966), based on three years of fieldwork with addicts and non-addicts in Oakland, and, especially, Edward Preble and John Casey's classic "Taking Care of Business" (1969), which grew out of street research in New York. The primary objective of much of this literature was the holistic description of the people for whom drug use was said to be the central organizing mechanism of their lives. For example, in an effort to counter simplistic stereotypes of drug users, Preble and Casey argued:

> Their behavior is anything but an escape from life. They are actively engaged in meaningful activities and relationships seven days a week. The brief moments of euphoria after each administration of a small amount of heroin constitute a small fraction of their daily lives. The rest of the time they are actively, aggressively pursuing a career that is exacting, challenging, adventurous, and rewarding. They are always on the move and must be alert, flexible, and resourceful. (1969, 2)

In constructing their description, ethnographic researchers of this period tried to understand and represent the world as it was actually seen, lived, and experienced by hardcore drug users. To a large degree, this literature consists of fascinating and detailed accounts of the survival strategies used to sustain a drug-focused lifestyle, the underground economy of drug acquisition, processes of socialization into drug use social networks, the social settings that comprise drug users' social environments, the folk systems used to classify drug users in terms of their social statuses within the subculture, and the special street argot that developed to communicate issues of concern to drug users as well as a sense of in-group membership (and, equally importantly, to hide this information from outsiders, including the police). In short, the ethnographic literature on street drug use from the 1960s onward emphasizes that the lives of drug users are not without considerable cultural order and socially constructed meaning. Obtaining drugs and drug use as social activities provide the framework for this order. As Preble and Casey commented:

> The heroin user walks with a fast purposeful stride, as if he is late for an important appointment—indeed, he is. He is hustling (robbing and

stealing), trying to sell stolen goods, avoiding the police, looking for a heroin dealer with a good bag (the street unit of heroin), coming back from copping (buying heroin), looking for a safe place to take the drug, or looking for someone who beat (cheated) him—among other things. He is, in short, *taking care of business*, a phrase which is so common with heroin users that they use it in response to words of greeting, such as "how you doing?" and "what's happening?" *Taking care of biz* is the common abbreviation. Ripping and running is an older phrase which also refers to their busy lives. For them . . ., the quest for heroin is the quest for a meaningful life. . . . And the meaning does not lie, primarily, in the effects of the drugs on their minds and bodies; it lies in the gratification of accomplishing a series of challenging, exciting tasks, every day of the week. (1969, 2–3)

In addition to structural behaviors and social meaning, researchers identified a set of distinctive values. For example, Sutter noted that, within the subculture, "prestige in the hierarchy of a dope fiend's world is allocated by the size of a person's habit and his success as a hustler" (1966, 195). Sutter also observed that heroin users at the peak of the drug status hierarchy worked hard to maintain their position and lifestyle. More broadly, on the street, Harvey Feldman found that heroin users were seen as having

positive qualities of creativity, daring and resourcefulness that provide the impetus for the top level solid guys (persons of established status) to rise to the top of the street hierarchy. Rather than retreating from the demands of their environment, they utilized the risks of heroin to ensure (or strive toward) a leadership position. Their use of heroin solidifies a view of them as bold, reckless, criminally defiant—all praiseworthy qualities from a street perspective. (1973, 38)

These accounts, shaped by an emergent "drug use as subculture" paradigm (Johnson 1980), took researchers a long way from earlier conceptions of drug users. As summarized by Friedman and colleagues with reference to drug injectors:

In contrast to views that see IV drug use as simply a matter of individual pathology, it is more fruitful to describe IV drug users as constituting a "subculture" as this term has been used within sociological and anthropological research. . . . This calls our attention to the structured sets of values, roles, and status allocations that exist among IV drug users. . . . From the perspective of its members, participating in the subculture is a meaningful activity that provides desired rewards, rather than psychopathology, an "escape from reality," or an "illness." Although there are regional and ethnic variations, it is nonetheless possible to analyze those who inject cocaine and/or heroin in the United States as constituting a single subculture in this sense. (Friedman, Des Jarlais, and Sotheran 1986, 385)

In short, ethnographers of drug use working in the period just before the appearance of AIDS tried to show that even under difficult circumstances—or more precisely, because of difficult circumstances—a subculture can emerge that is as meaningful and dear to its participants as it is alien and repugnant to "outsiders." Further, they attempted to counter earlier images of the urban drug user framed by the paradigms of psychopathology and the sociology of criminal deviance. Often, in so doing, however, they turned their attention away from the wider social context that fosters drug use and the intense social suffering it often expresses, and instead emphasized the microsocial world of the drug users in holistic culturalist terms (Waterston 1993).

Anthropological and Sociological Rapprochement in Drug Ethnography

Before long, a growing number of sociologists, including individuals such as Howard Becker, Peter Adler, James Inciardi, and Harvey Siegal, came to the realization that not only were they interested in studying drug use but they preferred the face-to-face contact with drug users that ethnography demanded over the administration of survey instruments devised for use in probability samples. Their involvement in ethnography from the platform of sociology built a cadre of sociological ethnographers with whom anthropological ethnographers compared notes and began to collaborate. As Howard Becker recalled, "Michael Agar was a member of the NRC [National Research Council] committee. Marsha Rosenbaum and that whole gang, I knew out here, Sheigla Murphy and Dan Waldorf. We all overlap so much" (Campbell 2005a). In this way, the disciplinary divide that had characterized earlier periods in the ethnographic study of drug use began to diminish.

Becker's own interest in drug use began in 1943 at age fifteen, when a fellow member of a student band offered to share a joint with him. As a young musician, Becker met many drug users, and he learned about drug use directly. He recalled:

I knew a lot of junkies. In fact one of the drummers I worked with, he wanted to be a junkie, he thought it was really quite romantic, but he had a physiological thing, he really couldn't tolerate opiate drugs so every time he'd inhale heroin, he'd run off and vomit almost immediately. He finally had to give it up. There were a lot of junkies around. It just never tempted me because I could see how much trouble it was. (Campbell 2005a)

When he read Alfred Lindesmith's book *Opiate Addiction* (1947), and later befriended Lindesmith, Becker's interest in the topic grew. After getting his Ph.D. at the University of Chicago (at age twenty-three), where he was strongly influenced by the Chicago School perspective on urban life, Becker got a job at the Institute for Juvenile Research, which was an Illinois state agency. Two senior delinquency researchers at the institute, Clifford Shaw and Henry McKay, had been awarded a large NIMH grant to study teenage opiate addiction. Driven by his enduring interest in marihuana use, Becker proposed a substudy of that topic, which Shaw and McKay initially thought was unimportant because marihuana was not seen as habit-forming and, hence, did not pose a social problem. Becker nonetheless gained approval for his idea.

Becker's research on marihuana use led to his book, *Outsiders* (1963), which became a sociological classic. This book, which examined both marihuana users and musicians, mobilized (and helped to create) labeling theory as an approach to the study of deviance. Labeling theory stresses that deviance is not an expression of an individual's internal qualities, but it is the result of someone else—someone with the necessary public authority—who labels specific behavior, such as smoking marihuana, as naturally bad. As Becker indicated, "The deviant is one to whom that label has successfully been applied; deviant behavior is behavior that people so label" (1963, 9). Once labeled as "deviant," people are inclined to seek out others who bear a similar social label, leading to the emergence of a deviant subculture. Becker defined this subculture as a group sharing "a set of perspectives and understandings about what the world is like and how to deal with it" (1963, 38). Involvement in such a subculture offers the labeled deviant social justification for his or her behavior, making it "more likely than ever before [for the deviant] to continue in his ways" (Becker 1963, 39).

Before leaving the drug field for other pursuits, Becker wrote two papers on the use of LSD in which he addressed a topic that had long interested him about marihuana: How do people learn to interpret and provide meaning for their own internal, and often ambiguous, sensations under the influence of drugs?

Components of the drug-use-as-subculture tradition were carried on by a second generation of researchers whose drug research careers often began just before and then extended into the era of the AIDS epidemic. Several seminal ethnographic studies were produced by this second generation, including Michael Agar's *Ripping and Running* (1973), Dan Waldorf's *Careers in Dope* (1973), Bill Hanson, George Beschner, James Walters, and Elliot Bovelle's *Life with Heroin* (1985), the volume by Bruce Johnson tellingly titled *Taking Care of Business: The Economics of Crime by Heroin Abusers* (1985), and Feldman, Agar, and Beschner's *Angel Dust in Four American Cities* (1980). Each of these studies, primarily written in a normal science voice from a "drug user lifestyle perspective," made important ethnographic contributions to the drug field. In so doing, however, as is common in scientific research, they produced findings that called into question aspects of their guiding paradigm.

Michael Agar: The Dope Double Agent

Agar's study, a formal (or ethnosemantic) ethnography of heroin addicts and the categories of cognitive organization for everyday events, was based on two years of fieldwork with patients at the NIMH Clinical Research Center in Lexington, Kentucky, a federal drug treatment hospital. He described his approach as follows:

> I would spend time hanging around in the patients' areas of the institution, listening and trying to learn how they viewed the world by attending to how they talked about it. . . . After doing this for several months, and after conducting several informal interviews and assembling a dictionary of slang, I began to worry about being more systematic. So I worked up three interlinked methods to help me display my understanding of the junkie world view. (1996, 137–138)

These methods, which were suggested by a wider anthropological turn toward viewing culture as a shared cognitive template for enacting socially appropriate behavior, were: the *simulated situation* (recording drug user enactments or simulations of real street drug-related behaviors like "copping" [buying] drugs and "getting off" [using drugs]), the *frame elicitation* (a fill-in-the-blanks approach in which the study participant was handed a card or read a statement about some aspect of drug use and asked to use his experience to complete the sentence), and the *hypothetical situation* (in which the participant was told about a life situation drawn from prior data collection and asked to select from possible courses of action). Based on these methods (both formal and informal), Agar was able to construct an "experience like" account of key scenes, concepts, relationships, artifacts, activities, and experiences that comprised the street drug user's lifestyle. Later, Agar was able to test the ethnographic validity of his understanding in New York City (Agar 1977) and became a pioneering proponent of intense street ethnography among heroin users. For example, one of the issues of interest to Agar in his Lexington study was life-event analysis.

> One event that I heard discussed was "hanging out." By listening and later asking questions, I learned that hanging out was a filler, a sort of nonevent while waiting for other things to happen. . . . When I worked in the streets in New York, I found myself actually hanging out with junkies on street corners and coffee shops. They were usually waiting for something else to occur, but hanging out served many useful purposes. While they hung out, they exchanged information critical for "getting over" on the streets. . . . The street scene was a social environment that could

change rapidly because of outside pressures beyond one's control. Hanging out was used to keep posted on the current state of that environment. . . . In this case, then, the observation on the streets corrected the account I received in the hospital. (Agar 1996, 108–109)

In other words, Agar came to realize that "hanging out" was not just a "filler" at all, but it was instead a vital survival activity. This insight helped to explain part of the reason why inner-city drug users spend so much of their day moving about on the street (hustling, or raising money to buy drugs, is the other primary reason, although "scoring" [finding and buying] desirable drugs can, on occasion, take up street time as well).

Another component of Agar's study was an attempt to understand the lives and behaviors of drug users as patients in drug treatment. In other words, in addition to eliciting information about life on the streets, he also was concerned with the experience of life in an institution. Here, Agar was able to address ethnographically some of the issues he encountered as he learned about staff attitudes and assessments of patients. One of his insights in this regard was that some of the very behaviors (e.g., strong skepticism, constant suspicion, and testing of dependability) that staff cited as evidence that patients were maladapted and lacked appropriate values, goals, and rules of proper social behavior, were in fact quite appropriate to survival on the streets where there are many threats that often come in human form.

In subsequent years, after moving away from drug studies for a time, Agar turned his attention to understanding trends in drug use patterns over time. In examining cocaine, for example, he pointed out that shifts in patterns of cocaine production, such as out-sourcing of tasks to smaller drug groups by the large illicit drug corporations, and the movements of populations, including the migration of people from the Caribbean to Miami, Los Angeles, and New York, were important social changes that helped to foster the development and spread of a new product like crack (2003). The invention of crack marked the beginning of a shift in the cocaine trade from an emphasis on the high-end marketing of expensive snortable powder to a reliance on poor and working-class people as the primary cocaine market. As Agar and Reisinger pointed out, producers lowered their risk of being caught by locating needed production processes, such as mixing ingredient chemicals, producing Ecstasy tablets, and preparing tablets for international shipments, in different sites. Agar and Reisinger maintained that a "fluid and modular structure," within and across allied drug-dealing organizations and internationally with players of diverse nationalities (in contrast with the ethnic-centered Mafia model), is the post-modern style of the Ecstasy industry (1999, 367). With regard to the War on Drugs, Agar argued: "Drugs are great for what I call chemical scapegoating. The anthropologist Lévi-Strauss once described totemism by saying 'animals are good to think with' [i.e., they provide readily available symbols to use in organizing conception]. Drugs, on the other hand, are good to *blame* with" (2007, 20).

Heath and Marshall

While Agar examined street drug use in the city, other anthropologists of this period, such as Dwight Heath and Mac Marshall, continued on the path blazed by Lowie and La Barre and initiated ethnographic studies of drug use in non-Western and nonurban cultural settings during the mid-twentieth century.

Dwight Heath's ethnography of alcohol use among the Camba, a *mestizo* population that, when he began studying them, were engaged in slash-and-burn horticulture in a forested area of eastern Bolivia, called into question the view that drug use is inherently disruptive and that continued use is inevitably addicting and damaging to health when consumed in strong preparations and in high volumes (1958, 1991). In his research on traditional drinking patterns among the Camba, which involved the consumption of 186-proof rum during festivals and rites of passage, Heath found that most adult Camba drank and became intoxicated for several days in a row on at least two occasions per month. Further, getting drunk was socially valued and was the explicit goal of drinking. Nevertheless, neither alcoholism (as defined in the literature) nor any antisocial patterns such as aggression, sexual disinhibition, or alcohol-related failure to fill social responsibilities, was found by Heath. Instead, he reported that alcohol made integrative and functional contributions to the group's social health, including facilitating "rapport between individuals who are normally isolated and introverted" (Heath 1991, 76). As a result, and based on the examination of the literature on groups, Heath promoted, and over the years continued to develop, a positive sociocultural model of alcohol use as an alternative to moral, criminal, and disease models of heavy drinking.

Notably, however, Heath found that patterns of drinking changed. Among the Camba, these changes occurred as the forests were cut down by the lumber industry—to fund large sugar refineries and to clear land for large-scale cotton and cattle-raising enterprises—and their traditional way of life became untenable. As a result, many Camba lost their land and, with it, their customary patterns of drinking. At the same time, the Camba economy was "displaced by the illegal trade in coca and cocaine paste" (Heath 2004, 132). In other words, Heath's work suggests that while traditional, community-controlled, and socially integrative drug use occurs, it tends to be in settings where the drugs in question are produced for use (not as commodities sold on the market) and in which community social life has not been disrupted by the forces of globalization.

Mac Marshall, in his studies of tobacco and alcohol use in Micronesia and Melanesia, noted that both of these legal drugs had entered the cultural contexts in question as internationally produced and marketed commodities (1979). He used formal ethnographic methods to characterize the disruptive and potentially health-threatening patterns of drinking found in young Micronesian males. His conclusions, in retrospect, provided a perspective that complemented Heath's, anticipating Heath's own findings about the latter-day Camba. The young male drinkers described in *Weekend Warriors* (1979) approached alcohol use as a behavior not circumscribed by community ritual, available for sale, and unrestricted by rules of comportment or decorum. Likewise, the Melanesian drinkers described in *Through a Glass Darkly* (1983) exemplify the growing pains of modernization as seen in the use of alcohol in Papua New Guinea.

Marshall's first works on alcohol use in the western Pacific focused primarily on the behavior of males and, in that sense, did not offer a gendered approach to the complex of alcohol-consuming behaviors. In *Silent Voices Speak* (1990), however, he and Leslie Marshall took advantage of an ethnographic opportunity to study a major social change in the form of Truk alcohol prohibition—a process in which women played a major role. The dynamics of gender relations in deciding the desirability of consuming drugs are important in detecting the signs of dysfunction and need for reform. These issues received a thoughtful and thorough treatment in *Silent Voices Speak.*

Ethnographers of Non-Western, Shamanistic Drug Use: One at a Time

Whereas Schultes attempted to characterize as many patterns of drug use as he could, the ethnographers described in the following narratives conducted intensive ethnographies of a single pattern. Marlene Dobkin de Rios intensively described the use of ayahuasca among *curanderos* in Iquitos, Peru, emphasizing the use of this hallucinogenic preparation as a strategy for identifying the cause of disease. In a demonstration of ethnographic immersion and commitment that is not uncommon for anthropologists, Dobkin de Rios married her key informant, making possible highly intense, extensive, firsthand learning about the complex of *mestizo curandería* associated with ayahuasca in eastern Peru (1970, 1971, 1972a, 1972b). Drug ethnographers such as Dobkin de Rios achieved an intimate understanding of specific cultural complexes of drug use and usually linked their practitioners' beliefs about the drugs' efficacy to accomplishing the stated objectives of use. She recognized the potentially life-changing impact that a dose of ayahuasca could have for an individual and attempted to understand that impact in terms of the cultural context from which the users came. On the other hand, she did not venture into the realm of theory about the relationship between ayahuasca use and the large-scale social and economic processes in which it took place.

Similarly, Peter Furst's work on the Huichol and peyote involved a highly focused ethnographic investigation of peyote use patterns among a Native

American group in Mexico, including detailed descriptions of the process of procuring the cactus buttons and the ritual connected with their consumption (1972). Beliefs about the healing impact of the peyote consumption ritual also received attention in this account. Despite the lack of theoretical orientation, Furst's work gives the student of drug use patterns some exotic examples of drug using behavior. He simply leaves it to others to find relationships between the Huichol peyote complex and other manifestations of drug use among humans.

Johannes Wilbert deserves mention here as an ethnographer of non-Western patterns of tobacco use. In its noncommodified cultural context among the Warao of Venezuela, tobacco has very different uses and meanings from those seen in the United States and Western Europe. Without generating influential theories about drug use and its origins, he provided a provocative counter example of how people approach what we would call a "commodity drug." The Warao patterns he described resemble those of the Camba in Heath's baseline reports—ritually circumscribed consumption of a drug preparation that is not commodified, yielding very different effects from the ones familiar to Western readers. The high potency of preparations used in the Warao tobacco use patterns also parallel the potency of the Camba's high potency alcohol.

Although they did not generate overarching theories on drug use among human beings, the modernist ethnographers of the mid-twentieth century contributed some new perspectives on these behaviors. The cultural contexts characterized by Dobkin de Rios, Furst, Wilbert, and others added valuable knowledge of how the human condition varies in its interaction with plant-derived drugs.

Drug Use and Public Health: Early Initiatives

Political action seldom is driven by scientific curiosity, and the initiative to document the ill effects of marihuana on users was no exception. In reconstructing events of 1971–1973, we can surmise the following sequence of events. (1) The Shafer Report (1972), produced by a blue ribbon panel that reviewed marihuana use in the United States, questioned its legal status as a schedule 1 narcotic. (2) Richard Nixon, who regarded marihuana use as a characteristic of his political "enemies" (subversives and antiwar zealots), rejected the Shafer Report. (3) John Mitchell, Nixon's attorney general (who would later be convicted), suggested to Nixon that the problem with detecting severe consequences of marihuana use in U.S. populations of users was the relative inexperience of the users, who tended to have no more than four or five years' experience with the drug. Mitchell convinced Nixon to direct his secretary of health, education, and welfare to fund studies of long-term marihuana smokers on the assumption that, with use histories greater than ten years, populations of Cannabis users outside of the United States would demonstrate all kinds of deficits in comparison with nonusers. (4) Eleanor Carroll, a project officer for the about-to-be formed National Institute on Drug Abuse[1] was asked to find prospective contractors for two or three large studies of Cannabis use in countries that had truly long-term users. This sequence of events set in motion a scientific process that would eventually demonstrate features of Cannabis use about which President Nixon did not want to know.

Ms. Carroll contacted the Research Institute for the Study of Man at Columbia University and the Center for Latin American Studies at the University of Florida. Vera Rubin and Lambros Comitas had already identified project sites in Jamaica where they would test *ganja* users and nonusers in Kingston and conduct in-depth ethnographies of drug use in rural villages to develop an understanding of that drug's impact on health and its place in rural Jamaican life. They therefore received the first contract to study long-term Cannabis use, and they presented their findings in a book, *Ganja in Jamaica* (1975).

Feasibility inquiries were conducted before deciding where to conduct the study, and conditions were checked in Brazil, Colombia, and Costa Rica before deciding on Costa Rica (Carter 1980). All three countries had medical facilities capable of conducting the tests that the contract offer demanded, but Brazil, at the time under control of a military junta, had death squads operating in the streets of its cities, and this condition made fieldwork too risky a prospect. In Colombia, the population of long-term users (characterized in Partridge 1974) lived near sea level, but the medical facilities were in Bogotá at a considerably higher altitude (3,000 meters). Given the highly sensitive tests to be conducted, the altitude differential would have presented a confounding variable that, along with the logistical problems of transporting study participants to Bogotá, would have made the tests very difficult to accomplish. In Costa Rica, the feasibility determinations were completely favorable—a population of long-term users, a new, well-equipped hospital in which to conduct tests with the help of well-trained physicians and staff, and a relatively easy commute from users' homes to the hospital.

The difference between this study and the one conducted in Jamaica involved the recruitment and testing of the same people for both the medical and the ethnographic phases of the study. Both studies had extensive ethnographic components; the Jamaican study followed the traditional anthropological model of finding a community and studying its people's use of *ganja* in a cultural context (Rubin and Comitas 1975), and the Costa Rican study attempted a contextual study in various urban neighborhood settings (Carter 1980). These ethnographic components had several scientific uses: In the Jamaican study, the ethnography gave the reader a sense of the link between mind-altering and medicinal uses of the plant in a traditional setting, as well as adaptations used to determine whether *ganja* was suitable for certain individuals' use (Rubin and Comitas 1975). In Costa Rica, the research team relied on ethnographic findings to determine whether or not users and nonusers met the criteria for inclusion in the medical phases of the study. Self-reports of Cannabis use or nonuse were verifiable by observation and by asking other neighborhood residents (who may or may not smoke Cannabis) to corroborate these reports. Ethnographers also kept track of where to find participants for follow-up studies and collected observational data on household conditions and nutrition. Finally, after developing a rapport with the study participants through all of these study processes, the ethnographers conducted in-depth interviews on the life and drug use histories of all 84 participants in the matched-pair phase of the study (Carter 1980).[2]

The third study in this cohort of Cannabis studies focused on hashish smoking in Greece (Stefanis, Dornbush, and Fink 1977). It did not employ ethnographic methods to the same extent as the other two, but Lambros Comitas served as a consultant on that study, bringing some cultural insight to the proceedings.

In terms of the political landscape in which these studies developed and presented their results, a new commitment by the National Institutes of Health began with the initiative to study the consequences of Cannabis use. Before 1971, most of the NIH's time and resources were dedicated to identifiable (if not fully characterized) disease complexes, such as infectious diseases, cancer, and mental illness. In the case of Cannabis, the problems related to its use remained questionable and ill-defined, and the executive branch of the federal government set out to clarify them through science. This approach backfired, because both the Jamaican and the Costa Rican studies pointed out that, in different cultural contexts, the effects suggested by initial studies in the United States (e.g., lowered serum testosterone in males—Kolodny et al. 1974; amotivational syndrome—McGlothlin and West 1968, Smith 1970) could not be verified, even at relatively high levels of use.[3]

Not long after the Cannabis researchers began to publish their findings, NIDA established committees for the review of support-of-research applications, engaging, as had been the pattern in the NIH for several decades, extramural reviewers (i.e., non-NIDA employees), including Lambros Comitas. For about four years during the middle and late 1970s, he advocated in review committee meetings for support of applications that had strong ethnographic components, sometimes aided by additional anthropologists and sociologists. In addition, Eleanor Carroll served as a project officer and advocated for ethnographic research on drug use (until her death in 1977). These factors did not result in a burgeoning field of ethnographic studies of drug use, but they succeeded in supporting a core of ethnographic researchers, including Michael Agar, James Inciardi, J. Bryan Page, Harvey Siegal, Wayne Weibel, Patricia

[Cleckner] Morningstar, Dan Waldorf, Marsha Rosenbaum, and Sheigla Murphy, who continued and elaborated a subfield of drug ethnography that met the specific criterion for funding by the NIH: The study must have relevance to health. As this pattern of support developed in NIDA, the agency experienced growth in its available funding.

Dan Waldorf's Career in Dope

Despite the conservative impetus to provide information on drug use for the purpose of preventing it or stamping it out, investigators funded by NIDA engaged in studies that did not necessarily assume deviance among users of illegal drugs. Dan Waldorf's *Careers in Dope* (1973) was based on a concept introduced into the Chicago research tradition by Everett C. Hughes and first applied to drug use by Becker in his important study of the pathway to becoming a marihuana user and the social contexts and relations that perpetuate drug use (1953). The "career" concept in drug research implies that, like a professional in a field of employment (like drug research), it is possible to identify standardized stages and transitions in the processual development of a drug user's life. The heroin drug use career in the inner city, argued Waldorf, begins early in life.

> Heroin is seemingly everywhere in Black and Puerto Rican ghettos and young people are aware of it from an early age. They know of heroin and addicts through close scrutiny—they see the endless trade of money for white power; they see the user nodding on the front stoop; they watch him "get off" in the communal bathroom down the hall; they see his theft of the family TV set. It is a wonder, not that so many ghetto dwellers become users and addicts, but that the majority, somehow, someway, resist this powerful drug that offers relief from the oppressive environment. (1973, 6)

Waldorf noted that large numbers of youth from disadvantaged households had few experiences of legitimate employment upon which to build a "straight" lifestyle. Instead, they developed "elaborate deviant identities and ideologies" centered around drug use (Waldorf, Reinarman, and Murphy 1991, 220). Waldorf examined the survival strategies and established subcultural roles in the drug use world upon which these alternative identities and ideologies were based. He observed that street drug users had to spend many hours each day planning and carrying out some form of income-generating hustle. Drug dealing, he noted, was considered one of the better hustles available to street drug users, although the primary "career path" open to them in the drug trade was as a low-level street "juggler" who sold small quantities of drugs to fellow addicts.

Waldorf found that not all lifestyles had equal status among heroin users. For example, he described the following case of an individual who was ostracized even by fellow addicts:

> After leaving prison . . . he became addicted once more and started to steal from home, pawning his mother's new radio and shoplifting. His mother forced him out of the house, and he started to sleep in cellars, which he had always hated, and developed pustular fungus sores all over his body. Although he had formerly been very careful and neat about his appearance and bathing, he now no longer cared, went downhill, and did all the things he had previously loathed. He slept in a rat-infested cellar that frequently drained human waste from overflowing toilets down on him. He lived this way for nearly three years going home on and off, until he became an outcast among junkies, no mean feat. They could not understand how he could live the way he did and described him as disgusting. (1973, 148)

At the terminal end of the "dope," Waldorf examined untreated natural recovery from heroin addiction, a transition out of drug use, or "retirement" in the career model, that many had assumed was not possible, or at least extremely rare (Waldorf and Biernacki 1981). He found that many former heroin users "drifted out" of drug use without significant problems because they had never been highly committed to the drug or the drug user lifestyle. Some of the untreated former heroin addicts studied by Waldorf intentionally tried the drug after quitting and successfully proved to themselves that they were no longer addicted and could elect not to resume regular use despite reexposure. Waldorf also led one of the first modern ethnographic studies of cocaine use (Waldorf et al. 1977) and later used an ethnographic approach to study long-term careers among cocaine users. One important finding of the latter study was the identification of a protracted career path among some cocaine users that involved continuous controlled consumption.

> Cocaine is an alluring drug. It has many uses. It has become widely available. For all of these reasons users often escalate their doses. But approximately half of our subjects sustained a controlled use pattern for periods ranging from a year or two to a decade. Our definition of "controlled use" is a pattern in which users do not ingest more than they want to and which does not result in any dysfunction in the roles and responsibilities of daily life. (Waldorf, Reinarman, and Murphy 1991, 265)

Multisited Drug Ethnography: Addiction as a Way of Life

The Heroin Lifestyle Study (HLS) that led to the writing of *Life with Heroin* (Hanson et al. 1985) was carried out in the inner-city areas of Chicago, New York

City, Washington, D.C., and Philadelphia. Study participants consisted of 124 African American men. All were regular heroin users and most had "never received or wanted any form of drug treatment" (Hanson et al. 1985, 1). This disinclination to enter treatment was a primary focus of the study. Specifically, the study was designed to "accurately pass on the rich, descriptive firsthand accounts of the daily lives of Black heroin users . . .; and second, to search for and analyze emergent patterns which reveal the complex social and psychological mosaic that comprises the contemporary Black inner-city heroin lifestyle" (Hanson et al. 1985, 2). Ironically, one important finding of the study concerns the validity of assuming that there is a distinctive heroin lifestyle that is separate from the basic lifestyle pattern of the surrounding inner-city community. As two members of the HLS research team noted:

> An unexpected finding is that the HLS men live rather structured lives in which successive daily time periods are spent engaging in a variety of fairly predictable and even conventional activities. Like men in straight society, they arise early in order to spend many of their waking hours "on the job"—but in their case, this usually means hustling in pursuit of the wherewithal to maintain their once-a-day, relatively controlled heroin habits. (Bovelle and Taylor 1985, 175–176)

Importantly, it was the "pursuit of normalcy" (under conditions of marked social inequality and lack of opportunity) rather than escape or exhilaration that was found to drive the continued use of heroin among study participants. Also noteworthy was the control that participants exercised over their drug habits, a refutation of the common assertion that regular heroin users "have an insatiable and uncontrollable appetite for heroin and that they therefore shoot up as many times as possible each day" (Bovelle and Taylor 1985, 177). In short, as Waldorf and coworkers had done among cocaine users, the HLS identified a stratum of daily heroin users who did not fit reigning stereotypes about this population nor even ethnographic descriptions of other inner-city heroin users, revealing both the changing nature of the heroin scene and a notable heterogeneity of drug using populations.

One insight of the Preble and Casey study (1969) was that street drug users are key players in a street economy that involves the redistribution of goods that are stolen from stores, warehouses, or other locations and sold on the streets or to local stores and restaurants at discount prices. Bourgois, in fact, credited this "enormous, uncensored, untaxed underground economy" with being one of the main factors that allows the poor to avoid rampant malnutrition and high rates of morbidity and mortality in oppressed inner-city areas (2003, 3). Ethnographically exploring the drug user role in the underground economy was the focus of the research presented by Johnson in *Taking Care of Business* (1985). Working from field research stations set up in East Harlem (Spanish Harlem) and Central Harlem in New York City, the project staff, composed of researchers and recovering drug addicts, recruited 201 active drug users and interviewed them concerning income generating and spending patterns. Each participant was interviewed for five consecutive days and then once a week over the next month (with additional follow-up interviews at the East Harlem site). Specific issues of concern were legal and illegal sources of income, types of illegal activities, arrest records, and daily expense information. The study produced a massive amount of data, which was synthesized by Johnson and his team to clarify the size, scope, and character of the underground economy and its interrelationship with the aboveground economy. The team found a wide range of illegal income activities including burglary, robbery, forgery, con games, prostitution, pimping, stripping abandoned buildings, drug sales, and many legal "hustles" such as panhandling and the collection of discarded items. Notably, they found that daily heroin users had an average yearly income of $18,710 (all of which they spent fairly quickly after it was "earned"), although included in this total was "income" gained by avoiding expenses (e.g., jumping over the gate at a subway station to evade paying the fare). With the economic data that were collected, Johnson and coworkers performed various calculations to assess the economic impact of the drug use–driven informal economy. Unlike other researchers who sought to demonstrate only the negative effects of drug-related crime, Johnson and his team identified benefits to the community. For example, they assessed the economic impact involved in a drug user stealing a $400 color television from someone's home and selling it to a merchant (who, in turn, sells it to a customer) for money to use in buying drugs. According to Johnson, "one person—the individual victim—had a substantial loss, but that loss was offset by the direct and immediate gains to four other parties: the burglar, the purchaser of the stolen television, the retail merchant, and the drug seller" (1985, 117).

Central to this argument is the idea that even when an item like a television is stolen, it does not necessarily disappear from the economy; it is merely redistributed (even if most of the monetary profits of drug sales are extracted rather than recirculated in poor neighborhoods). Importantly, this study revealed how the underground and aboveground economies are, in fact, one economy. This was an important step away from thinking of drug users as comprising a self-contained microsocial world.

Angel Dust: An Ethnographic Study of Phencyclidine Users (1979) was a particularly important contribution to the literature on drug use for a number of reasons. The edited volume was a product of a collaborative multisited ethnographic study carried out simultaneously in four cities (Miami, Philadelphia, Chicago, and Seattle) using a common research protocol. The study was initiated because of reports that PCP (phencyclidine, an animal tranquilizer with hallucinogenic properties) was becoming popular among some youth as a regularly consumed psychoactive drug. However, little was known about the recreational use of PCP, including when the substance had made its way into youth drug use networks or its role in such networks. Agar casually described the origin and evolution of the study in the following terms:

> A NIDA staff member with ethnographic tendencies (he had been a street worker in New York) decided to try an ethnographic study. He asked that a small team of ethnographers be assembled to get some preliminary feel for the situation. Because of the time rush and money constraints, four ethnographers were selected who had done good ethnography with drug users in the past. Further, because of their ongoing work, they all had rapport so that they could begin work immediately. . . . The group met for 2 days to work out a strategy for doing the ethnographies. Informal interviews were to be the focus. In addition, the group came up with a four-page guide to specific items of information that would be easy to get from each informant. (1996, 200)

The study found that PCP had entered youth drug networks in all four target cities in 1973, increased in popularity through 1974, and began to lose its appeal the following year (although it never completely disappeared from the youth drug scene and continues to have periods of renewed popularity [Holland et al. 1998]). An examination of NIDA's annual national survey of drug use among high school seniors for the mid-1970s, however, did not include findings on PCP use. As Feldman and Aldrich remark, "the PCP phenomenon entered the world of youth and diminished without the national data system ever identifying it" (1990, 22). When questions about PCP were finally added to the Monitoring the Future Study in 1979, lifetime prevalence for use among 12th graders was found to be 2.4 percent (falling over the years to 1.4 percent in 1991) (Johnston, O'Malley, and Bachman 1997).

The Angel Dust study also found that exclusive PCP use was rare and that its greatest appeal was among especially restless youth who found life to be generally boring and uninteresting. The participants in the study appeared to be quite familiar with the drug's effects and how to modulate them by controlling dosage levels. Of special concern to regular PCP users was a state they referred to as "burn out" in which the user exhibits memory loss and incoherent thoughts. Cutting back on consumption of PCP emerged as the folk strategy for controlling burn out.

One consequence of the PCP study was the realization that ethnography, a method commonly seen as requiring a protracted period of rapport-building and ever-more-penetrative data collection, was found to be especially useful for the rapid assessment of emergent drug trends. Wayne Weibel, who carried out the Chicago arm of the four-city PCP study, noted:

> Generally speaking there appear to be two factors that contribute to the importance of qualitative methodologies in the field of substance abuse

research. First, continually evolving patterns and trends of substance abuse within our society foster a fluid situation in which emergent and novel phenomena are integral facets of today's drug scene.... When attempting to construct a meaningful data collection instrument for drug-related research, the researcher must gain sufficient a priori familiarity with the topic to frame appropriate, meaningful questions. Such knowledge is the province and product of qualitative methodologies.... The second factor confirming the value of qualitative methods in the substance abuse field relates more to the types of information required of research.... Clearly, qualitative research is often the only appropriate means available for gathering sensitive and valid data from otherwise elusive populations of drug abusers. (Feldman, Agar, and Beschner 1980, 4–5)

As Bourgois pointed out, the productivity of ethnography in drug use research stems from the fact that the reason drug users are elusive is that they "live on the margins of a society that is hostile to them" (2003, 13). By design, ethnography is a methodology that incorporates rapport-building, self-disclosure, nonjudgmental sensitivity, genuine concern with the insider's perspective and experience, and involvement in the lives of study participants into its approach to data collection. These features of ethnography provide a basis for the establishment of "relations based on trust . . . [that allow the researcher] to ask provocative personal questions, and expect thoughtful, serious answers" from individuals who have learned to be extremely wary (Bourgois 2003, 13). In addition, ethnography offers a means of accessing hard-to-reach populations of drug users and background information on them that is useful in the construction of good surveys. By taking the researcher into the world of the drug user, it also fosters the development of important hypotheses and research questions and empowers the researcher to produce interpretations of findings grounded in the social, cultural, and experiential realities of the study population. Recognition of these strengths by at least some research sponsors helped set the stage for a public health agenda that dramatically influenced street drug studies during the last decades of the twentieth century.

Lessons from Ethnography

The pathway into a drug use research career varied considerably among leaders in the field. Some, such as Becker, developed an interest because drug use among friends and peers raised questions that they hoped to answer through research. For Becker and others, drugs *per se* were not the primary issue of interest; rather, they offered an arena through which to explore more general questions: "For a lot of people, drugs was [*sic*] not really what we wanted to do, but it was a good field to do what we wanted to do. So it worked for us"

(Campbell 2005a). Others, such as Bruce Johnson, had little personal exposure to drug use prior to taking it on as a research topic.

> Looking back, to say that I was naïve about drugs would be a rather considerable understatement. I'd never used drugs. I didn't even drink alcohol going through college. I didn't smoke. I came from parents who didn't use drugs. Everything was against my being involved with drugs. But I began to look for a topic of interest and decided that illegal drugs looked promising as a field to study. (Campbell 2005b)

Often, such questions hinged on the availability of money for research, most of which came from the federal health research budget and depended on changing Congressional interests in the issue.

Depth of involvement in ethnographic methods also varied among the key figures of this era. In some cases, design of ethnographic research and the analysis of ethnographic data was more important than actual field immersion. Bruce Johnson noted the following about his own career:

> [Edward Preble] trained me in ethnographic research (which I had only had a brief exposure to at Columbia sociology). Now, I've never done fieldwork nor ethnographic research myself—but I have gained a substantial reputation in the field because I'd gotten very good at writing applications and getting funded by NIDA and [the] National Institute of Justice to engage in ethnographic research. Then I would hire good ethnographers, train them, review their work, conduct ethnographic data analysis, and help get articles published. I really have gained the essence of being an ethnographer without ever doing any actual field research. (Campbell 2005b)

Others, such as Preble, were far more skilled at face-to-face interviewing of active drug users (often in a storefront interview setting) than in assembling their very detailed and contextualized knowledge about drug user behavior for publication. Still others, such as Agar and Bourgois, combined notable skills in on-the-ground ethnographic research with insightful analyses.

The ability to focus on drug use behaviors for all of these researchers was dependent on funding, most of it from the federal government, and thus always influenced by shifts and flows in societal interest in and concerns about drug use. In this sense, it is appropriate to suggest that the course of drug ethnography has been shaped by a federal agenda, although at different points in time this course has fallen to changing attitudes about the value and contribution of ethnography or related qualitative methods. Also of importance was the particular configuration of key people in federal institutions, especially (but not limited to) the National Institute on Drug Abuse and the National Institute on Alcohol Abuse and Alcoholism. At times, strategically located proponents of ethnography, especially at the National Institute on Drug Abuse, played critical roles in sanctioning the methodology and promoting federal funding of ethnographic studies of drug use and related issues.[4]

Conclusion

There has been not only a history but a politics of ethnographic alcohol, tobacco, and drug studies. With its track record, it is not always clear why ethnography continues to generate dubiety in the drug research field (or, for that matter, why the ethnography of drug use garners only limited recognition in the broader social and behavioral sciences). Agar maintained that an important part of the problem was that many quantitative researchers continued to be "unfamiliar with . . . how ethnography works" (1996, 197). Bourgois suggested that the problem lay in the fact that ethnographers "violate the canons of positivist research; we become intimately involved with the people we study" (2003, 13). Waldorf and colleagues asserted that the key issue was that drug research ethnographers attempted to give voice and legitimacy to people who "have been defined as deviant by the dominant forces in society" (Waldorf, Reinarman, and Murphy 1991, 14). Very likely, all of these are true and mutually reinforcing.

4

Drug Ethnography since the Emergence of AIDS

Before the medical/scientific community understood the mechanisms that caused collapses of patients' immune systems, interviews with people who had the mysterious syndrome initially called Gay Related Immune Deficiency (GRID) and then, later, Acquired Immunodeficiency Syndrome (AIDS) indicated that some complexes of behavior might be related to its presence. The first two patient subgroups identified in the United States had at least one behavioral characteristic that set them apart from other people: if they were not men who had sex with men (MSM) or people who received regular transfusions of blood products, they were people who reported that they injected illegal drugs into their bodies. The scientific community's understanding of the relationship between HIV infection and patterns of injection behaviors was in its early stages of development when Des Jarlais and Friedman wrote to the editor of the *American Journal of Public Health.*

> We do want to emphasize, however, the need for continuous ethnographic research and careful pre-testing of questionnaires and debriefing of subjects of survey research in studies of AIDS among IV drug users. As the AIDS epidemic continues, we should expect it to generate social change within the IV drug use subculture and increase the potential communication difficulties between researchers and respondents. (1988, 1498)

This passage, crafted by two researchers who became internationally known experts on drug use and HIV infection, reflects the realization that survey interviews needed to be informed by ethnographic research. Its authors were in position to notice AIDS through their studies of methadone programs and the impact of those programs on addict populations. The emergence of HIV among IDUs (note the previously employed term, IV drug users, which was changed in

1989 to Injection Drug Users—IDUs—to reflect the fact that not all illicit drug injection is intravenous) led to a shift in focus for both Des Jarlais and Friedman to the new phenomenon of AIDS. As they attempted to make sense of the AIDS cases that they studied among methadone clients, it became abundantly clear to these two sociologists that behavioral trends among IDUs were not going to be accessible by means of survey instruments. Their letter to the editor expressed their realization that the investigation of AIDS among IDUs at the beginning of the epidemic needed to employ ethnographic means to complement the practice of interviewing AIDS patients in order to understand not only the condition's origins and epidemiology, but also the shifts in behavior that might develop spontaneously in response to the emerging understanding of the epidemic.

The field of behavioral research on drug use had established great familiarity with the same kinds of dilemmas that faced would-be AIDS researchers: How do you find people who practice the behaviors of interest if those behaviors are covert and/or private? What is the best way to elicit information on those behaviors from the people who use drugs? In New York City, where Des Jarlais and Friedman were working, for example,

> IDUs were living in a particularly hostile legal and sociopolitical environment. The Rockefeller Drug Laws, passed in 1973, posed a constant threat of long-term imprisonment. New York City government's fiscal crisis led to the closing of many social services. Partly because of this, massive waves of arson-induced and other fires ravaged impoverished and minority areas of the city, leaving behind considerable community demoralization, overcrowding, and many half-destroyed structures that became the sites of shooting galleries in which HIV spread rapidly among IDUs. (Friedman et al. 2007, 108)

In this context, the pre-AIDS drug ethnography experience gained in the Cannabis studies (Carter, Coggins, and Doughty 1980; Rubin and Comitas 1975), heroin studies (Agar 1973; Preble and Casey 1969), and phencyclidine (PCP) studies (Feldman, Agar, and Beschner 1980) provided templates for how the investigators of AIDS among IDUs needed to proceed. This process led to transformations in the ethnography of drug use after 1980 in response to the AIDS epidemic, bringing distinctive features to the field as well as a large number of new drug ethnographers (whose careers are examined in chapter 6).

Chronology of Ethnography and AIDS among Drug Users

Only a handful of fully trained and productive drug ethnographers were active in the United States in 1980. The revelation that "certain risk groups," including heroin users, had developed an immune disorder variously called GRID or AIDS (among other names) eventually led to the conclusion that any effort to understand and arrest the spread of this malady would need more drug ethnographers than were currently available.

The National Development and Research Institute (NDRI) in New York had established an active group of drug use researchers by the late 1970s, including ethnographers and ethnographic supervisors such as Paul Goldstein, Bruce Johnson, Ed Preble, and Doug Goldsmith. Because New York soon became an epicenter of the AIDS epidemic among IDUs, these individuals were exposed to this consequence of self-injection early in the epidemic's history. Publications on this topic, however, came predominantly from Des Jarlais and Friedman, also affiliated with NDRI. According to Friedman (personal communication), they at first relied on a combination of retrospective interviews and reports by ex-addicts, hired by NDRI as outreach workers, to assemble their information on how IDUs incurred risk of exposure to AIDS (also see Des Jarlais et al. 1989). Through the efforts of David Strug, an anthropologist, they quickly developed a perception of risk among IDUs that included enhanced ethnographic insight (Des Jarlais, Friedman, and Strug 1986). They also enlisted the help of Doug Goldsmith, an ethnographer who had worked at NDRI for several years on research related to drug use, in expanding preventive outreach based on the ethnographic assessments of risk conducted by Goldsmith and Strug. Brief articles in *Medical Anthropology Quarterly*, when it was still a newsletter, made it clear that Des Jarlais and Friedman were both in contact with anthropologists (and clearly were reading Agar) as they thought about approaches to the AIDS epidemic (Des Jarlais 1986; Friedman 1986). This was due to the fact that they regarded ethnography as an essential part of the effort to understand drug user behavior, in addition to other behaviors that involved risk of HIV infection.

Drug ethnographers' involvement in the effort to understand and mitigate the AIDS pandemic began in at least three different locations: New York, San Francisco, and Miami. Des Jarlais and Friedman were engaged in studies of the interaction between IDUs in New York and methadone maintenance treatment centers. Strug conducted ethnographic study among IDUs, although the book chapter reporting on this work (Des Jarlais, Friedman, and Strug 1986) did not specify that he had conducted "shooting gallery" observations (see also Hunt et al. 1985). The chapter indicated that Strug had developed an understanding of some aspects of risk involving needles/syringes, but he applied a concept of "sharing" as an accepted standard of behavior. The chapter's narrative on sharing did not indicate that the ethnographer ever saw anyone "shooting behind" (i.e., using the same needle/syringe just after someone else has used it) anyone else. In this very early "first take" on behaviors that were not well understood, interview materials, rather than direct observations, appear to dominate the conceptualization of sharing.

Robert Broadhead and Eric Margolis reported that an ethnographic project in San Francisco, aimed at identifying strategies for preventing infection among IDUs by the AIDS virus, received support from the NIH in 1985 (1993). This effort reported on street-based outreach to IDUs and used the word *ethnography* to describe the methods. The ethnographic analysis of their work appeared at least twice in the peer-reviewed literature (Broadhead 1991; Broadhead and Fox 1990). Another funding initiative took place in 1986 through a consortium of institutes including NIMH and NIDA. In a first wave of funding, the NIH supported four research centers in San Francisco, San Diego, New York, and Miami. The Miami center had a component that engaged in ethnography of injecting drug use, and its initial revelations about self-injection behavior provided a model for subsequent ethnographic studies (Chitwood et al. 1990; Page, Chitwood et al. 1990; Page, Smith, and Kane 1990).

Between 1987 and 1988, forty-one projects in sixty-three different sites were funded to conduct outreach research on HIV among IDUs (Schuster 1992). The approach used by these projects was formulated by social and behavioral scientists in drug abuse, who, when faced with the opportunity to obtain new sources of funding by focusing on AIDS among IDUs, conceived research strategies that combined ethnography, HIV testing, catchment surveys, and intervention trial technologies into overarching research plans aimed at stemming the spread of AIDS in IDU populations throughout the United States (McCoy et al. 1990; Schuster 1992). These investigators realized that, in order to engage street-based IDUs in a research study and enable them to respond candidly to one-time, short-answer surveys, the questions had to reflect the researchers' informed understanding of the behavior patterns and contexts of interest. The researchers therefore designed a study model that investigators in various cities could emulate, a model that emerged from a collaboration among Carl Leukfeld, Clyde McCoy, James Inciardi, and Robert Booth based on a strategy for testing an intervention while maximizing the number of IDUs contacted by broad-net street contact techniques. Ethnography was to be a key component of the model, because the framers correctly surmised that the potentially varying patterns of injecting drug use in different cities would require researchers to obtain local-specific information on how IDUs injected themselves with drugs.

The model proposed by this group, and adopted by the National Institute on Drug Abuse, had the ethically attractive feature of offering all IDUs who participated in a local project exposure to a preventive intervention, regardless of their assignment to experimental conditions. The national project that put this model "into the field" was called the National AIDS Demonstration Research (NADR) project. Its framework called for formative research carried out by drug ethnographers who established contact with networks of IDUs in their respective home cities and learned as much as they could about the local patterns of self-injection behavior. This knowledge could then be used to establish rapport with participants who could be recruited into the survey/intervention phase of the project.

Once recruited into the project, each participant responded to a structured survey and was assigned to an intervention condition. In order to achieve ethical equipoise in the treatment of human study participants, the framers of the NADR model defined both conditions as interventions—one a "standard of care" intervention and the other an "enhanced" intervention. The former involved a one-on-one counseling session before and after HIV testing and distribution of printed literature on how to avoid further risk of HIV and other diseases transmitted through drug injection. The enhanced intervention involved attendance at a number of group discussions that intensified the exchange of risk information and attempted to train the participants to avoid risk of HIV infection.

As originally planned, the survey used in the NADR projects was to be informed by the local formative work of the ethnographers, but some prominent AIDS researchers insisted that the survey have uniform content across all sites. The content chosen for the survey did not please some local ethnographers, whose criticisms of the survey instrument reverberated throughout the life of the NADR initiative (Clatts 1994). Among the individuals who participated in NADR as ethnographers during the first wave of funding were Page in Miami, Stephen Koester in Colorado, John Watters in San Francisco, Wayne Weibel in Chicago, and Michael Clatts in New York. Page, Watters, and Weibel had been drug ethnographers for years before the NADR initiative, but Koester, who had previously done ethnographic research in St. Lucia (not drug-related), was new, recruited by the principal investigator in Denver. Clatts, who had been an AIDS ethnographer with other populations in New York, began to make ethnographic contact with IDUs in the late 1980s (Clatts 1994). Neither the new nor the veteran ethnographers were happy with the survey's final form, but their objections were overruled by the NADR projects' principal investigators.

Perhaps more important than the discontent over the survey instrument was the fundamental error involved in assigning participants to experimental and control conditions on the basis of random selection. Given the ethnographers' experience in observing injection behaviors, they could see that personal influence on the part of a "house man" (the individual who "hosts" a shooting gallery; he may or may not be a proprietor) or a "running partner" (a person with whom the IDU shares drugs and coconspires to obtain money for drugs) may be the ultimate driver of decisions to take or avoid risks, rather than the influence of an intervention (Page, Smith, and Kane 1990). Therefore, the randomization of individuals into "standard" and "enhanced" conditions could lead to placement of influential individuals in settings populated by participants in the "standard" condition. This placement could result in the "enhanced" intervention exerting influence on the "standard" condition, or conversely, the "standard" condition prevailing over the "enhanced." Some NADR sites attempted to control for this interbleeding of conditions by randomizing running pairs or groups of simultaneous enrollees into the same condition if the recruiter was aware of social linkage among new recruits. In fact, the analysis of the intervention's impact in Miami (where participants who presented for screening together were inducted into the same condition) showed no difference between intervention conditions (personal communication). Nationwide, the results of standard versus enhanced conditions were summarized thus:

> For the most part, not-in-treatment IDUs in the locally enhanced interventions have demonstrated more risk reduction than their counterparts in the standard intervention—although often not significantly better. For example, in II NADR sites, IDUs assigned to an enhanced intervention were more likely than those in a standard intervention to report reduced or continued low frequency of drug injection, but the difference was statistically significant in only one case. Evaluations of other enhanced models of AIDS education for drug users reported to date have also yielded mixed results. (Stephens et al. 1993)

NADR had two more waves of funded projects, eventually including 63 sites. Each site was required to hire an ethnographer, and this requirement offered gainful employment to people who otherwise might never have ventured into the ethnography of drug use. Some participants in the third wave had experience in studying some forms of drug use (e.g., Robert Trotter, the principal investigator in Flagstaff), but others (e.g., Robert Carlson in Dayton, H. Ann Finlinson in Puerto Rico) had conducted no studies of drug use prior to their hiring as project ethnographers.

While the component sites were collecting and analyzing data, the researchers in these projects were given regular opportunities to meet, share experiences, and compare findings. This process did not always result in the formation of alliances among the ethnographers working in the various sites, and some conflicts and tensions emerged. Nevertheless, an approach to drug ethnography (namely, establishing standards of research and interpretation) developed out of the regular meetings that had a generally positive influence on the subfield of drug ethnography. Techniques for collecting and analyzing data tended to converge as the ethnographers shared experiences with each other. By 1995, eight years after the funding of the first NADR projects, ethnography of street drug use had established a set of practices that became widely accepted. There also developed a shared focusing of ethnographic research attention on the specific configuration of behaviors that comprise the acquisition and use of drugs, the social and physical contexts in which these behaviors are enacted, the role of broader structural factors in shaping everyday life patterns among drug users, the nature of relationships among drug users and other people in their social worlds, the relationship of behavior and context to health risk, and risk prevention and drug treatment issues.

Two collections of articles published as part of the NIDA monograph series, one edited by Elizabeth Lambert, Rebecca Ashery, and Richard Needle (1995) and the other edited by Richard Needle, Susan Coyle, Sandy Genser, and Bob Trotter (1995) compiled several issues in which the drug ethnographers had developed something of a consensus. The research monograph edited by Needle and colleagues focused on the role of networks on the relationship between HIV infection and drug use. The monograph on the uses of ethnography in the study of drugs and HIV included an overview of qualitative methods (Carlson, Siegal, and Falck 1995), uses of ethnography in the study of men who have sex with men who use amphetamines (Gorman, Morgan, and Lambert 1995), ethnography in the study of women's drug use (Sterk 1995), advanced ethnographic methods (Trotter 1995), use of research teams in studying emergent patterns of drug use (Ouellet, Weibel, and Jimenez 1995), multimethod studies that use ethnography (Bluthenthal and Watters 1995), and the use of ethnography in the evaluation of community intervention strategies (Singer et al. 1995). Both of these research monographs were remarkable in the degree to which the participating anthropologists and sociologists agreed on basic questions of method and procedure. A consensus article on the reuse of potentially contaminated injection equipment also emerged from this process (Needle et al. 1998). This article relied heavily on ethnographic perspectives to trace how individual IDUs come to use contaminated paraphernalia, despite exposure to dire warnings of danger.

After its first three waves of funding, the federal initiative to fund projects aimed at preventing HIV infection among IDUs morphed into a somewhat different entity in the form of a cooperative agreement. Whereas the NADR projects were separate grants in which the principal investigators responded to a request for proposals that specified key aspects of the research plan, the cooperative agreement left the approach details up to the qualifying applicants, most of whom had been funded by the NADR initiative. These applicants then attempted to agree upon a set of research procedures to be enacted at each participating site. The fundamental problem with this approach, with respect to further development of drug ethnography, lay in the limited involvement of the local site project ethnographers, who tended, with a few exceptions (e.g., Singer), not to be principal investigators. Fortunately for the ethnographers who continued to pursue studies of IDUs, most had by then or within a few years thereafter become sufficiently familiar with the federal research funding system to become funded investigators in their own right, usually through grant applications to NIDA.

One notable aspect of the cadre of drug ethnographers who emerged from the NADR projects was a well-developed sense of the roles played by ethnography in large-scale multidisciplinary projects. Consequently, the drug research projects that they subsequently developed employed varieties of data and analytic strategies not previously associated with ethnographic studies. Most notably, it was evident from their projects that they understood what ethnographic research could and could not contribute to the overall process of inference in a research project. For example, the essential contribution of molecular biology in the determination of HIV and HCV (hepatitis C virus) infection risk led to collaborations in the work of Singer and Robert Heimer on the presence and viability of HIV in needles/syringes (Buchanan et al. 2006; Singer et al. 2000; Singer, Romero-Daza, et al. 2005), HCV contamination of injection paraphernalia by Koester and Heimer (Koester et al. 2003), HIV in needles/syringes by Clatts and Heimer (Clatts et al. 1999), and contamination levels in ancillary injection paraphernalia (e.g., cookers, cottons) by Page and Shapshak (Page et al. 2006). Multicity investigations of these questions led to broad collaborations among ethnographers and molecular biologists for comparative purposes (e.g., Bluthenthal et al. 2004).

Contributions of AIDS Ethnographies

Drug ethnographers contributed numerous published works on the relationship between drug use and risk of HIV infection. Page's studies of HIV risk among IDUs in Miami were the first to utilize direct observation of self-injection behavior in settings where IDUs gathered to inject (Page, Smith, and Kane 1990; Page, Chitwood et al. 1990). These observations and the studies that complemented them (e.g., Chitwood et al. 1990; Shapshak et al. 1994; Shah et al. 1996; Shapshak et al. 2000) lent a perspective on the nature of HIV risk among IDUs that carried understanding of these behaviors well beyond the vague "sharing" gloss used by Des Jarlais and Friedman (1988). This perspective was subsequently adopted in HIV prevention initiatives.

In fact, as of 1987, no social/behavioral scientist had conducted observations of injection behavior since the advent of disposable syringes, and this deficiency of information led to the formulation of "sharing" as a principal manifestation of risk behavior. In defense of the early publications on AIDS and syringe-mediated risk, it is clear that the researchers involved were scrambling, in light of the deadly nature of the epidemic, to put together available information on use of needles and syringes from whatever sources they could find. Agar's accounts of self-injection in the era of glass eye-droppers and baby pacifier bulbs (i.e., IDU homemade injection equipment) as components of a set of "works" (i.e., full complement of drug injection paraphernalia) were the best accounts available (albeit not based on actual observation) in 1987. Combined with AIDS patients' accounts of "sharing," the authors (e.g., Des Jarlais et al. 1989) may have felt that they had the best possible description of risk behavior related to HIV infection. After all, they had interviewed people who had injected for a long time, and they had obtained corroboration from ex-injectors who worked as outreach staff for studies of IDUs. The problem with this reliance on descriptions provided by ex-users had nothing to do with the interviewees' evasiveness or poor memories, but rather with the question of taking some aspects of their experience for granted. With regard to certain contextual and behavior factors in injection activities and sites (e.g., all the potential risky components of injection equipment "sharing"), it simply did not occur to researchers yet that these factors might be extremely important. That is why direct ethnographic observations of behaviors of interest are essential to understand those behaviors.

Page's observations, beginning in 1987 and published in 1990, gave first-hand accounts of the areas of risk as they occurred in sessions of self-injection behavior in Miami "get-off houses" (Inciardi and Page 1991; Page, Chitwood et al. 1990; Page, Smith, and Kane 1990). The areas of risk included the use of a needle/syringe that originated in a pooling receptacle (i.e., syringes that were not directly shared, but likely contaminated by previous users); use of a common, pooled source of water for mixing drugs; use of a common, pooled source of water for cleaning syringes; sharing drugs from the same receptacle, or "cooker"; sharing drugs via "frontloading" or "backloading" techniques; and use of a previously used drug filter, or "cotton." Page also was able to acknowledge efforts by proprietors of get-offs in Miami to reduce risk by instituting bleach rinsing of needles/syringes and, in one case, providing new, packaged needles/syringes for use by clientele (Page, Smith, and Kane 1990). These findings contributed needed insight into the details of self-injection behavior, but more importantly, they pointed out the significance of cultural context in the framing of risk behaviors. Subsequent research on IDUs contributed extensions of the scientific community's understanding of those cultural contexts in which self-injection and other risk behaviors occur.

A newly recruited anthropologist in the NADR projects, Stephen Koester, had received training to become a Caribbeanist anthropologist. Having experienced the typical difficulties in obtaining a regular university faculty position, Koester responded to an advertisement placed by Robert Booth, a social psychologist, and became a drug ethnographer. In ethnographic studies conducted in Denver, Koester added to our understanding of why IDUs are unwilling to carry personal needles/syringes (1994a, 1994b; Booth et al. 1991). He conducted the observations and in-depth interviews necessary to delineate personal histories of IDUs in which there was no room for error when one intended to inject drugs. Because most of his interviewees had extensive and often unresolved histories of petty crime, their possession of a needle/syringe could, if they were detained for any reason, lead to the invocation of some or all of the prior charges, leading to extensive jail time. Rather than risk what for an ordinary citizen would be a minor inconvenience, the IDUs interviewed and observed by

Koester and his associates preferred to rely on whatever needles/syringes their associates might have available at the locale where injection took place (Koester 1994b). Koester's work also verified Page's observations of what have come to be called indirect sharing behaviors, and his publications and presentations on these behaviors contributed to the recognition of their importance in HIV risk (Koester and Hoffer 1994).

The second round of NADR-funded studies included Hartford's Hispanic Health Council as a research site, involving Singer and his colleagues in a project in which ethnographic findings took the forefront. Whereas other sites in NADR used ethnographic findings primarily to inform the process of gathering data from IDUs recruited into standard and enhanced interventions, the Hartford site used ethnographic findings to inform the construction of a culturally appropriate enhanced intervention (Dushay et al. 2001; Weeks et al. 1996). This variant of the NADR projects therefore featured an intervention that included an additional degree of enhancement over the group sessions and counseling received by NADR participants elsewhere: cultural appropriateness. Language used in the sessions was specific to the Hartford drug scene, and the vignettes described in the sessions included familiar place names and sequences of action derived from the ethnographers' findings (Singer et al. 1991). Comparing this intervention with the standard-of-care intervention yielded significant differences in the risk behavior of the participants in the enhanced intervention. On the strength of this project's findings, Singer and his colleagues, allied with other groups that sought to prevent HIV contagion, including Robert Heimer and Ed Kaplan (Heimer et al. 1993), who had conducted research on a trial exchange program in New Haven, to lobby the Connecticut State Legislature successfully for establishment of a program that gave IDUs fair access to sterile syringes (Singer, Romero-Daza, et al. 2005). Singer's team subsequently evaluated the Hartford syringe exchange program using ethnographic and other methods.

Also included in the second round of NADR funding recipients, the group from the University of Puerto Rico (headed by Rafaela Robles) incorporated significant ethnographic components in its research. In Puerto Rico's case, the AIDS epidemic had very different demographic contours than the ones seen in Africa, the United States, and Northwestern Europe. About 60 percent of the identified AIDS cases in Puerto Rico had reported injection of illegal drugs as their principal source of risk, compared with about 25 percent in the United States and Europe (although some U.S. cities, such as Hartford, Connecticut, had the same pattern as Puerto Rico). This difference implied that the process of the epidemic had cultural dynamics that needed acute ethnographic examination, and the Puerto Rico group responded by producing exemplary characterizations of risk behavior (Finlinson et al. 1999) and useful evidence-based intervention guidelines for drug users (Finlinson et al. 1993). Ethnographic research played a

major role in the Puerto Rico project's production of findings related to procurement and distribution of needles/syringes, patterns of drug sharing and
their impact on infection risk, identification and mapping of drug copping
areas, techniques for recruiting IDUs on the street, culturally appropriate prevention of injection-related risk for HIV infection, and suggestions for changing
the ways that IDUs handle their drug use paraphernalia.

National meetings in which the principal investigators of the NADR
projects included their project staff led to various collaborations among drug
ethnographers. One group, which included Stephen Koester, Bob Trotter, Laurie
Price, Richard Bluthenthal, and Michael Clatts, among others, attempted to gain
multisite perspective on the use of injection paraphernalia by comparing
directly observed instances of self-injection collected in different cities, including Denver, Flagstaff, Los Angeles, and New York City. Their summary results
revealed that the common use of ancillary paraphernalia, especially cookers,
cottons, and sources of standing water, was far more frequent (about 80 percent
per item, but 94 percent in aggregate) than the common use of needles/syringes
(14 percent) (Needle et al. 1998). Richard Needle, a member of the NIDA staff
who became a particularly effective advocate for the use of ethnographic methods in AIDS research, organized this effort.

Although publications that contained cross-site, ethnographic comparisons
of IDU behavior did not subsequently dominate the literature on injecting drug
use, the process of pooling information on observable behaviors taking place in
very different parts of the United States, and in very different contexts, showed
ethnographers and their audiences that the methods used to gather ethnographic information were in fact being applied consistently to produce compa-
rable findings. Prior to the NADR and later Cooperative Agreement projects,
ethnographers had tended to work in their own microenvironments, producing
the insights that come from immersed up-close study, but not comparing their
findings with those of other ethnographers until they had been published or presented at professional meetings. The NIDA initiatives not only provided gainful
employment to many ethnographers, but they also led to cross-site comparisons
of ethnographic methods and findings that had not been previously attempted.

Some unique bodies of ethnographic work developed in the years following the initiation of the NADR projects that also had an impact on the social/
behavioral science of AIDS. Especially unique among these was the study of networks among IDUs in Flagstaff, Arizona, conducted by Bob Trotter and his
research team (Trotter, Bowen, and Potter 1995). In a small city such as Flagstaff
(about 50,000 people in the early 1990s), the setting for injecting drug use was
very different from that found in large cities of the East and West Coasts or the
metropolises of the Midwest. Trotter obtained funding for his research team to
work through the networks of informal social relations among IDUs living in
Flagstaff and its environs.

Trotter and his field ethnographers found various patterns of interaction in these networks. First, the networks had lasting and well-defined links among their participants. These properties may have been due to the limited choices that IDUs in a small town have when choosing associates with whom to share their covert behavior. Second, the establishment and maintenance of the networks were of utmost importance to the ongoing business of obtaining and distributing drugs, because in a small town, all drug marketing had to proceed via networks in which customers and sellers knew each other well, rather than via the open emporia of drug sales seen in big city neighborhoods. Third, and most important to the efforts to prevent the spread of HIV among IDUs, the morphology of the networks featured key individuals who could be targeted for preventive intervention. According to the team's findings, some individuals represented the lone links between large groups of IDUs aggregated in either centralized or amorphous networks. These amorphous networks featured irregular distribution of relations among individuals. If an amorphous cluster of IDUs included some who might already be HIV seropositive, the linking individual represented an opportunity for stopping the spread of HIV into another network. Centralized networks found in Flagstaff afforded another opportunity for targeting preventive intervention, because the focal person in a centralized network could exert influence on the risky injection behavior of everyone participating in that network (Trotter, Bowen, and Potter 1995). The Flagstaff group's findings added a strong local context perspective on the behavior of IDUs, a theme also seen in comparisons between sites (Singer, Jia, et al. 1992).

HIV Natural History

The recruitment and follow-up study of IDUs led in some cases to opportunities for characterizing progression of HIV infection to disease. Page and colleagues used these opportunities to study the effects of viral coinfection, dietary deficiencies, and cognitive impairment among IDUs.

In 1988, evidence that some IDUs were infected with another lymphotropic virus, HTLV-II, led Page and his research team to test stored blood from IDUs to determine exposure to HTLV-I or II via radio-immune assay (RIA) assessments. That study indicated that a substantial percentage (about half) of the participants in a longitudinal study of IDUs showed evidence of coinfection by one of these two viruses. As the research team attempted to inform the study participants of their results, it became apparent that several of them had either already died or were gravely ill. Using a proportional hazards model to compare coinfected IDUs with those infected only by HTLV, the team found that coinfected individuals were about three times as likely to die in a given period of time as were people with only HIV infection (Page et al. 1990). This transdisciplinary finding illustrates the utility of having an ethnographic component in a

longitudinal epidemiological study. Findings such as this, suggesting the importance of disease interactions in marginalized social groups, led to the development among ethnographers of the concept of syndemics (Singer 1996b, 2009),
which subsequently gained recognition as a significant factor in contemporary
public health at the Centers for Disease Control and Prevention. The initial syndemic described in the literature, SAVA (substance abuse, violence, and AIDS
risk), came to be recognized because of street-based ethnography suggesting
the frequent co-occurrence of these elements.

Additional findings from a subsequent cohort in Miami revealed the
importance of immunoglobulin G as a predictor of health outcome (Page et al.
1996) and the importance of selenium deficiency in the survival of HIV-1 positive IDUs (Baum et al. 1997). In all of these cases, the capability to find, engage,
and follow street-based study participants was only possible because of the
ethnographic approach used by the investigators to initiate the study.

The methodological features of contemporary ethnography include not
only participant observation, informal and formal interviewing, and focus
groups, but also, as described in greater detail in the next chapter, ethnographic
mapping, network analysis, data triangulation, and consensus theory building.
If a research team engages in transdisciplinary studies of people over time (e.g.,
longitudinal data gathering at regular time intervals), all of these features contribute important information. Participant observation of the contexts where
people engage in behaviors of interest give the observer perspective on the
people in the drug user's immediate social surroundings, allowing opportunities to meet and talk to the people who surround those under study. These
people become essential to the process of conducting a longitudinal study in
which participants return for regular follow-up assessments (in the case of HIV
natural history, this may involve a blood draw for immunological and virological assays, assessments of psychological state, and assessments of cognitive
function). The field team in such a study may resort to these people to locate the
study participant for his or her next periodic assessment. The ethnographic
process of recruiting study participants makes this level of follow-up inquiry
possible.

In many cases, however, the ethnographic approach has already helped to
assure regular follow-up of the study participants because of the rapport built
during the recruitment process and the treatment of participants during the
study's data-gathering procedures. Street-based, drug-using study participants
appreciate when the people who ask them questions and perform assay procedures treat them with dignity and respect, communicating empathy with their
life experiences, in that such experiences are rare in the punitive social world
they inhabit on a day-to-day basis. In longitudinal projects with ethnographic
components, this feature is usually present in all phases of the study's contact
with its participants.

The Crack Epidemic

As HIV became prominent in the study of street-based drug use, a form of cocaine previously unknown in the United States emerged in the inner cities and spread rapidly—ready rock, or crack cocaine. This form of cocaine appeared just as powder cocaine had begun a cyclical downturn in popularity, a phenomenon seen at least twice before in the history of the leaf-derived alkaloid. Manufacture of crack was simple enough to be accomplished by anyone with access to an oven. Cocaine hydrochloride, the chemical vehicle for making the cocaine alkaloid water soluble, could be stretched by combining it with baking soda and water and cooking the mixture in an oven. The chunks of material that remained in the baking pan provided a variety of freebase cocaine in smokeable form. Its pricing structure made available an effective dose of cocaine at as little as two or three dollars.

Cocaine hydrochloride was first introduced to European and North American markets in the mid-nineteenth century as an energy booster in products such as Mariani's Coca Wine and, possibly, Coca-Cola (Singer 2006b). The Harrison Act of 1914 had the effect of removing cocaine from tonics and elixirs, but enthusiasm for those products had by that time waned, as had Sigmund Freud's enthusiasm for cocaine as a treatment for depression. Cocaine's next emergence as a widespread drug of choice did not come until the 1960s and 1970s, during a period known as the youth drug epidemic, when large numbers of people experimentally used illegal drugs. In the general context of illegal drug use, cocaine developed a following among people who were largely unfamiliar with previous generations' negative experience with the drug. Cocaine has a tendency to develop a negative reputation among users, who eventually lose interest in it. This process takes ten to fifteen years, and the cycle of use that began in the 1960s had just about run its course when inner-city entrepreneurs in Los Angeles introduced a new hardened form of cocaine. Ethnographers began almost immediately to notice this new form, which gave access to cocaine to a whole new segment of the U.S. population—the poor and marginalized. Studies on crack, however, were not published until the late 1980s (e.g., Carlson and Siegal 1988), and the relationship between crack and HIV was not published until the early 1990s (e.g., Inciardi 1995)

Crack's relation to the HIV epidemic was not obvious, because its mode of consumption was not intravenous. Nevertheless, ethnographic studies of crack use began to point out that increased sexual activity was a major aspect of the growing crack epidemic (e.g. Carlson and Siegal 1988). This activity implied risk of sexually transmitted HIV, and subsequent investigations confirmed this risk (e.g., Cohen and Metzger 1994; Edlin et al. 1994). The ethnographic investigations described a vortex of crack use and sexual activity, in which participants engaged in highly frequent sex acts in exchange for money to buy crack or in direct exchange for crack (Inciardi 1995). Because a dose of crack only produces acute effects for five minutes or less, the drug is a very demanding mistress to maintain (hence the name "girl" used for cocaine, with the ephemeral crack as a "high-maintenance girl"). When a crack user's high dissipates, he or she is left with a dysthymic feeling thought to be caused by lack of dopamine in the synaptic spaces between brain nerve cells. Under those conditions, the user will do whatever it takes to make that terrible feeling go away, including the provision of sexual services (or, as Carlson and Siegal found among crack users in Dayton, "personal favors") to anyone willing to buy them with money or more crack. Bourgois and Sterk produced textured ethnographic accounts of the cultural contexts in which consumption of and traffic in this form of cocaine took place. These book-length accounts gave the authors opportunity to achieve an understanding of crack's meaning and risk far beyond that of descriptive articles on the subject. Their titles, *In Search of Respect* (Bourgois 2003b) and *Fast Lives* (Sterk 1999), reflect the experiential aspects of crack use described in these exemplary in-depth studies. The former emphasizes the adaptive process in Spanish Harlem, where socially legitimated opportunities and potential sources of self-esteem are scarce, and the latter emphasizes the speed with which women become so enmeshed in cycles of crack and sex that it dominates and often significantly damages their lives.

Conclusion

By the time the scientific community made its first characterizations of the AIDS epidemic, drug ethnographers had developed skills that would prove to be crucial to understanding the behaviors that powered transmission of HIV. Prior successful studies that employed ethnographic methods paved the way for the relatively rapid acceptance and encouragement of ethnographic approaches to studying the spread of HIV in drug using populations. This appreciation resided not just at the institutional level (i.e., the funding agencies) but at the level of fellow social/behavioral scientists who had seen first-hand the fruitfulness of ethnographic studies in developing an understanding of drug using behavior. In the midst of an epidemic in which self-injection behaviors represented a clear opportunity for the spread of HIV, researchers and interventionists working in communities across the United States and in many other countries needed the kind of information that ethnographers could obtain through their methods. Early ethnographic investigations of risk behavior among IDUs and crack consumers led to information that would not have been acquired by any other means, improving approaches to preventive efforts and culturally informed community-level interventions.

The power of these contributions is reflected especially in the blossoming of ethnographic research efforts (and the necessary hiring of ethnographers) supported by the National Institute on Drug Abuse. Interventions to prevent the spread of HIV in drug using populations have reported success in affected communities both in the United States and elsewhere, and these interventions owe much to the information gathered by ethnographers. Advances in methods have resulted from the creation of a critical mass of drug ethnographers who have had the opportunity through multisite projects and informal networking to exchange ideas and approaches, producing compendia of methods and conceptual clarifications which advanced the field of drug ethnography (e.g., Lambert, Ashery, and Needle 1995; Needle et al. 1995).

Transdisciplinary research on questions of disease progression has also benefited from the contributions of ethnography. These kinds of studies need to be able to follow patients over time, and the ethnographer's focus on cultural context facilitates this perspective on the conditions of people living with HIV/AIDS. Not only does the ethnographic component of transdisciplinary projects help to keep track of difficult-to-find individuals, it also provides a holistic perspective on the lifeways and activities of study participants, which may contain information crucial to the health question under study, as in Baum and colleagues' work where ethnographic perspective on drug use and daily food intake contributed to the study's conclusions (1997). Thanks to these and many other developments in the extension of ethnographic research that took place between 1981 and 1999, the field of research on drug abuse continues to benefit.

5

Drugs and Globalization

From the Ground Up and the Sky Down

This chapter examines drug ethnography from a global perspective. Its subject is the impact of globalization on drug use and the conduct of contemporary drug ethnography. Framing the dynamic interface between macro-structural and micro-observable processes, behaviors, and relationships is a critical challenge for contemporary ethnography. The chapter assesses how ethnographers understand drug use in a rapidly globalizing world and the concepts and constructs they use in this process. As part of this examination, the chapter presents ethnographic research on and the contribution to understanding of (a) supply-side issues in the flow of drugs (i.e., trafficking), including drug markets and patterns of distribution; (b) demand-side issues that emerge from particular drug using populations and their social contexts; and (c) intermediate-level issues, including the impact of punitive anti-drug policies and the development of alternatives to the criminalization of drug use. This examination begins with several snapshots of contemporary drug ethnography in light of globalization.

Case Studies in a Globalizing World

Drugs are a truly global commodity, but not all parts of the world are equally affected by the flow of various drugs across national borders on their way from production, to refinement, to repackaging and shipment, and ultimately to the most lucrative terminal markets, where high demand and risk inflate prices to consumers and profits to distributors. At the same time, global transformations of other sorts, such as international labor migration, can reshape drug consumption patterns while workers are abroad and when (and if) they return home. Other global processes, such as transnational natural resource extraction, can reshape the physical environments and subsistence strategies of local populations and have an impact on motivations for and patterns of drug consumption. Expressions of these drug-related global restructurings can be seen in the following ethnographic cases:

- Writing about illicit liquor consumption in Sri Lanka, Michele Gamburd noted that, traditionally, women worked in the domestic sphere and provided economically critical but unpaid household services for their families. The significant economic challenges that now face poor families, including the inability to make enough money to buy land and build a home, have led to the decision, at the family level, to respond to the call for housemaids in countries like Kuwait, Saudi Arabia, and the United Arab Emirates. In 2005, for example, Gamburd reported that more than a million Sri Lankans participated in international labor migration, two-thirds of them women. Often, women were hired on two-year contracts and left behind their husbands and children. Women—for the first time—became household breadwinners and men became homemakers. Consequently, older gendered divisions of labor and social roles had been thrown into severe question. As a result, Gamburd asserted, many men turned to illicit alcohol consumption to self-medicate their damaged identities and diminished sense of self-worth. As explained by one of Gamburd's key informants, ". . . I was home while my wife worked in the Middle East as a housemaid. I was drinking then. . . . [Men drink] because they have no job. They can't help their kids. While their wives are abroad, the husband is doing the housework. Then this goes to his head and he gets confused and upset. . . . Then men drink and forget" (Gamburd 2008, 116)

- Enrique Desmond Arias spent time across several years in an ethnographic study of violent drug trafficking gangs in three of Rio de Janeiro's *favelas* (shantytowns). During this period, wars raged among drug gangs over control of the cocaine that flowed from Colombia and over command of the *favelas*. One drug war that Arias described raged for seven years. Central to his research was the question "How can violence in the *favelas* remain so high? The answers lie in the political connections traffickers maintain with civic leaders, the police and politicians" (Arias 2006, 61–62). Writing about one of the *favelas*, Arias noted, "Violence remains at high levels in Santa Ana because of an active network that brings police, traffickers, policymakers, and civic leaders together in perverse and undemocratic ways. At its core, the illegal network that operates in Santa Ana links across from different sectors of state and society to perpetuate illegal activity" (2006, 128). Thus, he argued, politicians engage in exchanges with drug traffickers, allowing them to maintain their illicit operations, and the traffickers, in turn, provide certain benefits (e.g., some services) to *favela* residents in exchange for their voting support of the implicated politicians. Only by

paying attention to all of these sectors, their connections, and their somewhat different expressions in each of the *favelas* could Arias develop an
understanding of the drug/violence nexus in Rio.

■ In the popular imagination, drug abuse is a behavior common to urban settings. In her ethnographic research for her doctoral dissertation, however,
Angela Garcia (2007) examined a rural Hispanic population, in New
Mexico's Española Valley, with the highest per capita rate of heroin addiction in the United States. In 2003 alone, 41 people in the valley died of drug-
related causes—a striking number in a rural area with a population of only
20,000. In accounting for this striking pattern, Garcia examined intergenerational relationships among heroin users, local discourses of remem-
brance and addiction, and the impact of unequal ethnic social relations. In
this, she linked on-the-ground behavioral patterns among Hispanics to the
encompassing and difficult political, economic, and social history of the
region. Garcia argued that the district's heroin phenomenon is a contemporary culturally shaped response to a historic pattern of communal land
expropriation, the resulting fragmentation of intimate personal and familial connections, and the corporal and existential desire to escape from
resulting socially structured suffering. In the valley, inequality is palpable,
as the rich and poor live close together with wealthy white families (many
who have come to work in the space industry) occupying land that once
belonged to impoverished Hispanic families. As one of her informants
explained, little by little they had to sell their land, often at depressed
prices, just to survive. As the family acres melted away, her informant's
heroin addiction spiraled out of control. Of course, all of the land lost to the
Hispanic community did not disappear. "The ultimate irony is that which
was 'lost' is still *there* for Hispanos to see—it's all around them in the mountains, rivers, mesas, and buttes," and in the property now owned by others,
explained Garcia (2008, 734). Many of Garcia's informants felt that they
were forced to trade away their self-esteem and most everything else of
value they ever had. Pondering this painful dilemma, she found, sets off a
craving for drugs to cope with their distress. Thus, painful emotion is tied
through contemporary drug ethnography to social history and regional
political economy.

In each of the cases described above, the conduct of local drug ethnography
in a globalizing world, and in complex national and transnational space,
requires a shift in the traditional on-the-ground ethnographic gaze upward
and sideward to include diverse social strata and groups; broad structures of
(generally unequal) social relationships; intricate histories of regional, national,
or transnational connections; and the flow of drugs over great distances, across
multiple borders, and through many hands. Doing this requires what Paul

Stoller has called a "globalizing method." Stoller maintained that a "street-level approach [remains] central to grounding transnational studies in concrete ethnographic detail [but] it is methodologically insufficient" (1997, 91). Data are also needed on the connections of local users and dealers to the wider political economy of the drug trade and to the impacts of the War on Drugs, to the activities of the police and the relation of prison life to street life, and to the making and enforcing of health and social policy. Consequently, ethnographic research in transnational spaces is, as Michael Watts characterizes it, "a tall order" (1992). But in the process of exploring this composite space, a new broader framework is emerging that affirms that an ethnographically grounded approach to drug research remains viable and vital in a changing world. Indeed, in light of the oft-mentioned homogenizing effects of globalization, a method that draws the attention of researchers to local distinctions, and hence reveals the limitations of (and resistances to) homogenization, is of enhanced value. Further, given the dynamic nature of human social life, an approach that can quickly identify emergent change (e.g., appearance of a new drug, drug combination, method of consumption, new populations of users, content of substances used to "cut"/dilute drug content, drug distribution patterns) is likely to retain utility under transforming circumstances.

Coming of the Global Ethnographic Gaze

Globalization is a complex term with various meanings, including the ever-increasing transnationalization of production, marketing, and consumption; the development of closer global linkages made possible by the speeding up and enhanced accessibility of transport and rapid transportable communication; and the growing global power and presence of transnational corporations. While sometimes described in purely economic terms, at its heart globalism is a social process involving transformations in the structure and nature of human relationships. Thus, as William Waters emphasized, globalization involves the "creation of new economic, financial, political, cultural, and personal relationships through which societies and nations come into closer and novel types of contact with one another" (2001, 8). The social and cultural consequences of these emergent global relationships on the lives of people around the world, especially as these relationships and their impacts involve and provoke the production, flow, and consumption of drugs, is an issue of primary concern to contemporary drug ethnographers.

The term *globalization* has been common in anthropological and sociological texts and discourse since about 1990, ultimately achieving a frequency of inclusion—in book titles, journal articles, and conferences—approaching ubiquity. Still, the social reality it labels presents a significant challenge for ethnography generally, and drug ethnography specifically. At issue, especially, is a tension between the primacy of "the local," the exploration of which was the *raison d'être* of ethnography, and the need to study world society in light of our progressively more interconnected lives. While all of the issues heightened by globalization are not, in fact, new ones for ethnographic research, such as addressing the infirm, the shifting nature of social boundaries and personal identities, and the conceptualization of culture as a dynamic and processual phenomenon, globalization does require that ethnography:

- Incorporates a wider array of materials and data (e.g., with reference to drug research, attention to global anti-drug policies, operations, and institutions).
- Rethinks the depth and duration of relationships with key informants/cultural consultants that are possible as researchers observe and participate in wider social and geographic arenas and spend time in multiple locations (e.g., when studying the changing social life of drugs as they move along a complex, transnational flow).
- Adopts an expanded approach (characteristic of traditional ethnography) to exploring emic perspectives and the daily experiences of insiders to include a far wider range of insider understandings encountered at multiple sites and at diverse levels of social complexity (e.g., when studying complex issues like syringe exchange that unfold at national, regional, and local levels and involve multiple and often conflicted social groupings at each level). This approach also significantly increases the focus on macrolevel and cross-cutting processes that develop across time and place (e.g., in the study of the role of the pharmaceutical industry and its products in the reshaping of street drug use patterns in diverse local contexts). (Eriksen 2003).

Similarly, Michael Burawoy and colleagues (2000) stress three shifts in the ethnographic gaze inherent in the development of global ethnography that have high a relevance for drug research:

- A focus on "external forces" (such as global economy and polity that impact local possibilities), which in the case of drugs includes the emergence of global drug corporations and the global War on Drugs.
- An examination of connections between sites (as seen below in the discussion of drug flows and the ties that link drug movements across borders, but also population movements that can significantly affect drug use patterns).
- A focus on global imagination, including the movement of ideas, cultural images and understandings, and norms around the world (such as movies and music that have diffused Western drug use models to diverse international locations).

Establishing and assessing the linkages between local behavioral trends in several sites (that often are contrastive across some key dimension) with the impress of external forces and the movement of cultural elements provides a foundation for a "grounded globalization" perspective in contemporary ethnography, an approach that fits the needs of twenty-first century drug research (Burawoy et al. 2000).

Flows: Ethnographic Mapping of the Movement of the Drug Trade

Most drug ethnographies spend much of their descriptive space on the issue of drug demand. Consequently, this literature, reviewed in previous chapters, is focused on the lives and behaviors of drug consumers. These ethnographies characterize more than addictive behavior. Their holistic perspective includes a range of different types of drug consumers, including nonabusive drug users whose activity in drug consumption constitutes a large proportion of the demand for illegal drugs. However important the demand-side of the drug equation, supply-side studies are equally valuable in understanding drug use and drug-related health and social risks for individuals, communities, and whole societies. This section describes the social topography of transnational drug flows and drug markets as they have come to light through the work of drug ethnographers, other researchers, and some journalists.

Notably, the ethnographic record on international drug flows is somewhat limited given the importance of this topic to understanding drug use in the world. In contrast, a fair amount of work has been done by ethnographers on local retail drug markets. Given the traditional focus of ethnography on observable behaviors and local configurations of meaning and experience, traditional ethnographic methods are useful in documenting changing patterns of drug production in a targeted area and to the linkage of proximate producers to global distribution networks. Newer, multisited forms of global ethnography are critical to studying the various roles and subgroups that facilitate drug trafficking along longer flows, the targeted marketing of drugs to specific consumer populations, and varied local retail networks of street drug sellers in a region.

Historic analyses suggest that drugs have played a far greater role in the construction of local, national, and international social relations and, as a result, in the creation of broad social worlds than generally is recognized (Courtwright 2001). The starting points of this process in the modern era were the globalizing changes introduced by Europe. The colonial administrations of England and France, for example, made significant contributions to the international spread of drug production and use throughout Asia and other parts of the world (e.g., parts of Europe, European colonies in the New World). Drugs such as heroin and cocaine, derived from plants that previously were grown for domestic consumption in indigenous communities and micropopulations around the world, were refined as drug commodities for worldwide sale within the global economy (Singer 2008). Subsequent efforts at international drug control and the criminalization of possession and use in core countries created the opportunity for illicit drug corporations—entities that often emerged out of illegal gangs among subordinate populations previously engaged in other illicit or hidden activities—in peripheral areas of the world system to address and expand global demand for psychotropic drugs. The ongoing struggle between control efforts and drug trafficking has led to the development of complex and continually changing routes of illicit drug flows.

Drug flows are characterized by four main points along a dispersed continuum: regions of production, corridors, regions of transshipment, and regions of targeted sales and consumption; although consumption, to some degree, takes place all along a drug's international itinerary. For illegal drugs, developing countries in the periphery of the world system commonly are sites of production, passage, and transshipment, while legal drugs tend to flow in the opposite direction. For example, Afghanistan has become widely recognized as a major production site for opium-based drugs derived from its massive poppy crop, and it has a significant local problem with opium and heroin addiction. It is rapidly developing, however, an even bigger problem with the misuse of pharmaceutical drugs, including analgesics such as morphine-based cough syrups, sedatives (especially phenobarbital) and benzodiazepine tranquillizers (diazepam and lorazepam) (Macdonald 2008). As areas and peoples are incorporated into an activity site along an international drug pathway, there are often dramatic health and social consequences.

Regions of Production

While, internationally, drugs are controlled by wealthy individuals who head the shadow corporations that oversee key components of the trade—while outsourcing other necessary activities, such as cross-border transport and street sales, to specialized groups—direct involvement in illicit drug production has also become an important source of income for many poor individuals and families with limited access to alternative sources of income. Opium production, for example, is the biggest employer in Afghanistan (Barker 2006). Elsewhere, in places where opium poppies and the highly psychotropic latex (i.e., raw opium) they produce bring a higher price than alternative legal crops, drug production is a critical resource among the rural poor. Thus, among poor farming families in Myanmar, ethnographer Jean-Paul Grund noted that growing opium poppies "pays for what most people in developed countries take for granted." In the words of one Myanmar man, "Opium is our food, our clothes, our medicine, the education of our children" (Grund 2004, 2). Likewise, cocaine production in South America has attracted thousands of families fleeing extreme poverty in other parts of the region to coca-growing areas—coca being perhaps the only cultivated plant they could make a living from in places where the soil is not well suited to intensive agriculture.

Elsewhere, the production scene is quite different, as seen among the Tarahumara Indians who live in the isolated canyons of Northern Mexico's Sierra Madre Occidental Mountains. As the drug trade in Mexico has grown, many parts of the country (especially in the north, close to the biggest drug market in the world) have become embroiled in the flow of drugs. Even the seemingly remote Tarahumara, who fled into the rocky crags of the Sierra Madre canyons centuries ago to avoid Spanish conquest, have not gone untouched. Enrique Salmon, an anthropologist and Tarahumara Indian, noted:

> Narco-traffickers force and coerce indigenous farmers to grow marihuana and opium in their fields in place of the traditional crops of corn, beans, squash, and many other endemic domesticated plants. The illicit plants become new cash crops replacing the . . . domesticated plants that have thrived in the Sierra [Madres] for centuries. People are often murdered if they refuse to grow the drug related plants. At best, they are forced off their small milpas (small planted plots on the edge of steep canyon walls) and other plots of land and move to urban areas looking for work in an economy that is already suffering. (Salmon 2008)

Whether they begin as drug plants (cocaine and heroin) or are the products of complex chemical mixtures (methamphetamine), the drug lab is a necessary station in the flow of many drugs. Like drug fields, the labs are also a source of employment among the poor, although they are often places that contain many risks to the health and well-being of those who work in them. In her ethnographic account of women who work in crack cocaine production labs in Atlanta, Sterk noted that individuals who are part of a drug dealer's "kitchen staff" (i.e., who work as "cooks" making crack from cocaine powder and baking soda) commonly must offer free sexual services to their employer. In addition, these women are themselves crack users (1999). Others who work in drug labs, pouring and mixing chemicals (some with significant toxicity levels), resemble Nilofar, a teenager from a small Afghan village. After her parents and her husband died, Nilofar and her younger sister found work in a heroin lab. As a result of the chemicals that they breathed and got on their skin, however, both sisters became ill. In fact, many of the staff at the illicit laboratory where Nilofar worked suffered from significant health problems, including stubborn skin rashes, asthma, blood deficiencies, and frequent upset stomach and diarrhea (PakTribune 2006).

Corridor Regions

Corridors are the ground pathways of international drug movement. They are of interest to ethnographers not so much because they are used for the movement of drugs but for the effects of drug movement on local populations, including the ensnarement of local people in facilitating the flow of drugs and in the diversion of some quantity of drugs for local consumption. Exemplary is the Amazonian region along the Solimões River where Colombia, Peru, and Brazil share a triple border. Cocaine flows through the dense rainforest in this area on its way to the significant drug markets of Brazil, including the wealthier southern coastal cities and smaller municipalities. The tri-border region is the traditional home territory of the Tikuna Indians, and their communities feel the effects of living in what has become a drug corridor. Increasingly, in recent years, younger Tikuna—individuals with firsthand knowledge of the rivers and forest trails—have been lured into serving as mules (transporters) in the drug trade and into the use of drugs as well. João Pacheco de Oliveira, an anthropologist at the National Museum of Brazil, noted that, as a result of globalization, non-Indian culture is reshaping the world inhabited by the Tikuna (1990). As a result, drug use has come to be defined as a significant problem among the Tikuna, as has the tendency of Tikuna young adults to commit suicide under the influence of drugs and alcohol.

Regions of Transshipment

To reach their final destination successfully, drugs may have to be repacked several times, moved from one size and type of container to another to avoid police detection. Repackaging occurs at transshipment sites, important way stations on winding clandestine drug-trade routes.

In recent years, the former Portuguese colony of Guinea-Bissau, a small country wedged between Senegal and Guinea on the West African Atlantic coast, has emerged as a transshipment site for cocaine that originates in the Andean region of South America and is on its way to the urban markets of Europe. Guinea-Bissau is a typical transshipment country in that it is a poor nation—the fifth poorest nation in the world—and has a weak central government with limited law enforcement, poorly monitored borders, and a largely unguarded coast. Along its craggy coastline there are arrayed a string of small islands and inlets that make the country an ideal place for drug smuggling. As a result, it is estimated that as much as 350 pounds of cocaine land on the coast of Guinea-Bissau nightly, part of the almost 300 tons of cocaine believed to be moved annually through West African nations en route to Spain and Portugal, and ultimately to the rest of Europe. In Guinea-Bissau, Aladje Baldé, head of Plan International, commented that "drug traffickers found an ideal spot to transport drugs to Europe" (De Queiroz 2007).

Airplanes and ocean-going vessels bring the cocaine to Guinea-Bissau; some of it is dropped at sea and retrieved by small boats, and some is offloaded at small airstrips on the coastal islands. The cocaine is then divided into smaller lots and moved on to Europe in small planes or by human mules. Given the lack of jobs in the country, a growing number of Bissau-Guineans have become involved in the transshipment process. For small amounts of money, they can be induced to retrieve drug packages dropped from the air, unload airplanes, cart drugs to transshipment warehouses, repack drugs, or serve as body carriers hauling small packages of drugs to Europe. Often, people living in transshipment sites have little prior experience with illicit drugs and no awareness of how dangerous or addictive they can be. This lack of experience results in explosive addiction rates which follow the development of a transshipment site in a new location. This pattern has begun to emerge in Guinea-Bissau as well. The country's only drug rehabilitation center was opened in 2002 for people suffering from problems related to the use of alcohol or marihuana. Today, most of its patients are addicted to cocaine (Sullivan 2008).

Retail Sales: Local Drug Markets

Ultimately, despite intensive and well-funded efforts to interdict them along the way or at their final border crossing, huge quantities of drugs reach their intended destinations (in part because of the sheer volume of drugs being moved, in part because of drug traffickers' creative skills in hiding and clandestinely moving their product, and in part because the great wealth produced by drug sales can be used to purchase law enforcement and political cooperation). Upon reaching the United States, for example, a shipment of drugs, such as heroin from South America or methamphetamine from Mexico, is filtered through drug networks, from larger scale dealers capable of "moving a lot of weight" to local groups that sell drugs directly to consumers. In cities, towns, and even small rural settlements, such networks convert cocaine, heroin, methamphetamine, marihuana, and other drugs into a multibillion dollar consumer industry.

One of the earliest ethnographic examinations of local drug markets was carried out in New York City by Ed Preble and John Casey during the late 1960s and published in 1969 (Preble and Casey 1969). Since then, there have been a number of ethnographic or other qualitative studies, primarily of very local illicit drug markets (e.g., Adler 1993). Nicholas Dorn, Karim Murji, and Nigel South, using ethnographic methods, initially described seven types of trafficking "firms" in the United Kingdom: (1) groups that are guided more by an ideological commitment to drug use than by a desire to reap great profit; (2) friendship networks of user-dealers; (3) entities involved in other activities that engage in the drug trade as a sideline; (4) full-time illicit groups that engage in diverse money-generating activities, including drug sales; (5) opportunists who take advantage of short-term opportunities to acquire and sell drugs; (6) groups that specialize in drug marketing and have set drug distribution roles; and (7) state-sponsored traders that emerge out of collusive agreements between law enforcement and drug sellers (1992). By the end of their fieldwork, however, these researchers realized that diverse drug corporations and small-time operations were highly fluid, with groups changing types and people weaving in and out of the trade, in large part because of pressures from law enforcement. They also found that local drug distribution was highly decentralized rather than controlled by a rigid, top-down hierarchy. In a subsequent spatial ethnography of four drug markets in the United Kingdom, Tiggey May and colleagues described differences in the ways and degree to which drug markets are connected to their "host" commercial and residential communities, the extent of local concerns about the presence of a drug market, the contribution of a drug market to the promotion of other kinds of local crimes and violence, and the profile of street behavior among drug dealers (2005). These researchers found that some drug markets are closely linked with the surrounding legal and illegal economies of their respective neighborhoods, and in some instances markets were controlled by cohesive groups with local family ties and broad networks of friends. Other drug markets, they discovered, were populated by individual entrepreneurs with few local ties in the communities where they operated. In one of the communities that they studied, local drug dealers were in the process of being displaced by outsiders.

Ethnographic research in the United States by Mangai Natarajan and Mathieu Belanger (1998) identified four types of entities involved in drug marketing: freelance operations, family businesses, communal businesses, and corporations. In this and other studies, Natarajan and coworkers have emphasized that drug markets are primarily composed of small groups of loosely linked entrepreneurs rather than large, highly structured criminal syndicates (Natarajan 2006). Variation in drug markets, by neighborhood, has been described by Ric Curtis and Travis Wendel for New York City (2000). They found that changes in the way drugs are marketed is not the consequence of a natural progression of distributional styles nor a reflection of developmental cycles in patterns of drug use, but rather a response to a complex array of neighborhood features and the ways and degree to which drug markets are embedded in neighborhoods. Thus, they found that corporate dealers who see neighborhoods primarily as just places to make money tend not to be well integrated and are subject to police "buy and bust" enforcement tactics. In more integrated markets, such approaches are less successful. Further, these researchers stressed that

> markets not only reflect the supply and demand for particular drugs, they help shape them. Besides being places where commodities were bought and sold, the market places observed in this research were also arenas where the socialization of neighborhood youth took place, often superseding in importance such places as playgrounds, parks, gymnasiums, and clubs. They were also places where trends were set: in the process of

buying and selling drugs, styles in clothing and music were established. Being a drug distributor was not entirely about making money, it also provided distributors with a very public forum where a persona could be molded to help achieve noneconomic ends. (Curtis and Wendel 2000, 145)

As the work of Dorn and coworkers suggests, all typological approaches to portraying drug markets are troubled by the dynamic character of the drug trade. Tiggey May and Mike Hough, for example, described patterns of change in the U.K. drug market over a ten-year period, including transition from an open street-based market to a closed market, a pattern seen in other locations as well (2004). Researchers found that this change was tied to the adoption of cell phone communications that allowed mobility and rapid buyer/seller contact in the retail drug market without an active presence in public space. May and Hough also described the connection of the retail market to what they call the "middle-level" markets and the latter of two types of higher level distributions systems—traditional hierarchical markets that were prevalent during the 1980s and a fluid, nonhierarchical entrepreneurial market that gained a degree of prominence thereafter. Ultimately, May and Hough were unable to determine which of these two structures predominates.

In their study of drug trafficking across the United States / Mexico border, Patrick O'Day and Rex Venecia found that "conversation concerning the trade's overt dynamics, as well as its fine points, typically took place within group settings. . . . In such group settings, established traffickers would seek to educate and impress wannabe smugglers" about the tricks of the trade (1999, 423). Further, in the course of their ethnographic research, they came to the conclusion that "the Mexican law enforcement establishment is anything but a thinly disguised commercial enterprise" that is heavily invested in the cross-border drug trade (1999, 422).

More recently, Howard Campbell ethnographically studied the growing role of women in the United States / Mexico cross-border drug trade (2008). With few exceptions, there has been limited focus on the role of women in the ethnographic study of drug trafficking. Campbell described the lives of several female drug smugglers, including a woman he called Zulema who had a high-level position in a heroin and cocaine smuggling ring. He argued that women such as Zulema, like her male counterparts in the trade, derived more than economic benefits from involvement, and she enjoyed the excitement and adventure of participating in an illegal activity. In addition, Campbell observed, involvement in the drug trade allowed Zulema a level of freedom from male social dominance that was unavailable to many other women of her social background. At the same time, many other women participated in drug smuggling as low-level drug-carrying "mules" and received limited economic benefit and considerably less social power than Zulema; although, in some cases, they were able to use their drug roles to gain some independence from male domestic control.

In Australia, Lisa Maher described an ethnographic study conducted in the city of Cabramatta in New South Wales that revealed an important dimension within the local drug market based on the "size" of the drug transaction (1996b). Depending on the customer, Maher found that different types of "half-weight" measurements would be used (e.g., Asian halves and Aussie halves, with the latter being underweight and reserved for low-status "aussie junkies"). Maher was also able to collect ethnographic data on nuanced aspects of the drug trade, including the frequency of larger and smaller purchases, the mean purchase price for various weights of drugs, and that women appear to pay significantly less than men for both larger and smaller amounts of drugs. In-depth, journalistic accounts of the drug trade, such as a series on Ecstasy smuggling into Australia by Nick McKenzie (2008), can also provide an ethnographic glimpse of the industry. McKenzie described the smuggling of 4.4 tons of Ecstasy (15 million tablets) hidden in 3,000 tomato cans in Italy, transshipped through Mauritius, and ending up in Sydney, Australia (McKenzie 2008; McKenzie, Houston, and Arup 2008).

As these brief accounts suggest, ethnography is able to provide detailed accounts of the organization, operation, and dynamics of drug markets, including descriptions of the behaviors of participants, features of drug transaction, the various roles in the drug trade, the relation of markets to local communities and law enforcement, how interactions between drug markets affect drug availability, styles of distribution, types of crime and violence associated with particular kinds of drug markets, smuggling routes and strategies, the changing sociodemographic composition of consumer groups associated with drug markets, and the importance of gender issues in the operation of drug markets. A critical finding of the ethnography of drug markets is the degree of change over time and location, and the resulting danger of overgeneralizing the nature of these illicit social spaces.

Drug Ethnography and Risk

Discussion of research on drug trafficking raises immediate questions about risk and safety, given the real dangers inherent in this kind of scholarly work. In this regard, Alison Liebling and Betsy Stanko drew attention to a conference presentation by a leading criminologist in which he mused that life would have been easier if he had chosen to be a professional bird watcher instead of a criminologist. They go on to ask, "What is wrong with us that we have had sleepless nights from doing the kind of work we do?" (Liebling and Stanko 2001, 422).

As a few ethnographers have commented (although usually not at great length), the kind of work they do and the places it takes them, as well as the kinds of things they see and hear about, can be the stuff of sleepless nights and stressful days. In part, the risks are emotional and involve witnessing and learning in great detail about the suffering of their informants, including tales of brutal child and intimate partner abuse and observations of interpersonal and street violence. During his fieldwork in Hartford, for example, Singer watched members of a drug-involved street gang chase down, knock to the street, and proceed to wantonly beat an individual who had run afoul of their expectations. On another occasion, one of his key informants suddenly pulled open his shirt to reveal a long, jagged, and swollen cut across the entire width of his chest that had recently been inflicted by the henchmen of a drug dealer whom he had crossed. Similarly, Janie Simmons and Kim Koester described the hidden emotional injuries and potential for "burn-out" they encountered while regularly hearing self-reports of physical abuse and suffering during ethnographic interviews with drug users on the role of violence in their lives (2003). Additionally, there is inherent in drug ethnography the daily potential for direct encounters with threats and danger. Bourgois, for example, described a mugging he endured while studying crack cocaine sellers in New York, as well as the experience of hearing the staccato echo of gunshots fired nearby as he went about his street research (2005). As these examples indicate, there are unavoidable risks of doing drug ethnography because of the places this kind of research often is conducted and the violence that, while not as routine as popular imagination and Hollywood movies suppose, is nonetheless real and potentially deadly. As a result, questions that must be on the minds of every drug ethnographer are: Will this research lead to violence? Am I at risk? If so, how do I keep safe in the field?

Gary Craig and his colleagues addressed some of the potential dangers of doing research as social scientists and have advocated the development of a Safety Code of Practice (Craig, Corden, and Thornton 2000). They and others have stressed the importance of always alertly assessing the risks of a field site, the need to take certain precautions while conducting research, the need to have a back-up rescue/escape system in place when problems arise, training for the deescalation of interpersonal tensions, safety planning, experienced and close supervision of field team members, and other strategies of self-protection (e.g., carrying a mobile phone, making your planned whereabouts known to coworkers, being prepared to leave an unsafe situation, working closely with "street smart" key informants who can provide social entree to new settings and recognize and defuse dangerous situations, acknowledging that no data are more valuable than the researcher's or the informant's safety. In the end, drug ethnographers tend to reach a point at which their "safety instincts" are sufficiently sharpened for them to feel reasonably safe in the field while believing that the value of this kind of research for addressing human social problems outweighs the actual level of risk in most settings (and that some drug-related settings are unfeasibly dangerous and should be avoided).

Ethnography and the Law: Studying Legal
Drug Use and Criminalization

The Ethnography of Legal Drugs in a Global Perspective

Most of the discussion thus far in this chapter has been about illegal behaviors involving drugs. Yet most drug use is legal, if subject to various social controls. Ethnography of prescription drugs, alcohol, and tobacco focuses on the availability of these drugs and the relationship between problematic use and legal sources of supply, as well as on the sometimes ill-defined borderlands between legal and illegal behaviors (e.g., the diversion of pharmaceutical drugs to illegal consumption; the selling or providing of legal drugs to those not allowed to have them or at times and places they are not allowed to be distributed or possessed; and the smuggling of legally manufactured drugs, including cigarettes and pharmaceuticals, to get around bans, tariffs, and other controls).

Like illegal drugs, those that are legal in most nations have become significant global commodities, and they have emerged as momentous sources of global health risk. Tobacco serves as the most powerful and poignant example of this emergence, which according to the World Health Organization causes 1 in 10 deaths among adults worldwide (more than 5 million people a year) and which, by 2030, may be responsible for an annual toll of 8 million lives internationally (2008). While tobacco has been used in New World societies since pre-Columbian times, and worldwide since the colonial area, as Kenyon Stebbins emphasized, many of the traditional smoking practices described by ethnographers in earlier decades have all but disappeared because of "aggressive marketing by transnational tobacco companies" (2001, 148). Consequently, recent ethnographic research on tobacco use has been framed by a global perspective on the production, distribution, and marketing and other promotional efforts of "Big Tobacco" and their impacts on behavior and health.

Stebbins, for example, has undertaken grounded globalization studies of smoking behavior in Mexico, including the role of transnational tobacco companies in smoking and health. Of special concern has been the effort by the tobacco industry to replace the profits lost—because of continually falling sales of tobacco products in the United States and Europe—by fostering markets in developing nations that are already struggling with infectious, nutritional, and other diseases. Stebbins's research shows that transnational tobacco corporations see markets in developing countries as particularly appealing because their governments often are in need of revenue, have enacted very limited—if any—tobacco control legislation, may have difficulty enforcing tobacco control laws that have been passed, can be tempted by the ostensibly philanthropic provision of resources (e.g., a tobacco company offered to set up a police station in Fiji and to provide vehicles to NGOs if they would display the company logo), may have an incomplete understanding of the health risks associated with tobacco consumption, or may choose to ignore available information. As a result, tobacco industry advertising and other promotional campaigns (e.g., cigarette giveaways) can be quite effective in gaining access to local markets and recruiting new smokers, often, in the process, playing off of a globalization of images that has led to a glorification of Western imports that are linked to Western lifestyles. Under these conditions, a handful of superrich transnational tobacco corporations have forged ahead to capture and expand tobacco markets in the developing world.

These patterns are seen, for example, in the Pacific island nation of Fiji (composed of 106 inhabited islands). In recent years, in response to both growing evidence of tobacco-related health problems and the international circulation of World Health Organization tobacco control information, the Fijian government began to put together a legislated program to control tobacco consumption that resulted in the Tobacco Control Act (TCA) of 1998, designed to be implemented several years later. The bill, which made Fiji the third country in the world and first developing country to adopt the WHO Framework Convention on Tobacco Control, banned tobacco advertising, sponsored public antismoking campaigns, restricted smoking in public places, and prohibited the sale of tobacco to persons under the age of 18 (Cornelius 2001). During this period, however, other events were also unfolding that affected smoking control in Fiji. One of these was an influential World Bank report issued in 1993 about the causes of "sluggishness" (i.e., a slow rate of growth in per capita income) in the Fijian economy. As a solution, the Bank pressed Fiji to adopt structural adjustment policies to increase foreign investment, including measures that would remove trade barriers and promote multinational investments (Lal 2001). Consequently, the Fijian government developed a series of reforms that promoted trade liberalization, privatization, and deregulation and taxation on foreign investment. Central to this effort was the introduction of the Pacific Island Countries Trade Agreement (PICTA) in 2001 (Institute for International Trade and Pacific Trade Consult 2007). One effect of PICTA was to open up the Fijian market to the global tobacco industry, most notably the British American Tobacco (BAT) company, which undercut the country's tobacco control initiatives. Signaling the company's subsequent stature in the country, BAT was awarded the 2007 Fiji Business Excellence Award, presented by Joni Madraiwiwi, the vice president of Fiji.

As a result of developments such as this, worldwide tobacco consumption is increasing at the rate of 1 percent per year. In developing nations, sales are growing at least three times faster than elsewhere. In some Third World settings, Stebbins observed that smoking is ubiquitous, even among physicians (2001). As would be expected, rising rates of lung cancer and related diseases have been identified in heavy smoking communities in Pakistan, South Africa,

Malaysia, Bangladesh, and Brazil. Stebbins also discussed the serious environmental costs of tobacco cultivation and curing, such as deforestation, erosion, and desertification.

Ironically, at the same time that the United States pressured the governments of South America to control the production and export of cocaine, U.S. administrations used their economic and political muscle to open up South American markets to the import of U.S. tobacco. Stebbins examined the hardline tactics employed by tobacco companies to gain access to South American markets. As he noted, transnational tobacco companies "have been making a killing (in more ways than one)" in South America (Stebbins 2001,164). These companies have successfully fought antismoking legislation and have been able to get some smoking-control laws vetoed or rescinded in some countries, such as Argentina. From the emic perspective of many people in Argentina, "the veto was the result of industry bribes at the highest level" (Stebbins 2001, 162).

In related work at the global level, Mark and Mimi Nichter and colleagues pointed out that while the United States has played an important role in fostering child-survival (e.g., through oral rehydration and immunization efforts) and safe-motherhood programs on a global scale, these efforts are contradicted by the complicity of the U.S. government in promoting Third World cigarette sales (Nichter and Cartwright 1991; Nichter and Nichter 1994). Indeed, these researchers maintained, an international focus on child health diverts attention from the political and economic dimensions of illness in a world of enforced inequality.

Noting that 75 percent of tobacco cultivation occurs in the Third World, the Nichters pointed out that international lending programs such as the World Bank and the Food and Agriculture Organization of the United Nations actively make loans, extend advice, and provide seed and pesticides to small farmers to help them enter into tobacco growing. While claiming to be committed to the development of Third World nations, these programs will, in the long run, help the Third World develop significant tobacco-related health problems. Contributing to this outcome is the fact that cigarettes marketed by transnational tobacco corporations in developing countries often have much higher tar (a primary chemical source of health problems in cigarettes) and nicotine (the chemical source of addiction to tobacco) levels than those sold in industrialized countries. As the Nichters stressed, the median tar level in cigarettes sold in the United States is 20 milligrams per cigarette, while in Indonesia it is almost double this amount.

In light of the importance of external forces on the distribution and health impacts of tobacco use, in their call for tobacco ethnography, the Nichters (1994) supported a research approach that was not narrowly focused on studying individual motivations for smoking or the array of behaviors and understandings characteristic of smokers in particular settings but rather one that was guided by the kind of grounded globalization approach advocated by Burawoy and colleagues. Noting that tobacco use "is not just a lifestyle choice" but "a behavior aggressively promoted by a global industry that profits off of the poor with little concern about the damage it causes" (Nichter 2008, 159), they urged adoption of an approach that pays keen attention to the actions of governments, international organizations, and the tobacco industry in shaping smoking behavior everywhere. They also argued for the study of the social relations of consumption and the semiotics of consumables (i.e., the social meanings invested by people in consumed items and the communication of meanings enacted through their consumptive behaviors) within a broader political-economic framework. In other words, the Nichters believed that it is essential to understand how the tobacco industry acquires new markets and with whose help, at the same time as we analyze how people come to invest tobacco products with particular cultural meanings and respond to these cultural meanings as if they had the same material reality as the products themselves.

A similar turn to a grounded global approach has developed in ethnographic research on alcohol (e.g., Gray and Saggers 1997; Singer 1986; Saggers and Gray 1998) and in the unified field of alcohol, tobacco, and drug studies (ATOD) (Singer 2001), suggesting the general recognition among drug ethnographers of the need to address the processes and effects of globalization on their domain of research.

Criminalization of Drugs and Its Effects

Drug policy in the United States since the mid-1930s has shown little tolerance for drug use, except, ironically, for two of the most deadly drugs: tobacco and alcohol. This official lack of forbearance, as expressed in the ongoing War on Drugs, has had a significant impact on the behaviors in which illegal drug users engage, the lives they lead, and the risks they take (including the ways they conceptualize risk) (Singer and Mirhej 2004). Depending on the will (and capacity) of local governments to enforce the laws that reflect this intolerance (as well as the ability of drug trafficking organizations to corrupt this will), users of forbidden drugs may be forced to go underground in order to procure and consume supplies of their drugs of choice. Any attempts to gain understanding of these secreted cultural contexts, as discussed in chapter 1, demand laborintensive approaches that involve the discovery tools of ethnography and the skill of individual ethnographers. In addition, ethnography has proven to be a useful tool in the development of representative samples when the population under study is not well defined (because it tries to hide its activities and its members from the criminal justice system). Both of these points are elaborated below.

The Necessity of Ethnography

Criminalization presents a formidable barrier to the acquisition of knowledge about drug use. Where there are laws to punish drug users, drug-involved individuals develop and share a set of protective strategies (which vary by location), including the use of somewhat secret sites for drug acquisition and use, escape strategies, and in-group jargon for disguised communication. As Lee Hoffer noted about his ethnographic research among street drug users in Denver: "The people I knew on the streets knew how to meld into the background of ordinary society and become inconspicuous" (2006, 37). Ethnography represents a way for social scientists to gain access to such hidden populations and the social scenes they construct, inhabit, and hide in.

After establishing contact with populations engaged in socially and/or legally disapproved behavior, and developing a research relationship with some individuals in the target group, ethnographers learn the form that their behavior takes in cultural contexts and how to talk about and describe that behavior. This is a gradual process that takes considerable investment of time, energy, and commitment. The payoff is the slow accumulation of an ever-deepening understanding of the drug use issues that are of concern (including new questions that emerge in the course of the research). Without the knowledge that ethnography provides, the level of understanding of drug using behaviors is often limited and lacks contextual insight. As Bourgois stressed, ethnographic approaches are especially well suited to drug research and to

> documenting the lives of people who live on the margins of a society that is hostile to them. Only by establishing long-term relationships based on trust can one begin to ask provocative personal questions and expect thoughtful, serious answers. Ethnographers usually live in the communities they study, and they establish long-term organic relationships with the people they write about. In other words, in order to collect 'accurate data,' ethnographers violate the canons of positivist research: we become intimately involved with the people we study. (2003, 13)

For the very reasons noted by Bourgois, ethnographers are able to collect full and detailed accounts of drug-related behavior and eventually face the challenge of extracting themselves from the field. Relationships develop, obligations emerge, and mutual concerns can grow. Noted Hoffer: "After completing my research, I did nothing with my data for months" (2006, 110). The reason that Hoffer became stalled was that he felt torn between his obligations to the drug users he had gotten to know, some as authentic friends—because one cannot fully control what becomes of the published findings of research—and his professional responsibility to write up and publish his data. In recent years, one factor that has helped ethnographers negotiate the rough passages incumbent in tacking between intimacy and distance is that their work contributes to the effort to address the pressing—indeed life-threatening—health and social issues faced by drug users.

Ethnography and Representative Samples in Unknown Universes

A challenge of drug user research is that, as a hidden population, they are not well defined as a group or readily available for enumeration (Braunstein 1993). The concept of *hidden population* implies two somewhat different but connected meanings. First, as noted above, some sectors of any drug using population may be difficult to find and recruit into a research sample. Second, the boundaries of any drug using population, including population size and distribution, are not well known. As a result, it is difficult for researchers to know if the conclusions they reach studying a sample of drug users can be generalized or if they reflect a sampling bias that resulted in skewed findings. For example, street outreach recruitment of drug users often leads to a sample that is approximately 25 to 35 percent women. Is this because women constitute this percentage of the total number of street drug users, or is there a tendency of outreach workers to over-recruit men because they are easier to find on the street? Ethnographers have come to play an important role in developing procedures for addressing the problem of how best to sample an unknown universe. Researchers at a number of sites have contributed to this work. One of the most important early efforts was carried out by the MidCity Consortium to Combat AIDS in San Francisco (Bluthenthal and Watters 1995). Recognizing that drug injectors constitute a dispersed population, the consortium used street ethnography, key informant interviewing, theoretical sampling techniques, and chain referral sampling to develop a picture of specified geographic areas and the makeup of the drug users residing within each area. Study participants were then recruited from identified areas of the city. Ultimately, this approach developed into the construction of a targeted sampling plan. In Dayton, Ohio, drug ethnographers at Wright State University (Carlson et al. 1994) developed a sampling plan that combined various sources of data, especially ethnography, to estimate the density of the target drug using population in zip-code areas. This combination of techniques allowed researchers to use proportional sampling for high-, medium-, and low-density zones, enabling them to shape the sample to reflect the estimated characteristics of the local drug using population. In both of these cases, and in other locations as well, ethnography formed a central part of foundational data collection that helped to produce an account of the boundaries and makeup of the drug using population that could serve as a rough but defendable sampling frame. In more recent years, a growing number of drug researchers have adopted the use of respondent-driven sampling (Heckathorn 2002), a type of chain-referral sampling involving peer recruitment by members of the target group, as a means of establishing valid population samples of hidden populations. Ethnography can also inform this method by suggesting the distribution of features in the original small sample of "seeds" (individuals recruited and asked to nominate members of their social networks for a second level of interviewing) that will ensure a thorough sample of the target group (thought to be achieved by six rounds of network recruitment and interviewing).

Ethnographic Study of the Health Impacts of Drug Criminalization

The size of the U.S. jail and prison population has increased six times since the 1970s, making the country the international leader in per capita incarceration. Rates of incarceration in the United States are five to ten times greater than those found in other industrialized nations. Drug convictions are the primary legal force driving up the U.S. incarceration rate. Incarceration on a nonviolent drug possession or sales charge accounts for over 50 percent of all people sentenced to prison between 1985 and 2000 (Fichtner and Cavanaugh 2006). Radical increases in the number of individuals imprisoned for drug offenses are, in part, a consequence of changes in the wording of the drug laws. Crack cocaine, for example, while not particularly different from powder cocaine, draws far harsher prison sentences for much smaller amounts. Ethnic minority populations, especially African Americans, have been disproportionately impacted by the War on Drugs, which, within the United States, has been carried out to a large degree through the arrest, prosecution, and imprisonment of street-level drug offenders from inner-city neighborhoods (Singer 2004). As Bourgois observed, with reference to the draconian marihuana laws in the United States,

> the greatest harm caused by marihuana comes from the collateral damage of its illegality. Criminalization has dramatically increased the profitability of marihuana and the violence surrounding its trafficking. Furthermore, millions of vulnerable lives are ruined as large sectors of poorly educated, destitute youth serve prison terms for selling trivial amounts of marihuana. (2008, 582)

While the consumption of drugs carries significant potential health risks, some of which may be intrinsic to the acute and chronic effects of the drugs themselves, the criminalization of drug use and incarceration of drug users have significant implications for the health of drug users, including their ability to lower HIV or other infectious risk, avoid drug overdose, and be exposed to the direct health consequences of incarceration given contemporary prison conditions. The ethnography of drug use has documented a series of health risks of drug criminalization as they are realized "on-the-ground" in particular social situations.

MULTIPLE-PERSON SYRINGE USE. As noted in chapter 4, Koester's ethnographic research in Denver indicated that it has become common practice to avoid carrying syringes in places where the police arrest drug injectors for being in possession of a syringe without a physician's prescription.

> Drug users spend a great deal of time thinking about and actively engaging in strategies to avoid detection. An injector summarized this common preoccupation by stating, "I never put my shit on the streets." In explaining this statement he said that he goes to great lengths to minimize his visibility and to reduce the number of reasons for which he could be arrested; not carrying drug paraphernalia is simply one of these ways. (Koester 1994a, 290)

Avoiding arrest for syringe possession is important to drug users for multiple reasons: it can lead to incarceration and being forced to go through the dreaded experience of drug withdrawal; it goes on the person's record as a drug-related offense, making it difficult to deny drug involvement in future arrests for more serious drug-related offenses; it can lead to a fine which, if not paid, will lead to the issuance of a bench warrant for yet another arrest; it provides arresting officers with leverage in eliciting information about other local drug users and sellers; and it can, if the person has prior drug-related arrests, convince a judge that he or she is incorrigible, resulting in extensive jail time. Consequently, for those addicted to drugs, the need to inject during the course of the day regularly leads to situations in which an individual must use someone else's syringe, a known pathway for the transmission of HIV, HCV, and other infectious agents (Feldman and Biernacki 1988; Singer et al. 1991).

INJECTING IN UNSANITARY ENVIRONMENTS. One aspect of avoiding detection by law enforcement among drug users involves concealing drug consumption. For homeless drug users or for those whose residence is insecure, institutional, far from drug acquisition sites, or where privacy is difficult, the tendency is to use sites such as abandoned buildings, deserted cars, wooded areas, parks, alleyways, rooftops, cemeteries, or similar sites that generally lack running water and offer only brief seclusion. When drug users inject in such locations, which police may raid at any time, they are often in a rush to complete the process of finding and penetrating a useable vein, injecting their drug mixture, and leaving the area. Injecting drugs under these kinds of conditions presents several health risks that have been observed and described by drug ethnographers, including failure to disinfect body injection sites properly, resulting in viral infections (Varga, Chitwood, and Fernandez 2006); use of unclean water mixed with drugs to create an injectable drug mixture (Page, Smith, and Kane 1990); use of syringes purchased or acquired on the street or at an injection location (Buchanan et al. 2003); and missed veins, resulting skin abscesses, and other soft tissue infections (Ciccarone et al. 2001).

DRUG OVERDOSE. Accidental overdose is a significant cause of death among drug users. Research by Lorraine Copeland and colleagues found that prior to the AIDS epidemic, the principal cause of death among active drug users each year was overdose (Copeland et al. 2004). According to the Centers for Disease Control, the frequency of unintentional fatal drug overdoses almost doubled between 1999 and 2004, behind motor vehicle crashes as the leading cause of accidental death in the United States by 2004 (Paulozzi 2007).

Various street drugs, especially those that slow central nervous system activity, present a special risk for overdose. Criminalization of drug use has contributed to a street drug scene in which the unregulated introduction of new drugs and drug combinations, the content of which is always uncertain, is quite common, sometimes with deadly consequences. Additionally, there are certain conditions that increase the likelihood of drug overdose. Experiencing a hiatus in drug use (e.g., during a prison incarceration) and then starting up again at the old dosage level (when the body's tolerance of the drug has diminished) is a common trigger of drug overdose. Consequently, the three-week period following incarceration is a quite common time for drug overdoses. The Urban Health Study in San Francisco found comparatively high rates of overdose in the twenty-one days following prison release or discharge from methadone maintenance. "Socially marginalized heroin injectors who lack a stable community, a safe place to inject, and a steady and known supply of heroin may be more likely to inject alone, rush injections because of fears of arrest, and to experience fluctuations in heroin purity and tolerance—all of which may culminate in a greater tendency toward overdose" (UCSF News Office 2001). While experience with drug overdose is common among drug users, it is probably most common when patterns and behaviors are changing and, as a result, user certainty about drug quality and content is diminished. A sudden spike in drug overdoses in a local setting is a sure sign that changes have occurred and users have not adjusted culturally or biologically. While common changes of this sort include the appearance of drugs of unusual purity or synthetic drugs of high potency (for various reasons—from new sources of supply to inexperience by those "cutting" and mixing drugs for sale), a particularly important change is the sudden imposition of an intense (if temporary) police crackdown in a specified neighborhood, a common strategy in the enforcement of drug laws (Singer 2007).

Incarceration and Risk

Whatever its failures in terms of stopping or controlling drug use, as noted, the War on Drugs has been quite effective at arresting an enormous number of people and putting them in jails and prisons. Moreover, a profile of those incarcerated on drug-related charges suggests that enforcement of drug policies is a better reflection of the "politics of race" than it is of a meaningful effort to stop the sale and consumption of illicit drugs. Overall, African Americans, who account for 12 percent of the U.S. population, comprise 55 percent of those convicted for illicit drug possession. One in fifteen African American males currently is incarcerated, primarily as a result of drug laws (Singer 2008). Moreover, arrest and incarceration carry with them significant health risks. While, as various ethnographers have noted (e.g., Kane and Mason 2001; Rhodes 2001; Wacquant 2002), the extent of prison ethnography is limited (by institutional control factors, the low status of this kind of research among social science researchers, and cultural stereotypes), it is evident that various features of prison life expose inmates to a range of risks. Notable among these in recent years is the reemergence within prisons of tuberculosis, including drug-resistant strains of this disease (Farmer 1999). HIV transmission is also a significant aspect of the carceral risk environment. As Stephanie Kane and Theresa Mason stressed, "imprisonment itself [should] be considered an HIV risk factor" (2001, 469). Drug use and violence are additional risks of incarceration. Loïc Wacquant, who has conducted ethnographic research among inmates in Los Angeles, noted that "prisoners like to say that there is more violence, hustling, and drugs 'in the joint' than outside" (2002, 374). Other research suggests that drug use in prison, while widespread, never reaches the level found in many inner-city street settings. Based on ethnographic research in the United Kingdom, Ben Crewe reported "drug use during incarceration . . . is common, though at levels lower than before imprisonment, and at rates that differ greatly between establishments" (2005, 458).

In sum, one product of the ethnography of drug use has been the documentation of the significant human costs of drug criminalization, findings that must be taken into consideration in assessing the War on Drugs as beneficial health and social policy. In the view of many drug ethnographers, in fact, the War on Drugs constitutes a notable example of unhealthy health policy (Castro and Singer 2004).

Ethnography and the Development
of Alternatives to Drug Criminalization

Drug Treatment

Ethnographic research on drug treatment has not been extensive but the work that has been done has produced mixed results about program effectiveness. In a review of the literature, Geoffrey Hunt and Judith Barker argued that drug users tend to be presented as passive individuals to restrictive social control, especially in therapeutic settings (1999). Their voice is rarely heard. Overall, the slant of the literature, Hunt and Barker argued, leaves the reader less than convinced about the beneficial nature of treatment. Geoffrey Skoll, for example, studied a therapeutic community treatment program based on participant rejection of drug culture through peer pressure and confession, and came away from the experience critical of the emphasis on destroying drug user culture and autonomy while building dependence on the treatment community (1992). Based on ethnographic research in an outpatient counseling program, Mark Peyrot developed the concept of "coerced voluntarism," which he applied to the micropolitics of treatment (1984). Patients in the program were pressured to "volunteer" for treatment by the criminal justice system. In response, the patients attempted to convince treatment personnel that they did not need treatment. Because they did not want to alienate the patients—who were needed for fiscal reasons to keep up the program's census figures—counselors seemed to side with patients and intervene on their behalf with representatives of the criminal justice system while trying to convince patients to become active participants in therapy.

Building on the Foucauldian concept of "governmentality" and work in the ethnography of methadone treatment, Steffen Jöhncke developed the notion of "treatmentality" for application to the assessment of drug treatment policy and practice (2008). He argued that the idea and practice of "treatment" requires ethnographic exploration as a cultural construction of one type of relationship between drug users and the rest of society. While the need for treatment and its potential benefit for drug users are self-evident from a societal perspective, Jöhncke suggested that treatment first of all serves to establish a particular relationship in which the logical solution (treatment) defines the problem (drug use) in a fashion that is both culturally and politically expedient. With reference to methadone treatment, which Jöhncke viewed as a quagmire of power relations that reflects an unhappy compromise between competing societal discourses on drug use, Bourgois concluded that this approach to treatment serves as a biopower mechanism for disciplining the poor while subjecting them, as patients, to impotence and suffering (2003a).

In another vein, more applied and less critical of the social roles of drug treatment, a number of ethnographers have sought to show how the use of ethnography can improve the matching of patients to appropriate treatment type (Singer 2000), as well as enhancing understandings of the nature of treatment processes and the meaning of treatment outcomes (Stahler 2003). On occasion, ethnographic approaches have even been used in the construction of drug treatment, such as the development of Project Recovery, a women's program in Hartford, Connecticut (Singer 2000), which sought to mobilize research findings in the creation of a comprehensive, culturally and gender sensitive approach to drug addition in social contexts. The inability to sustain many parts of the program because of funding challenges was seen as affirming the less-than-sincere societal commitment to addressing drug-related problems (Singer 2004).

Harm Reduction

Harm reduction is presented as a nonjudgmental public health-oriented approach to the issue of drug use that is anathema to the punitive attitude toward drug users that has characterized drug policy in the United States, although it has found great support in northwestern Europe, Canada, Australia, parts of Asia, and elsewhere. Central to the practice of harm reduction is the belief that some people always will engage in illicit or socially unapproved behaviors such as drug use but that it is possible to diminish the public health risks associated with these behaviors through well-designed, nonrepressive policies, low-threshold community prevention programs, and caring and respectful attitudes. Ethnographers have examined various harm reduction programs, targeted to drug users as alternatives to criminalization and related punitive orientations, including syringe exchange programs, pharmacy syringe access policies, harm reduction education, drug user support networks, drug substitution programs, court diversion programs, and medically supervised injection room programs (Bourgois and Bruneau 2000; Hong et al. 2005). In some instances (e.g., syringe exchange, pharmacy access), ethnographers have tended to find generally positive effects, while in other instances (e.g., drug substitution), accounts have been generally critical. With regard to syringe exchange and pharmacy access, for example, ethnographers have reported that, given the fact that at any point in time most injection drug users are not in drug treatment and are at risk of injection equipment-mediated HIV infection, syringe access programs that create linkages to drug users and provide them with the resources needed to lower infection risk to themselves and others warrant social and health policy support. These programs do not increase the frequency or spread of drug use, and they form part of a broader approach to risk reduction that includes health care, social support, and rapid access to treatment (Bluthenthal et al. 2004; Bluthenthal et al. 2008; Finlinson et al. 2000; Singer et al. 1995; Stopka et al. 2005).

Overall, ethnography has proven to be an effective tool in the description and assessment of harm reduction alternatives to punitive approaches to drug use.

Conclusion

Globalization has restructured the world, tying it together ever more closely and seemingly undercutting the initial rationale for the ethnographic project: the holistic study of distinct communities on their own terms. In drug studies, as elsewhere in ethnography, new approaches and conceptual frameworks have emerged to carry ethnography into the twenty-first century. The new ethnography is not only designed to meet the challenges of social research in a globalized world; in the arena of drug studies, as in other areas, it offers an approach to understanding—the relationship of the local to the global—that is essential to grasp the complexities of contemporary human society.

6

The Conduct of Drug Ethnography

Risks, Rewards, and Ethical Quandaries in Drug Research Careers

In this chapter, we are concerned with the process of doing drug ethnography as an approach to knowledge and as an intense personal experience that requires difficult moral decisions. Building on the brief discussion of key ethnographic methods presented in chapter 1, and the historically evolving approaches mentioned in chapters 2 and 3, this chapter both examines additional components of the ethnographic toolkit as they are put to use by contemporary ethnographic drug researchers and the roles these methods have come to play in multi-method and multisited studies of drug-related behavior. Further, as a consequence of ethnography's demonstrated utility in (1) studying behaviors that often are deemed illegal or seen as normatively or morally ambiguous, (2) the tendency for marginalized and illicit behaviors (e.g., drug use, violence, commercial sex) to cluster together in what might glibly be seen as "behavioral red light districts" (Cooper 2002; Ellickson et al. 2005; Malow et al. 2001), and (3) the participatory nature of ethnographic research, this chapter also is concerned with the often difficult ethical challenges encountered by drug ethnographers. Such challenges stem from the fact that ethnographers hear about or witness illegal behaviors, possess knowledge of risky behaviors (including risk of transmission of potentially lethal diseases), and put themselves at potential risk because of the kind of work they do. In short, this chapter will address questions about the conduct of drug ethnography as we move deeper into the twenty-first century and the array of moral and ethical issues encountered in this type of research.

Emergent Components of the Ethnographic Toolkit in Drug Studies

During the late twentieth and early twenty-first centuries, ethnography has come to entail more than just participant observation, in-depth and casual interviewing, and the convening of focus groups—the core methods discussed in chapter 1. Newer methods now commonly used in ethnographic research efforts are discussed in this chapter. The methods discussed below are network studies, systematic cognitive approaches, social mapping, use of field stations and community-based researchers, triangulation of diverse data sets, and multisited ethnography.

Network Studies

The systematic study of informal networks of social relations was not combined with the ethnography of drug use until the mid-1980s. Earlier ethnographic studies on socially integrated drug use, such as LeBarre's work on peyote consumption among Native Americans and Heath's studies of heavy drinking among the Camba (discussed in chapter 2), viewed drug consumption within a community context. The actual social networks—that is, the pattern of connections that link (or fail to link) study participants to each other, to other community members, and to individuals beyond the local community—and the impact of the configuration of network linkages on individual drug use patterns, drug-related beliefs and attitudes, and on other aspects of drug users' lives, including their health, were not part of the ethnographic research agenda until relatively recently. Most ethnographers who studied somewhat socially hidden street drug users prior to the mid-1970s did not vigorously investigate the personal networks of their participants. Rather, there was a tendency to see illicit drug users from the perspective of the larger society as social outcasts living marginal and fragmented lives. The lone exception to this tendency was the work of William True and colleagues (1980, based on research conducted between 1973 and 1976) in which personal networks of marihuana users were analyzed in terms of J. Clyde Mitchell's scheme for characterizing content and morphology of networks in urban settings (1969). This work preceded the burgeoning of network research during the 1980s, and it represents a first attempt by drug ethnographers at analyzing networks.

Early efforts to incorporate an examination of the web of ties that exist among drug users (and with non-drug users) involved the descriptive mapping of network features among individuals whose social connections were seen as avenues for recruiting new participants into research. Thus, the first ethnographers to use network approaches did so heuristically to broaden their reach into the dispersed population of illegal drug users and thereby include individuals who were hidden and hard to find using other recruitment strategies. In this process, the nature and importance of social and personal networks for understanding the lives, drug use, lifestyles, and drug-related health risks of drug users became increasingly evident. Since then, drug research ethnographers have applied formal and systematic methods to elicit information on the personal networks of individuals (e.g., all of the people with whom an individual acquires drugs, uses drugs, has sex, receives material support, and receives emotional support). This information is used to identify ties that link together sets of personal networks, leading ultimately to the identification of social networks that may include hundreds of individuals (Needle et al. 1995). This kind of understanding was achieved by recruiting and interviewing the individuals identified as network members by an initial study participant (sometimes referred to as a "seed") and subsequently asking these contact individuals about their own social connections. This approach extended and mapped complex webs of social ties through multiple layers of recruitment and interviewing. Further, researchers have analyzed the nature of these networks (based on the configuration of linkages they found and various concepts drawn from graph and network theory) to characterize the nature of drug user networks, components of networks, principles of network operation, and the health and social implications of network structures. As noted by Weeks and colleagues, "Social network research offers a means to map routes of potential viral transfer, to analyze the influence of peer norms and practices on the risk behaviors of individuals, and to trace communication channels through which prevention interventions might diffuse within a social group" (2002, 193).

Work in this area accelerated significantly following a meeting called by NIDA in August 1993 designed to explore the utility of the social network paradigm for examining the spread of HIV/AIDS among drug users. Participants at the meeting emphasized that the study of drug user networks would significantly expand insights gained through the traditional focus on individual risk behaviors, including nonrandom patterns of HIV transmission as well as innovative intervention approaches for linked drug users. Presenters at the conference noted the importance of assessing structural characteristics of networks, including their *density* (the proportion of direct ties identified among network members relative to the total possible number of ties if everyone in the network were connected with everyone else in the network); *reachability* (the proportion of network members connected by both direct and indirect pathways), and *centrality* (the total number of connections an individual network member has to other network members compared to the number of connections established by others in the network). Research has shown, for example, that HIV spreads more rapidly through a densely connected drug user social network than through one with a low density. Also, infection of individuals who are highly central to a network (i.e., having many connections to others in the network) results in a more rapid spread of HIV through the network than the infection of more peripheral individuals with fewer connections to other network members (Rothenberg et al. 1995).

As noted in the previous chapter, using social networks to recruit samples of drug users into research has led to the development of an approach known as Respondent Driven Sampling (RDS). The initial version of this recruitment strategy was developed by Douglas Heckathorn (1997) as part of a study of drug injectors in several cities in Connecticut, and has been elaborated in a series of subsequent studies with drug users and other groups. The objective of RDS is to enable the recruitment of reasonably representative samples when studying hidden and hard-to-reach populations. One of the challenges ethnographers face in studying drug users is that some individuals involved in drug use are much more accessible than others. For example, if drug injectors are recruited through a syringe exchange program or through street outreach at illicit drug buying sites, the resulting samples—based on syringe exchange use patterns and drug buying practices—are likely to be biased toward men and more experienced drug users (Heckathorn 2002, 2007; Salganik and Heckathorn 2004). The RDS methodology, which has been adopted in whole or in part by a number of drug use ethnographers, provides recruitment procedures (involving multiple waves of recruitment through drug user social networks) and a statistical means for calculating confidence intervals and weighting a sample to control for differences in network size and clustering across groups. Though some of the claims of RDS supporters have been disputed, the method has been widely implemented (Wejnert 2009).

Exemplary of this kind of research strategy, within a broader ethnographic approach to the study of drug users, is the work of Margaret Weeks and coworkers in Hartford, Connecticut (2002). With a grant from NIDA, Weeks and fellow researchers designed a multimethod study to:

- use street outreach to find, recruit, and interview a sample of drug users about their personal networks (i.e., the list of individuals, identified by nickname, described as having a significant relationship with the participant, including those with whom they use drugs, have sex, feel close, or have had conflicts during the previous six months).
- ask participants about the sex, ethnicity, and age of their identified network members, as well as the nature of their relationship with the participant (kin vs. nonkin), their HIV status (if known), frequency of contact, and trust they feel toward each of their network members.
- request that participants recruit two members of their identified network to also participate in project interviews.
- use all of this information to document the kinds and level of HIV-related risk behavior among personal (ego) network members, potential economic and social supports available to participants within the network, network size, ethnic/gender/age diversity, intensity and duration of interaction, and presence of HIV risk.
- link participants' personal networks to construct a macronetwork that connects multiple personal networks through individuals who appear in the personal networks of several participants.

- use the network lists and descriptions to recruit and train well-linked individuals as peer HIV prevention educators to disseminate, demonstrate, and support HIV prevention practices among their network peers.

Through these strategies, this research team was able to show that there were relatively few individuals in the personal networks of all of their participants but that network patterns differed somewhat by ethnicity (e.g., African Americans had larger personal networks and longer network relationships than Puerto Ricans had). The research team also found verifiable connections that linked two-thirds of the drug users in their study to each other in a macronetwork of interpersonal relationships. Further, the sharing of a drug use site (e.g., an abandoned building) was found to create additional linkages among study participants. Finally, they were able to use their approach to implement a successful HIV prevention program that, via the pathway of personal connections, could reach hidden and otherwise hard-to-find individuals. As noted by Trotter and colleagues, using a network approach to intervention confers several advantages:

> Once the first few individuals in [a] network have been recruited, the group itself can provide impetus for other members to participate. Rather than relying on individual-by-individual recruitment, group dynamics are in force beyond individual motivations. Once the group is assessed, the prevention or intervention program can be transmitted to a central individual in the network, with a good chance that it will subsequently be transmitted to part or all of the rest of the network. This use of networks makes the prevention effort more effective than prevention without network utilization. (Trotter, Bowen, and Potter 1995, 159)

Systematic Cognitive Methods

While classic ethnographic methods such as participant observation have been used in the study of drug users for more than seventy-five years, in more recent years a new set of approaches, primarily focused on cultural analysis, have been added to the ethnographer's toolkit and adopted by ethnographic drug researchers. These newer methods improve ethnographers' ability to analyze culturally defined cognitive systems by allowing ethnographers to examine narrowly delineated areas of culture rapidly and, as a result, contribute to the potential for rapid ethnographic assessment. Trotter grouped these approaches into three types: those that (1) help determine the content of specific cultural domains (e.g., drug consumption methods), (2) contribute to the analysis of the structure of cultural domains, and (3) allow a more accurate depiction of a cultural domain using a consensual framework (1995).

Exploration of the content of cultural domains commonly begins with the use of the free-listing technique, which involves asking members of a target group (e.g., street injection drug users) to list, off of the top of their heads, all of the elements that comprise a domain. For example, participants might be asked to list all of the drugs they know are mixed together before use (e.g., heroin and cocaine to make a speedball), to identify all of the reasons they use drugs, or to identify all of the components of the process of copping drugs (Agar 1973). This approach provides researchers with the natural language in use among study participants, including the names used for key behaviors, relationships, locations, or articles of interest. Knowledge of this information improves the cultural and communication competency of the ethnographer working in the target community. Free-listing also allows identification of intracultural varia- tion across subgroups, such as gender, age, or ethnic differences in beliefs, values, behaviors, and information. In drug use studies, this approach has been used systematically to identify cultural differences between injection and non- injection drug users. Additionally, this approach is used to generate ethno- graphic questions and to suggest the precise working terms that should be used in such questions to get at the information ethnographers are trying to gather. Moreover, free-listing has been found to be an effective discovery technique in that it often generates unexpected information that allows exploration of previ- ously unknown cultural domains.

Approaches for the analysis of the structure of cultural domains include pile sorts, triad tests, and sentence frame techniques (Weller and Romney 1988). Each of these approaches begins with a free-listing exercise to generate elements of a cultural domain followed by the use of these elements to clar- ify how they are ordered in the cognitive maps of study participants. Commonly, this process involves asking participants to make judgments about similari- ties and differences in the cultural elements that comprise a domain. In a pile sort, for example, Carlson and coworkers asked a group of young Ecstasy (MDMA) users to sort fifteen drugs in terms of their perceived similarities and differences in riskiness of use (2003). Contrary to their expectation—that users would discount the riskiness of Ecstasy—study participants classified Ecstasy as midway between drugs that were perceived to be most and least risky in terms of the damage they can cause users. Study participants expressed two popular myths about Ecstasy, namely the beliefs that it can drain spinal fluid and produce holes in the brain. Users also were found to be quite con- cerned about the impact of Ecstasy on memory. Notably, these researchers found that regular drug users did not necessarily think that the drugs they used were safe; rather, they used them despite harboring significant concerns about their riskiness.

Finally, consensus theory is an approach used both to establish a consen- sual description of a cultural domain (e.g., what injection drug users believe to be the best technique for targeting a vein and injecting drugs into it, an important area of knowledge given the risks of mistargeting or misinjecting outside of a vein) and to assess participants' cultural expertise (i.e., agreement or disagreement with most other members of the group about specific cultural information). Consensus models of culture are established by administering a set of questions to group members to examine the dominant (or consensus) and alternative answers to these questions. From the perspective of consensus theory, culturally correct answers are those offered by individuals who most commonly provide answers given by most other members of the group. Consensus theory approaches can be used, for example, to understand better the subcultures of drug users, such as the acceptability of particular behaviors used to raise money for or otherwise acquire drugs (e.g., begging, shoplifting, mugging, stealing from other drug users) or the culturally appropriate response to witnessing a fellow drug user overdose (e.g., run away because the police will come, call for help, splash water on the individual, make the individual drink coffee and walk around). Based on ethnographic research, Singer argued that, despite countervailing forces (e.g., interpersonal violence), a sense of community is developed among drug users who have similar folk knowledge and shared community values (2006c). Knowledge of how to load a crack pipe, mix different drugs together, avoid syringe clogging, and successfully "hit" a vein in intravenous injection is acquired socially—a process sometimes called "learning the ropes." Agar and MacDonald, for example, argued that conversation among homogeneous drug users flows easily because it relies on a body of shared knowledge that does not need to be explained (1995). Overall, drug ethnographers have tried to show that even under difficult circumstances—or, more precisely, *because* of difficult circumstances—a community of drug users can emerge that is as important and meaningful to its participants as it is alien and repugnant to "outsiders."

Consensus theory approaches are useful in drug ethnography because they extend research beyond a general assessment of community knowledge to the structured measurement of the strength of particular beliefs or values within a target group. Combined with social network methods, consensus research can be used to examine and attempt to explain patterns of knowledge or value distribution in a heterogeneous population. In public health–related research among drug users, for example, such an approach can be useful in determining the strength of both correct and incorrect information (based on existing science) held within the community, as well as identifying examples of misinformation that need to be targeted for change (e.g., the misunderstanding among many drug users that mosquitoes transmit HIV or that condoms are untrustworthy), as well as beliefs that should be reinforced through intervention strategies (e.g., those that promote prevention and harm-reduction behaviors).

Social Mapping

Although other fields, such as geography, have established clear dominion over this type of research in communities, mapping has come to play an important role in the course of ethnographic inquiry in and beyond drug-related research. Ethnographic mapping emphasizes the meaning of place in a community context, documenting in detail how people conceive and use space, who occupies particular space at what time of day / day of the week and for what purposes, and ways in which people are linked together within and affected by social locations. These dimensions of people, places, and times, described from an ethnographic, participant-observer perspective, can provide very useful information for purposes of intervention and problem solving. An example of this kind of work is seen in the High Risk Sites study directed by Margaret Weeks, an ethnographer and executive director of the Institute for Community Research in Hartford, Connecticut. This study focused on the examination and testing of drug use sites, such as shooting galleries, as potential HIV prevention venues. In the study, ethnographers and outreach workers scouted out, mapped, and routinely visited such locations, getting to know their physical and social characteristics, including the individuals and social networks of drug users who visited and used them (e.g., abandoned buildings used to inject drugs or smoke crack, have sex, and as temporary residences). In addition, they documented the natural histories of drug use settings in targeted neighborhoods (e.g., the range of uses they served, length of abandonment before demolition or refurbishment, police and property owner activities at the site) and determined the presence and receptivity of site gatekeepers (e.g., "house men" who regulate access) and site users to on-site prevention efforts.

Social mapping is also used by drug ethnographers to gain access to the emic (or insider) view of local settings. One approach for this involves providing drug users with poster board and markers and asking them individually or collectively to draw a map of the areas where they operate, including the location of the sites that are important to them and why (e.g., drug acquisition and use sites, soup kitchens and other resource sites, locations of police activity, community organizations, emergency rooms and clinics, drug treatment centers, syringe exchange locations, places to sleep). This approach allows ethnographers to gain access to the cognitive worlds of drug users, including their spatial conceptions and the types of culturally salient locations they value or avoid (Schensul et al. 1999).

In another example of the ethnographic study of the role of spatial issues in drug use, Page and Salazar (1999) elaborated a branching logic characterization of risk among IDUs in Valencia, Spain in which the primary drug injection sites, or *chutaderos*, had all of the necessary ingredients (i.e., discarded or contaminated needles/syringes, standing water, discarded lemon husks which provide the acid used to dissolve adulterants that are less water soluble than heroin, other injectors, isolation from the surrounding streets) to place the IDUs who ended up in them at maximum risk of exposure to HIV. These sites were located near major plazas and activity sites so that the IDUs could conveniently get money, buy drugs, and repair to the *chutadero* to inject the drugs, afterward returning to the plazas to pursue new ventures. Within the densely packed streets of Valencia, *chutaderos* were never far from the plazas. A significant outcome of this research was the recommendations it led to concerning the benefits of examining risk sites and their features in locally grounding HIV/AIDS prevention messages and approaches among drug users.

In the Community: Ethnographic Field Stations and Beyond

Street drug research presents a number of significant challenges for ethnographers, including protecting the safety of researchers in sometimes violent settings and identifying places to conduct confidential interviews with people engaged in illegal behaviors. In longitudinal studies, it may be quite difficult to relocate a street drug user for follow-up interviews. One solution to all of these problems, which grew out of the street research tradition initiated in New York by Ed Preble, is the ethnographic field station. The field station was defined by Paul Goldstein and colleagues as "a research 'outpost' in a community of interest to the researchers. It is a place where data are collected. It serves as a base of operations for the research staff, providing an environment in which research subjects and research staff may interact over an extended period of time" (1990, 80). Field stations are commonly located in rented storefront commercial locations or similar sites close to the places drug-related street life takes place and study participants reside. Goldstein, for example, reported that his Economic Behavior of Street Opiate Users study used three field stations in the East Harlem area of New York City while the Drug Related Involvement in Violent Episodes (DRIVE) study and the Female Drug Related Involvement in Violent Episodes (FEMDRIVE) study operated out of the same field site on the Lower East Side of Manhattan. All of these sites varied in their physical conditions, ranging from unheated space in tenement buildings that were hard to work in during winter months to well-maintained sites that neighborhood residents and former research participants would visit to share refreshments and stories with fieldworkers. The projects noted above found that having a permanent, fixed-location field station in the community facilitated the process of recruiting research participants because potential participants always knew where they could go to find the researchers. Such sites provide a reliable location in which researchers and participants can congregate in a protected environment. Moreover, researchers and participants commonly come to view the field station as a safe haven in an often hectic and occasionally threatening street environment. In addition, they offer researchers a physical place in the community "that negate[s] the perception of staff as strangers" while contributing to researchers coming to be "accepted as belonging to the local community" (Goldstein et al. 1990, 93).

Despite these advantages, field stations present their own set of challenges. Theft and the potential for on-site violence are two of the issues that station-based ethnographers have confronted. Small items with street value, such as tape recorders, clothing, money, and office equipment, may be taken by visitors if the opportunity presents itself. Such occurrences can be emotionally difficult for less-experienced project staff as this appears to reflect a lack of trust between participants and ethnographic researchers. Experienced ethnographers realize that opportunistic thievery is a well-honed and highly valued survival skill among street drug users. Part of the proficiency of experienced street drug users is the ability to offer a creative explanation when caught stealing from a field station. In fact, ethnographers have found that participants who steal from a research project in which they have been well treated may subsequently feel guilty and, as a result, avoid subsequent contact with project staff.

Another potential weakness of field stations is that they can lead to the development of complacency among field researchers, reducing their inclination to spend time on the streets in the natural venues of drug users, such as drug copping sites, drug use sites, resource locations (e.g., soup kitchens), and drug user residences. Presence on the street, which enables seeing events and interactions as they unfold in natural contexts, is one of the greatest strengths of the ethnographic study of drug use. Consequently, though field stations can be useful, they are not a substitute for traditional ethnographic participant observation in the natural settings of drug user populations.

Even though most ethnographic field stations are temporary, lasting the lifetime of one or more back-to-back studies, longer-term placement in communities is another approach to drug ethnography. In Hartford, Connecticut, for example, drug ethnographers have developed an approach that they refer to as the Hartford Model of practice / research collaboration (Singer and Weeks 2005). The cornerstone principles of this research model include (1) the ongoing location of ethnographers in nongovernment community-based organizations and research institutes; (2) long-term, community-based partnerships between researchers and research-informed community interventionists; (3) highly collaborative team efforts guided by a participatory action orientation to research and the transfer of research skills; and (4) closely linking community-based research with research-informed intervention. In drug use studies, the Hartford Model takes several aspects of the field station approach, such as working out of a fixed-site community location, but it extends the time frame of community involvement over several decades, allowing ethnographers (even if they are new to a project) to (1) gain rapid community access (through the reputation of the community organization), (2) participate over an extended period in community events and struggles, and (3) translate research findings into community-directed intervention initiatives. In the case of drug research, the fixed-site location has led to ethnographic findings used in the development of drug treatment programs, HIV/AIDS prevention tailored to drug users, and harm-reduction policy initiatives (Singer 1993, Singer, Romero-Daza, et al. 2005).

Multimethod Approaches and Triangulation

Rooted in the holistic view of the human behaviors that it studies, ethnography commonly incorporates the tools of a number of research disciplines. To systematize data on spatial relations among component parts of a cultural location, geographic information systems can provide drug ethnographers with a useful technology. To assess the distribution of particular beliefs or behaviors in a population of drug users, the survey methods utilized by sociologists and political scientists may be adopted. Psychometrics or nutritional study instruments may be useful in assessing the health status of drug users. Extant databases may already be available for the ethnographer's use in attempting to achieve a fully rounded perspective on the specific research question at hand. Consequently, drug ethnographers often employ multiple methods borrowed from other fields. To integrate disparate types of data, ethnographers employ an approach they have come to call *triangulation*.

The term *triangulation*, developed within astronomy, refers to the use of geometry (or trigonometry) to calculate the location of intersecting sides of triangles in order to measure the distance to another planet or celestial body. Within ethnographic research, triangulation refers to an approach to data collection and analysis that builds on and synthesizes data from multiple sources based on different data collection methods. In data collection, triangulation involves the use of data from one method to inform data collection using a different method (e.g., using field observations to suggest issues explored with in-depth interviews or surveys). In analysis, triangulation is like viewing the inside of a locked building through several different windows to develop a composite understanding of the internal environment of the building. In this case, triangulation is used to examine several different data sets (e.g., in-depth interviews, observations, participant diaries, survey findings) to validate the accuracy of the findings (data corroboration) of any individual method and to expand the overall level of understanding (data integration).

By examining information collected through the sequential or concurrent use of various methods, concurrent research by different but linked individuals or teams of researchers, and research conducted in different locations or populations/subpopulations, findings can be connected across data sets, both reducing the impact of potential biases inherent in any individual method (e.g., the limitations of self-report about risky behaviors) and extending insight into behaviors of special interest. In drug studies, for example, triangulation often involves combining information collected using various qualitative methods and wedding qualitative and quantitative methods and findings (e.g., linking observational discoveries of particular drug-related behaviors with quantitative findings from survey research on the frequency, social distribution, and correlates of these behaviors). Several drug ethnographers, including Claire Sterk and Kirk Elifson (2005), Robert Carlson and colleagues (1995), and Merrill Singer and Margaret Weeks (2005) have published papers on the uses of triangulation in ethnographic drug research. These publications affirmed the utility of combining data collection and analytic approaches to better understand the social and cultural worlds of drug users and to increase the validity of, generalizability of, and confidence in research findings, while noting the challenges (e.g., difficulties of combining different types of data) of complex, multicomponent research approaches.

Multisited Drug Studies

In 1995, George Marcus published a text arguing for the adoption of multisited approaches in ethnography. Marcus suggested that the value of such studies, which involve the tracing and describing of social connections and relationships among different locations previously thought to be incommensurate, was that it allowed ethnographic investigation of more complex issues. Further, multisited ethnographic research strategies offer "an opportunity to dislocate the ethnographer from the strong traditional filiation to just one group of subjects among whom fieldwork is done" to a broader field of social actors in different locations (Marcus 1995, 20). Although the multisited strategy proposed by Marcus was new to ethnographic research on other issues, the implementation of concurrently linked research on "the same behaviors" in several dispersed sites was already several decades old within drug ethnography at the time of Marcus's proposal. One of the earliest multisited drug ethnographies was discussed in chapter 2—the NIH-funded study of the impact of Cannabis on health in Jamaica, Costa Rica, and Greece.

Another early multisited ethnographic drug study focused on the use of the drug PCP and led to the publication of *Angel Dust: An Ethnographic Study of Phencyclidine Users* (Feldman 1979). This study was carried out in Miami, Philadelphia, Chicago, and Seattle using a common research protocol. The study responded to growing reports of the spread of PCP, an animal tranquilizer, among younger drug users. One product of this study was the realization that the ethnographic method, though traditionally seen as requiring long-term immersion in local settings to allow for the development of trust and the analytic penetration of complex and behaviorally dispersed social patterns, could be adapted under certain conditions for the rapid assessment of emergent trends in drug use behaviors.

A subsequent drug study that helped to affirm the value of qualitative multisited research in drug studies was the Heroin Lifestyle Study (HLS). This qualitative examination of the day-to-day lives and subcultural characteristics of African American heroin users was carried out in Chicago, New York City, Washington, D.C., and Philadelphia. Study participants included 124 men, all of whom were regular heroin users and the majority of whom had never received (nor wanted) drug treatment. This disinclination to receive treatment was a primary focus of the study. Specifically, the study was designed to present a descriptive account of participants' daily lives and to identify emergent patterns in their routine behaviors. The men reported that they first tried heroin, which was readily available in their local inner-city communities, for several different reasons: curiosity, heightened status among peers, strong peer encouragement, and media sensationalism. Commonly, they viewed their second shot of heroin "as the beginning of a long descent from the peak experience of their first injection" and "a futile attempt to recapture the first experience—in short, the beginning of a neverending search for the perfect high" (Beschner and Bovelle 1985, 87). Ironically, one of the important findings of the study was the falsification of the assumption that there was a distinctive heroin lifestyle that differed from the basic daily pattern of the surrounding inner-city community. While addiction, and the need to raise money for heroin, impacted some of the routine activities of the men, it was the "pursuit of normalcy" under conditions of significant social inequality and the general conventionality of behavior relative to local norms that characterized the lifestyle of study participants. Also of note was the degree of control that participants exercised over their addiction—a refutation of the common assertion that regular heroin users "have an insatiable and uncontrollable appetite for heroin and that they therefore shoot up as many times as possible each day" (Bovelle and Taylor 1985, 177).

With the appearance and rapid spread of crack cocaine and its linkage to HIV risk, researchers in New York City, Miami, and San Francisco launched the Multicenter Crack Cocaine and HIV Infection Study (Edlin et al. 1994). The study interviewed more than 1,000 crack smokers (18 to 29 years of age) and found that, overall, just under 16 percent were positive for HIV infection, with the highest prevalence among female crack users in New York (29.6 per cent); 42.9 percent of the men who had anal sex with other men tested positive for HIV infection. The common thread among those who were HIV+ across sites and subgroups was their involvement in risky sexual practices.

Indeed, as noted in chapters 3 and 4, the HIV epidemic among drug users helped to trigger the development of a series of multisited epidemiological studies, many of which included significant ethnographic components, including the National AIDS Demonstration Research Program and the Cooperative Agreement for AIDS Community-Based Outreach/Intervention Research Program. Overall, these two programs helped to confirm "the value of ethnographic and other field research techniques in social and epidemiological investigation" (Friedman et al. 1990, 104). Ultimately, they also helped to establish ethnography as an indispensible method in drug research and multisited ethnographic research as a useful approach to understanding the relationship of macronational to microlocal patterns of drug use and its health sequelae (Singer, Valentín, et al. 1992; Singer et al. 2007).

Research Ethics and Drug Ethnography

Ethnographers who study drug users face formidable challenges in ensuring that their work is ethically sound and does not harm the participating individuals and communities. The special ethical demands of this work stem from three primary sources: (1) the configurations of social conditions that often are faced by drug users; (2) the characteristics of the ethnographic approach to studying this population; and (3) the effects of powerful, psychotropic drugs on informed consent and other aspects of research involvement. In some settings, especially those in which the population of interest has been marginalized because their behavior is deemed illegal or inappropriate by the dominant society, drug users are a particularly vulnerable group. This vulnerability stems from the potentially intense craving for drugs among those who suffer addiction or dependence; a disproportionate suffering from mental health burdens such as depression and anxiety (which they self-medicate with the drugs they consume); a constant risk of arrest and/or police harassment or even harm; a disproportionate exposure (far greater in some settings than others) to trauma, including child abuse, domestic violence, street violence, and other forms of criminal victimization (the effects of which also may provide motivation for self-medication with drugs); common drug user involvement in the criminal justice system (based on prior arrests) as a result of local, national, and international wars on drug use; and the disadvantaged socioeconomic status of many drug users.

Involvement in ethnographic research puts drug users at heightened risk because of researcher transcendence of the cultural masks and social boundaries that separate them from participants in less intensively interactive research methods. Buchanan and colleagues (2003), for example, described the ethical dilemma faced by ethnographic researchers in deciding whether or not they should replace used syringes with sterile syringes (to eliminate their infectious potential) found during visits to abandoned buildings and other known drug use sites to conduct bioassay assessments for HIV and hepatitis exposure from "discarded" drug equipment (as an indirect measure of risky settings and levels of local infection). In this research, it was not always a question of whether or not identified syringes were abandoned or simply hidden for subsequent reuse. Furthermore, the "on-site" nature of ethnography may create risks for study participants. Drug ethnographers, for example, have expressed concern that their public contact with drug users might endanger the trust of drug dealers (and, hence, participants' access to drugs) because of fear that the ethnographer is an undercover police officer (Jacobs 1998). The exploratory nature of ethnographic research may also pose challenges to the ability, during the informed consent process, to identify fully the exact nature of the kinds of information that will be obtained or when confidential information could be disclosed because of unexpected circumstances such as court orders, confiscation of project data by police officials, or the enactment of new mandated reporting requirements (Marshall 1992a, 1992b; Singer et al. 2000).

In addition, ethnographers come to know a lot of things that other kinds of social researchers are not privy to about the lives and activities of the people they study, including a considerable amount of information that drug users may wish to keep private. The same may be true of the researcher. The blurring of personal/professional boundaries in ethnographic research can, as a result, pose significant ethical quandaries for both researchers and participants. Ethnographers studying drug use behaviors may become privy to participants' most intimate feelings and clandestine behaviors, including intentions to harm rivals or engage in other behaviors that put people at risk (e.g., have sex with a minor). Similarly, the participant may gain information about the researcher (e.g., place of residence) that could become a liability. Singer and another researcher had this experience when they encountered two drug-involved informants sitting across the street from the latter researcher's home. As it turned out, they coincidentally were repairing the roof of a house in the neighborhood, but the potential that the location of the researcher's place of residence had become known was briefly very discomforting because of the anxiousness drug users feel to constantly be engaged in income generation to buy drugs and avert withdrawal symptoms. Overall, the intimacy that develops during informal conversational interviews, participant observation, and prolonged contact with participants may create opportunities for mutual coercion, exploitation, or harm (Singer et al. 1999). Given the considerable amount of information that key informants provide ethnographers, for example, the possibility exists for them to insist on reciprocity and pressure researchers to engage in illegal activities (e.g., hide drugs to help protect an informant from an impending arrest, use the ethnographer's car or office to consume drugs safely away from the watchful eyes of police, or provide fiscal incentives prior to interviews—that may never take place—as a means of helping an informant avoid withdrawal symptoms). Consequently, the potential for ethical violations has many sources, including both researcher and participant vulnerability.

Beyond the risks created by research participation, ethnographic or otherwise, questions also have been raised in recent years about the full set of responsibilities researchers have regarding the discovered vulnerabilities of drug using populations (including those that have their source outside of research participation). This issue is of special concern to ethnographers because of the complex personal nature of the research/participant relationships that can grow out of this approach to research. In short, as a result of getting to know individual drug users, including sometimes detailed information about their mental health, emotional states, risk behavior, and vulnerability to the harm caused by involvement in dangerous settings, ethnographers acquire the responsibility to help protect participants from harm that may befall them outside of the research context (Singer et al. 2000). Of course, there are limits to the researchers' awareness of potential risks faced by their study participants and limits to the researchers' abilities to act on behalf of the perceived well-being of participants (e.g., because they may decline researchers' offers of assistance). Members of Singer's research team have come across situations in which known participants in ongoing studies appeared to be in extreme distress yet adamantly and unwaveringly refused assistance. In such instances, researchers must make careful and sometimes difficult judgments about the capacity of the individual to understand the dire nature of his or her situation and to make rational decisions about possible courses of action.

Limiting Ethnical Dilemmas

In addressing these challenges, ethnographers are assisted by disciplinary guidelines that specify accepted research ethics, such as those developed by the American Anthropological Association and the Society for Applied Anthropology, as well as by prevailing government standards designed to protect the rights and welfare of research participants. In response to a long history of abusive treatment of research participants—exemplified by the now infamous Tuskegee syphilis study with African American men—fundamental principles of beneficence, respect, and justice have been formulated by the U.S. National Commission (DHEW 1978) and have been operationalized as federal regulations (DHHS 2001, subpart A). These regulations require investigators to minimize research risks, maximize research benefits, obtain informed consent from research participants, protect participant privacy and confidentiality, and ensure that participation in research is always voluntary. Further, researchers are required to minimize the harm that research causes the study participants while they ensure that the benefits and burdens of research participation are equally distributed and not limited to specific subgroups of the study population (Levine 1986; Singer et al. 1999).

The Institutional Review Board (IRB) provides the key mechanism for protection of human subjects in research. Research institutions throughout the United States and in many other countries have established IRBs to approve, monitor, and review research with human subjects (as well as with animal subjects) and to protect their rights, safety, and well-being. In the United States,

IRBs receive their charge from the Department of Health and Human Services' Office for Human Research Protections under Title 45 CFR of the Code of Federal Regulations. Composed of experienced researchers, as well as representatives of communities and vulnerable populations, it is the job of IRBs to review and approve or disapprove all research procedures involving human participants proposed by members of the institution. Review of research procedures involves taking into account six factors that assess the ethical protections included in research: (1) provision of a detailed description of proposed human subject involvement in the research design, including specification of the characteristics of the subject populations; (2) identification of research information sources obtained on research participants (e.g., interviews, observations, anthropomorphic measures, biological specimens) and indication of whether these are newly collected data for the purposes of research or gleaned from existing records; (3) description of participant recruitment and consent procedures, including description of the conditions under which consent is to be obtained; (4) identification of the specific physical, psychological, social, legal, or other risks that participants will face as a result of their involvement in the research; (5) report of the exact procedures to be adopted to protect subjects against or minimize potential risks, including specification of the provisions to be adopted for ensuring necessary medical or professional intervention in the event that subjects experience adverse effects as a result of their participation in the research; and (6) justification of any potential risks to which participants will be exposed in light of the anticipated benefits to participants and in terms of the importance of the knowledge likely to be produced by the conducted research.

The craft of drug ethnography has given its practitioners opportunities to develop and review the practices of protecting human participants in research studies. Because research on illegal drug use has a history of eliciting concern from IRBs for the protection of human subjects, drug ethnographers are somewhat more used to providing adequate protections at the outset of their studies than their colleagues in other fields of social research. This protection involves anticipating all risks that are reasonably possible and building safeguards to minimize or eliminate that risk. Examples of this kind of preparation include:

- To ensure the maintenance of professional relationships with participants despite prolonged interaction, interaction ground rules are developed and research team members are monitored for adherence.
- To diminish the likelihood that researchers will use large cash incentives to lure participants who really would prefer not to participate, payments are set in terms of local prevailing levels (i.e., what is generally being paid for local research participation).
- To ensure that risks and rewards of research participation are equitably distributed, recruitment plans are developed that reasonably reflect the

target populations (with detailed explanations of necessary deviations from this practice).

- To limit the vulnerability of ethnographic research team members to participant coercion based on the cultural values of reciprocity, training is used to help research team members develop skills in resisting such efforts.
- To ensure that participation is voluntary and that participants are fully informed about the nature and demands of a study, consent documents are developed and reviewed for comprehension, completeness, and accuracy, and their use in the field is monitored.

One of the major challenges of ethnographic research with drug users involves the social status differences that commonly exist between academically trained researchers and drug user participants, including incongruities in class, education, resource access, and ethnicity. It is critical that researchers recognize how these disparities, which reflect wider social-structural inequalities, can, if addressed carelessly, be experienced by study participants as a violation of ethical principles of respect, beneficence, and justice. Many of the drug ethnographers whose work is described in this book, for example, had very different cultural backgrounds from the people they studied. Sir Richard Burton wore the costume (and artificial facial coloring) of the group that he was visiting to avoid apprehension and execution. Agar was a bearded graduate student as he visited the Lexington treatment facility populated by criminals from all over the eastern United States. Page's observations in Miami took place among a group that was 95 percent African American, while most of Singer's work in Hartford involved primarily Puerto Rican and African American drug users. In the vast majority of the cases of drug ethnography, white males (and, to a growing degree, white females) have attempted to study culturally and phenotypically different populations. This incongruity has advantages and disadvantages. In the advantage column, researchers are able to present themselves effectively as outsiders with no motivation to become involved in the internal conflicts and rivalries of the scene under study. In the disadvantage column, the ethnographer often must engage in a long, slow, and at times frustrating process of deciphering body language, slang terms, and nuances in the local cultural environment (e.g., learning when and how to break the rules in culturally sanctioned ways). Drug ethnographers, as a result, must be keenly sensitive to the populations they study and highly aware of their own beliefs and values. Ethnographers who lack these capacities—and they are encountered all the time in research initiatives with large field teams—tend not to have long careers in drug-related research. Indeed, insensitivity to the difficult life experiences and hidden injuries of everyday living among drug users is more likely to doom a career in drug ethnography than are poor initial research skills.

While the guidelines and training protocols developed for use in drug-related research are very helpful, they are far from clear-cut and do not fully address the array of troublesome and complex moral issues encountered in drug-related ethnographic settings (e.g., the impact of drug addiction on the voluntary nature of research participation). Further, federal provisions for the protection of vulnerable populations offer no special protections for drug users (Fisher 1999; NIH 1999). Finally, questions have been raised about whether ethnographic research should be held to the same standards that were developed for other research methods, such as biomedical research and clinical trials. Rayna Rapp, for example, argued that bioethics, the domain that has dominated the establishment of ethical research standards with human (and nonhuman) populations, tends to be "self-confidently unaware of its own sociocultural context" and often fails to consider whether the standards it advocates are harmonious with the values of non-Western populations (2000, 44). Exemplary of this problem is the fact that, while bioethics stresses the critical importance of respecting individual autonomy, free will, and self-determination, these values reflect the Western prioritization of individualism and may not be values in cultural systems founded on a belief in individual subordination to collective needs and top-down decision-making about appropriate behaviors. This kind of insensitivity to other normative systems has been criticized as a form of ethical ethnocentrism.

Some ethnographers have also expressed concern that prevailing ethical research standards at times require ethnographers to engage in behaviors that create rather than avoid ethical complications, such as mandating that research participants sign their names to informed consent documents. In the study of illegal drug use, this practice may cancel out the researcher's commitment to protecting the confidentiality of study participants. Further, ethnographers working with active drug users in high-crime neighborhoods may be subject to existing "duty to protect" laws and court decisions that oblige researchers to report the existing potential for harm (Appelbaum and Rosenbaum 1989). "Duty to protect" requirements of this kind give rise to ethical complexities in situations in which causing harm to others is interpreted by authorities as including involvement in HIV risk behaviors, such as the direct sharing of drug injection equipment by an individual who knows that he or she is infected (Fisher 2004). While federally funded researchers in the United States are able to apply for a certificate of confidentiality that is supposed to protect them from having to share their raw data (e.g., participant names) with legal authorities, this protection often does not exist for ethnographers working outside of the United States (and has yet to be tested in a U.S. court case). Further, even in the United States, the possession of a certificate may not dissuade local officials from challenging a researcher's effort to protect participant confidentiality by involving them in a time-consuming and costly judicial battle to obtain the desired research records (e.g., to prosecute a pregnant drug user for child abuse). Even with certificates of confidentiality, problems can arise. A participant in one of Singer's studies, for example, was arrested while in possession of his research diary, in which he had recorded several recent drug use events. Consequently, drug ethnographers have come to realize that de-identification of their research notes and interview records (by using pseudonyms or code numbers for participants) can help protect research participants. Similarly, it is possible to teach participants to use codes for illegal activities when keeping a diary for research purposes.

As a result of these issues, the relationship between ethics and ethnography has become an arena of strong concern and intense discussion in recent years. In an effort to address some of these issues, drug ethnographers have attempted to develop and promote targeted guidelines, including the creation of sets of "dos and don'ts" to be followed during street drug ethnography (Singer et al. 1999). Despite these guidelines, several significant breaches have occurred—as would be expected in any arena of human behavior—reminding drug ethnographers of the constant need to foreground and routinely discuss ethical issues in research.

Conclusion

As the discussion in this chapter suggests, research is never stagnant; new questions arise and are answered (sometimes), new methods are developed and refined, and new controversies and challenges, including emergent ethical issues, develop and must be addressed. This pattern is no less true with regard to the behaviors, contexts, populations, and psychotropics that comprise the social worlds of drug use studied by ethnographers.

7

Career Paths in Drug-related Ethnography

From Falling to Calling

$\mathbf{W}$ho becomes a drug use ethnographer? Why pursue this vocational path? What are the special appeals and distinctive burdens of this line of professional work? This chapter addresses these questions by reviewing findings from a study conducted by Singer, Page, and Melissa Houle of changing patterns in the development of anthropological careers in drug research.

In the past, the road to such a career was rarely a straight line leading from a carefully thought out decision to an established training program, and from there to professional involvement in the field. Recalling his own pathway into a drug research career, Michael Agar observed:

> My first teaching job landed me at the University of Hawaii in 1971. . . . It was bad enough that a new kid arrived working on book revisions. . . . But a book on *heroin addicts*? Anthropology was obviously going to hell in a handbasket. Most [of my colleagues] did books and articles, if they wrote anything at all, on villages in Asia and the Pacific. I wish I had a nickel for every time someone asked me, "Yes, but is it anthropology?" (2007, 51)

As reflected in this statement, when Agar began his career as a drug researcher in the early 1970s, there was far from universal acceptance among fellow anthropologists that such a career track was fully legitimate within the discipline (Bennett and Cook 1996; Page 2004).

Recognizing that, relative to other scientists or even other social scientists, anthropologists were considered a marginal group, unconventional in their methods and research perspectives. As an ethnographer of drug-related behavior, Agar found that he was "marginal in a marginal field" (Agar 2007, 48). At the time, drug research was not the quest anthropological dreams were made of (Singer 1986). Indeed, it was far from clear that such a career path existed in anthropology, and it certainly was not something many people planned in advance. In his assessment of anthropological careers in alcohol research during this period, for example, Dwight Heath observed that, traditionally, anthropologists who came to study drinking behavior rarely deliberately selected such a vocation from an array of well-considered alternatives (1976). Rather, they tended to "stumble into" such an off-the-beaten-path occupational track as a result of unanticipated circumstances. The same was true of illicit drug research, which was something anthropologists found themselves in "by chance or circumstance rather than [select] it intentionally because of its centrality to the discipline, the recognition and career benefits it would bring, or because of the productive impact findings were expected to have on policy makers and program managers" (Singer 2001, 210).

Certainly, this was the case with Agar, who applied to the U.S. Public Health Service when he discovered that it was a route for avoiding the draft and being sent to fight in the widely unpopular Vietnam War. From the pool of applicants, Agar was chosen for a commission in the public health corps when Jack O'Donnell, a sociologist, decided it would be interesting to have an anthropologist in the research office at the federal drug treatment facility in Lexington, Kentucky. O'Donnell actually wasn't quite sure what anthropologists did, but somehow he intuitively sensed that it would prove to be interesting. In retrospect, he was right. The volume that resulted from Agar's research with patients at Lexington, *Ripping and Running: A Formal Ethnography of Urban Heroin Addicts* (1973), is considered a classic in the field.

The career trajectories of many anthropologists and others who found their way into drug-related ethnographic research in the years before the appearance of the global AIDS pandemic followed a similarly unexpected, yet ultimately quite rewarding, pathway. Since AIDS, however, a new pattern has appeared that involves a conscious decision to become a drug use ethnographer. For some, such a career is also an avocation, a selected profession that allows them access to a line of personally meaningful and at times socially impactful work at the front lines of several intersecting epidemics.

In this chapter, we describe the ethnographic drug research career, how it has changed over time, and the essential role that NIDA and several other institutions, such at the National Institute on Alcohol Abuse and Alcoholism (NIAAA), have played in helping to create and shape this professional role in the health social sciences. The impact of the funding provided by these agencies has rippled throughout the research world and helped to shape the study of illegal drugs, including ethnographic studies of drug use. Researchers originally funded by NIDA have proceeded to conduct studies and train researchers in various countries, including Thailand, Spain, Russia, Ukraine, Botswana, Brazil, China, Vietnam, and Colombia. Because NIDA provides more than 90 percent of all funding for worldwide drug research, it is not surprising that it has had such a widespread international impact. Other U.S. funders, including the Department of Justice, state governments, programs like the California HIV/AIDS Research Program, private foundations like the American Foundation for Addiction Research, and funding bodies in other countries like the Canadian Institutes of Health Research and the Australian National Health and Medical Research Council, have also provided financial support for drug research. Meanwhile, investigators funded by NIAAA have joined in international efforts to assess drinking patterns that are informed by ethnographic studies.

Our Stories

Like Agar, unplanned detours into long-term drug research careers occurred in the lives of both of this book's authors. For Page, the process began at a party hosted by his eventual dissertation advisor which led to his recruitment to fill an empty slot on a research team that was assembled to study marihuana use among working-class men in Costa Rica. The study's principal investigators, observing his skills as a singer/guitarist (singing in Spanish), surmised that his abilities might help make connections with marihuana-smoking musicians. In Costa Rica in 1973, musicians tended not to use Cannabis at all, with the exception of a few who attempted to imitate the hippy lifestyle of the United States. Nevertheless, Page's guitar and repertoire of *rancheras* and *boleros* helped him to establish rapport with men who had a minimum of ten years' experience smoking marihuana—the requirement specified by the research contract under which he worked. The experience gained in this project helped Page identify a niche for further development in the study of human drug use, but he also recognized the need for complementary skills in statistical analysis. A one-year postdoctoral experience in the Gainesville Veterans Administration Hospital under the tutelage of George Warheit, Jeff Krischer, and Charles Holtzer taught Page the language of statistics.

Armed with this combination of street ethnography and quantitative methods, he entered the world of "academic hunting and gathering" in the Department of Psychiatry at the University of Miami. This position involved the infamous "soft money," but it paid better than any of the academic jobs available at that time ($20,000 per year for a twelve-month appointment versus $12,000 for nine months). From this platform, Page was able to devise projects that sustained his research for the next thirty years.

In Singer's case, his graduate research focused on the anthropology of religion, a subfield with a long tradition dating to the earliest encounters of European explorers with the diverse spiritual understandings and ritual practices of the world's far-flung populations. Having conducted ethnographic research with a Hassidic group in California for his master's thesis (leading to several of his earliest publications), exploratory research with a polygamous Mormon sect in Utah, and doctoral research in Israel with the Black Hebrew

Israelites, an emergent religious faction of African American origin, he sought an academic career focused on the social and cultural patterning of human religious beliefs and practices.

At the time he completed his doctoral degree, however, in the late 1970s, academic jobs in anthropology received hundreds of applications and many neophyte anthropologists faced the painful realization that times had changed: the academy—which only relatively recently (beginning in the 1960s) had become the primary arena of anthropological employment—could no longer absorb the many graduates who desired academic careers. As a result, when he was offered an NIAAA-funded postdoctoral fellowship to study family factors in abusive drinking at the Center for Family Research, George Washington University School of Medicine—the only offer yielded by his many applications—he leapt at the opportunity. Not much of a drinker and completely lacking in knowledge about the role of families in generating and sustaining problem drinking patterns among their members, he spent a year attending lectures, reading, and thinking about drinking behavior. Unlike the study of religion, it was evident and appealing that alcohol research addressed pressing health issues and had socially beneficial uses. During this period, Singer carried out several small studies on drinking, although his initially planned ethnography of a twenty-eight-day alcohol treatment center collapsed when government funding for the program ended the week his study began. Instead, he examined recidivism among so-called Skid Row alcoholics (Spradley's urban migrants) and the therapeutics of Christian Science healers (who treat people for alcoholism but do not believe such a material condition exists independent of the patient's belief that it does). Papers on these topics, as well as one based on the analysis of data he had collected on drinking behavior among the Black Hebrew Israelites, became Singer's first publications in drug studies. The paper on Black Hebrew Israelites reflected a key feature of ethnography whether or not the ethnographer set out to focus on drinking (or other drug use): if drinking is going on in the cultural context under observation and the ethnographer is taking detailed field notes, he or she can end up with sufficient data to characterize drinking in that cultural context.

During a subsequent second postdoctoral fellowship (again because academic jobs remained hard to come by), this one funded by the National Institute of Mental Health (NIMH) through the University of Connecticut Medical School, Singer carried out an ethnographic study of spiritual healing among Puerto Rican *espiritistas*, during which he found himself drawn to the question of folk treatment of alcohol-related problems. This study led to his involvement with a community-based health research and service institution, the Hispanic Health Council in Hartford, Connecticut. In light of expressed community concerns about problem drinking and its social consequences, Singer and colleagues at the Hispanic Health Council developed a research proposal designed to examine pathways into unhealthy drinking behavior among Puerto Rican youth. Funding of this grant led to employment at the Council, and to a research career that was for many years primarily focused on drug use and health issues, a turn that was strongly fueled by the emergence of drug-related behaviors as primary factors in the AIDS epidemic among inner-city ethnic minority populations.

Careers in Dope

In 1975, Dan Waldorf, a sociologist, published a book called *Careers in Dope*. His title referred to the utility of the career concept for the study of lifelong drug users. However, as the previous discussion of Agar, Page, and Singer indicates, there is also a "career in dope" that has emerged among ethnographers of drug-related behavior. Although there are a few individual and anecdotal accounts of how and why various anthropologists have become long-term drug researchers, and exchanges about these matters occasionally enliven anthropology conference conversations of fellow travelers in drug research, there has never been a systematic assessment of this career path in anthropology. Do most anthropologists (or ethnographically oriented sociologists) who work in drug research still arrive there serendipitously like Agar, Page, and Singer, or are some anthropologists now consciously seeking out such careers? If the latter, why? Moreover, how are drug research anthropologists received by their colleagues within the discipline or sister disciplines? Do anthropologists involved in drug research feel like they have an impact on the wider discipline or on the multidisciplinary domain of drug research? These are the questions we will address in the remainder of this chapter based on findings from a study of fifty-four anthropologists who completed a survey about their drug-related research careers.

Career Study Methods

In the summer of 2006, a forty-two-item questionnaire inquiring about anthropologists' involvement with, interests in, and experience with drug-related careers was developed and implemented through an online survey program. The survey included a variety of multiple-choice and open-ended questions, and respondents were asked to answer a range of questions, including how they initially entered the drug field, their coursework and training, what their influences were, their perceptions of the field, and how they think the field is changing and/or impacting other fields such as medical anthropology.

An invitation to respond to the questionnaire was sent via e-mail to two anthropology listservs: one operated by the Alcohol, Drug, and Tobacco Study Group and the other by the AIDS and Anthropology Research Group—both interest groups of the Society for Medical Anthropology. The announcement was sent with a letter explaining the research aims and included an embedded link to the survey. Potential respondents were told how their answers would be used, and they were asked if they would like a copy of the results upon publication. Anonymity was ensured as respondents were not asked to provide their names or any other specific personal identifier. No respondents' e-mail addresses were collected. After approximately two months, a general thank-you message was sent out on the listservs, and this generated an additional set of respondents who had missed the earlier announcement.

As noted, a total of fifty-four individuals responded to the online survey, constituting the sample for this analysis of drug research careers in anthropology. While the sample was not random, in that recruitment was by general announcement, respondents self-selected to participate or not, and the announcement certainly did not reach every anthropologist who works in drug research or related fields (e.g., those who are not members of the selected listservs), the sample size was sufficient, we believe, to gain a general sense of drug research career trajectories in anthropology.

Respondents were able to complete the survey at their own convenience by simply clicking on the link to the survey (or cutting and pasting the address to their Web browser) and answering the questions by clicking appropriate boxes. The data were automatically submitted and compiled into various frequency graphs.

Educational Patterns and Dissertation Topics

Of the survey participants, eight were still students, two had master's degrees, and the remainder (78 percent) had a Ph.D. Of those who had earned a Ph.D., seven received it during the 1970s, six during the 1980s, fifteen during the 1990s, and eleven since the turn of the twenty-first century. While this distribution may reflect participation in the listservs that were used to recruit respondents, it is more likely an indication of the increase, beginning in 1995, in the number of graduate students electing to work in drug research. Fifteen of the participants received their Ph.D.s during the twenty-four years between 1970 and 1994, while twenty-four received their degrees during the twelve years after 1994. The modal year for receipt of the Ph.D. was 1986, during which four participants completed their graduate educations.

The majority of survey respondents (87 percent) considered drug use and related topics to be a primary focus of their careers, although only 43 percent of those with Ph.D.s wrote their dissertations on a drug-related topic. Notably, among those who completed their Ph.D.s before 1995, 25 percent wrote their dissertations on drug-related topics, while this was true for 57 percent of those who finished their dissertations during or after 1995, further affirming an increase beginning in 1995 in the intentional selection of drug-related careers while still in college. It is likely that the key turning point for interest in drug-related issues among anthropology graduate students was the AIDS epidemic, which resulted in a significant increase in funding for epidemiological and ethnographic research on health-related drug use behaviors. As Tim Rhodes and David Moore observed:

> While the dominant methods in contemporary drugs research remain quantitative, the realisation that HIV epidemics among injection drug users posed a grave threat to public health was associated with an increased receptivity to qualitative research methods. . . . HIV and AIDS have had a major impact on the substantive interests as well as method-ological parameters of drug research, and have arguably been catalyst to greater methodological flexibility, experimentation, and innovation. (2001, 282)

About one-third of survey participants reported that the colleges and universities they attended offered courses on drug-related topics; of those who attended a college or university that offered drug-related courses, however, only 31 percent reported taking such a course. Half of that latter group had taken a single course on a drug use topic, while the rest participated in between two and six courses on drug use during their education. Various reasons were provided for not enrolling in drug-related courses even though they were available, including the following comments by study participants:

> I did not focus on drug use until after my dissertation which was HIV/AIDS focused. I took no courses on HIV/AIDS either, the focus of my dissertation.

> Interest in alcohol as a research topic emerged during fieldwork—after returning from the field, didn't take more courses.

> When I was taking courses, I didn't know I would be going into this field. Now I know that such courses are offered at times.

These responses suggest that the individuals involved did not think about taking a course on drug use because they did not acquire an interest in the topic until after graduation.

Only about one-third of the respondents reported receiving any training in research on drug use from any source. Furthermore, half of the recipients who received some training on drug issues characterized it as "informal." These training experiences ranged from postdoctoral programs and internships to casual contact with mentors. Despite the general lack of formal training in drug studies, a high proportion of the respondents reported that they were currently active in drug use-related conferences and organizations. Two-thirds were members of drug use-focused organizations, and four-fifths participated in drug-focused conferences. These proportions testify to the development of a significant commitment to the study of drug consumption. The majority of the respondents (88.5 percent) also said that they would recommend a career in drug studies to their students, further confirming dedication to this field. Their comments on this issue included the following:

> I think we need to grow the field and we can't do that without an increase in the number of grad students studying drug-related topics. Unfortunately, it doesn't seem to be as "sexy" as other topics. I think we need to publish data (such as yours [i.e., this study]) to show grad students that there is a career trajectory in drug studies. The field desperately needs the input of anthropologists.

> It is so needed particularly for communities impacted by health disparity issues.

> I would encourage them to also obtain training in Public Health (preferably by earning an MPH) so that they would have a range of employment opportunities available in and out of academe.

> Anthropologists still have much to offer the broader field of drug use and HIV prevention, locally, nationally and globally. They provide a critical edge to what are often not especially critical approaches to drug use prevention and treatment and can help explain the causes of drug use to a wider population in the service of social justice and a more equitable society/world.

> Again, the opportunities are there, we just have to know how to present our skills and create the vehicle for research/intervention. We need to teach our students how to write grants to fund their interests and we need to teach anthropologists in general how to be better Public Relations people, to let folks know what we do and why. Most people don't really have a clue what an anthropologist is, but most like our approach once they know what we do and why we do it. I think folks are tired of quantitatively-based research because it basically tells them what they already know, but we can provide people with much more context and emic perspective that gives real "umph" to what is going on and how people feel. That's powerful.

> I think in drug research you will almost by necessity learn solid enough skills, and acquire the right tools that will allow you to go into almost any [research endeavor].

Significantly, of the participants whose dissertations focused on drug-related topics, 73 percent attended a college or university that offered drug-related courses. Of those whose dissertations were not focused on a drug-related topic, only 45 percent attended a college or university that offered drug-related courses. Among some of those whose dissertations focused on drug use, however, this was not a result of intention and preparation made prior to beginning their research. Rather, it was only once they were in the field, and as a result of observations and experiences there, that this interest developed and they refocused the topic of their dissertations. This type of in-the-moment decision-making is not unusual in anthropology and reflects a disciplinary openness to serendipity in research. In the period before she began her seminal study, for example, Adler admitted that she had "no idea" she would soon launch what would become a study of illicit drug trafficking, smuggling, and use (1993, 11). Encouragement from a mentor, Jack Douglas, however, was significant in leading her to take advantage of a research opportunity that presented itself unexpectedly. Similarly, Bourgois reported that he was forced into crack research "against my will" (2003b, 1). Intent on doing a study of poverty and ethnic segregation, the explosion of the crack epidemic all around him made it hard to avoid making crack distribution, consumption, and social impact the focus of his research.

For those whose dissertations did not address drug-related topics, there was a wide range in the number of years after finishing graduate school that their careers shifted to a focus on drug-related topics. For some, the shift came soon after they graduated, very likely, it appears, because their first jobs after graduation were in the drug field. For others, the switch did not come for many years—as many as twenty—after graduation. For most (71 percent), however, the shift came within three years of receiving their Ph.D.s.

Career Paths: Choosing Drug Research?

Our initial hypothesis about what shapes drug research careers among anthropologists posited two basic pathways: those who became interested in drug use as part of their anthropological studies on other topics, and those whose skills and experience made them attractive to principal investigators who hired them as team members on funded drug research projects. Affirming our hypothesis, one-quarter (24 percent) of the survey respondents reported that they had made the decision to study drug use behavior during graduate school. The other three-quarters came into the field of drug research through some combination of available funding and support, the urging of mentors, or the discovery of drug use behavior during their dissertation research. These respondents describe the choices that faced them in the following ways:

Available support:

I figured there would always be research support available and I didn't have a love of my life professionally anyway so one thing led to another.

. . . it was simply an available job at the time, but now I have come to love the work.

Initially, I thought it would last just a few years. But publications led to other opportunities for further alcohol and drug research, and these eventually led me to a long-term commitment.

Available support plus mentorship:

. . . originally my career aim was to study more "diagnosable" health topics (e.g., . chronic or infectious diseases) as well as health disparities. Eventually my mentor pushed me into the HIV field, although originally I was focused on issues of HIV treatment. A job opportunity got me into HIV prevention, doing rapid community health assessments. This was my first direct involvement in drug research and led me to another job conducting behavioral surveillance of injection drug users. This in turn led me to my current position as an epidemiologist, charged with constructing a statewide drug information system . . .

I was interested in medical and recreational use of pharmaceuticals however through the suggestion of a mentor [and] wrote my honours thesis on an illicit drug. This later led to a job in illicit drug policy reform and now a Ph.D. in HBV [hepatitis] and IDU.

Multiple reinforcements:

I figured it would be a long-term involvement because I had job stability, I was consistently tapped for particular expertise (qualitative methods), and I could examine other issues I am interested in (mental health, trauma) while studying drug use.

Respondents who premeditated their direction toward the anthropology of drug use recognized the topic as having especially compelling aspects that drew their attention. The following quote reflects the participant's interest in solving a persistent problem among Native Americans:

I work with substance abuse treatment for Native Americans, a perennial topic of interest (as well as stereotype) among health researchers and policymakers in North America. The question of how to provide culturally appropriate services is complex and multifaceted enough to warrant long-term attention.

Another participant was interested in a wide variety of drug using patterns:

I define "drug research/application" very broadly—from misuse & problems with OTC [over the counter] & prescription drugs to tobacco, alcohol, & illegal drugs.

The following respondent found drug studies to carry opportunities to engage in applied anthropology:

> I wanted to stick to applied anthropological research and it was clear that there were many different directions to follow within the field of drug/alcohol research—enough for an entire career.

The authors' own experiences during the 1990s with NIDA's National AIDS Demonstration Research project (NADR), discussed in chapter 4, helped clarify the job-driven drug research career path as we witnessed a massive (by anthropology's job-market standards) infusion of anthropologists into several waves of NIDA-funded projects aimed at preventing the spread of HIV through injection or other drug use. These researchers, whose stories we eventually heard in some detail as we got to know them, began their professional anthropological careers with dissertation fieldwork in places as disparate as Tanzania, China, Mexico, and St. Martin, focusing on topics ranging from ecological adaptation to tourism to women's health. Given constraints on academic employment, however, they accepted jobs in applied research efforts such as the multisited NADR initiative and made the jump into drug research.

The data collected by the survey added a third career path to those included in our initial hypothesis. This professional trajectory was pursued by individuals who described a preexisting attraction to questions related to drug use, in several cases, as a response to experiencing the addiction of a parent or other significant individual in their lives. The following two respondents expressed this life circumstance:

> Having lived with an alcohol-abusing parent, I understood that there were multiple factors involved in his addiction/behavior as well as my family's response to it. As a result my work has expanded to take a look at trauma, adverse life experiences, intergenerational and historical trauma (specifically among American Indians), and other related health issues.

> I had worked for several years in needle exchange, and then began working in research regarding drug use and HIV. With this experience, and a history of addiction in my immediate family as well, I felt passionate about the importance of social research dealing with drug use and HIV and particularly well qualified to do such work.

We can derive a sense of process in the development of anthropological drug researchers from the responses of survey participants. One aspect of this process involved the discovery that, far from finding anthropology devalued as a discipline, participants in the survey discovered that the field of drug abuse studies had a growing appreciation for anthropological methods and for their power to produce valuable and useful knowledge that was appreciated by an NIH institute and researchers from other disciplines. Although the majority of our respondents had not become anthropologists in order to study drug use, they came to recognize how useful the anthropological view was in conducting such studies. Availability of funding was an undeniable stimulus to this recognition, but the fact that one could productively direct an anthropological lens at the problems posed by drug use held most of our respondents' interest for at least a period of time. That the immediate problem in question (i.e., the AIDS epidemic) initially was seen as being of great importance in the wider world was no doubt also an influencing factor. As a result, anthropologists in drug research began to garner the rewards of professional success (publication, recognition, advancement), which itself became a motivator for a continued focus on drug use.

We say "for at least a period of time" because the survey data clearly indicate that a subgroup of anthropological drug researchers have experienced burnout. They tend to be the ones, our data suggest, who focused on treatment of drug abuse or interventions to prevent consequences of drug abuse. As time passes, they find the consuming intensity of these endeavors wearing on their psyches. In his book, *Dope Double Agent* (2007), Agar articulates some of the specific causes of this burnout, including his decision (twice) to leave the field of drug research. Individuals such as Agar, who have already moved on to other research problems, were probably not reached by our recruitment method (and, hence, we did not collect much end-of-drug-research-career data). Other survey respondents were relatively recent arrivals in drug studies, having caught the wave of HIV-related funding, and some of them expressed intentions to move away from HIV studies, primarily because of the emotional intensity of this field. The open-ended responses to survey items elucidated some of the concerns of these individuals:

> This is something I will be interested and involved with for my entire life. But because of the stresses and negatives present in this field, I will need time away from it.

> After studying and writing about heroin addiction for my dissertation (approx 3 years), I am not sure I want to pursue drug-related research at the post-doctoral level.

Nevertheless, most of the respondents appeared committed to continuing their pursuits as drug researchers, although not to the exclusion of other health questions. In this, they appeared to approach the anthropological study of drug use as a way to take advantage of the set of features that comprise the anthropological orientation to research:

1. Detailed familiarity with behaviors of interest based on direct observation in natural settings and on informal interaction with drug using participants as

they engage in these behaviors (including activities carried out to raise money for drug use, drug acquisition, drug consumption, HIV risk and prevention, participation in drug using social networks, participation in treatment, and related behaviors).

2. Description and analysis of the immediate and wider contexts and structures that define and enable illicit drug use. This holistic orientation draws attention to behaviors that:
   a. affect and are affected by family structure and formation of households.
   b. are related to economics and labor.
   c. have implications for faith and religion.
   d. are related to sexual behavior and choices.
   e. are related to friendship and social networks.
   f. are affected by the surrounding political economy.
   g. affect diet and nutrition.
   h. affect and are affected by health.

3. Attention to social processes and change, which draw attention to emerging drug use behaviors and relationships that otherwise would take months or even years to detect by other approaches.

4. Interest in the insider perspective on behaviors, the lived experience of study participants and the meanings they invest in and derive from their activities, and a focus on participants' life histories and the individual, social, historical, cultural, and structural factors that shape peoples' life journeys.

Despite their commitment to drug research, most respondents reported considerable publication activity outside of drug-related publications. Well over half of the respondents reported that half or fewer of their publications dealt with drug-related issues. Apparently, the anthropologists who responded to the survey attended to a wide variety of interests besides drug studies. This combination of facts represents the quintessentially anthropological worldview: to commit to focusing on a single topic but retaining the right to address other aspects of the human condition as they present in the course of inquiry.

Acceptance of Drug Research in Anthropology

As noted, drug research has not always fueled the anthropological imagination. Has this changed in recent years? Survey participants appear to have mixed views on this issue. Almost one-fourth of respondents indicated that they felt drug research is well-accepted in anthropology. Typical responses among individuals in this group included: "Anthropology accepts it better than any other discipline I know," "increasingly accepted and valued," and "It seems to be a well-established area (assuming that alcohol is included in what you mean by 'drugs' along with other substances)." Still, even within this subgroup of respondents, recognized limitations of anthropology's embrace of drug research were voiced, as noted in the following comments: "Accepted, yes; valued: not much," "Accepted in medical anthropology, less so elsewhere," and accepted "in applied anthro: very; in academic anthro: marginal." The largest group of respondents (39 percent) gave answers that suggested an uneven acceptance of drug research within the discipline, although recognition of a growing level of approval over time is evident in this group: "I think it's becoming more accepted and valued, but for years was pushed to the side and studied by anthropologists in ethnobotany or public health," "I think it has been increasingly valued and accepted, but still probably seen as compromised by many anthropologists in Departments of Anthropology." Finally, 37 percent of respondents reported that they still see drug research as a marginal area in the wider discipline—unappreciated and undervalued. In the words of one participant, the area is "considered unscholarly by some." Others noted: "I feel it is relatively given little attention within anthropology," "Not hardly [accepted] at all, outside of those who study it," and "It's a fairly marginal topic in anthropology." As these comments suggest, there is a general sense of advancement in the acceptance of drug research as a legitimate arena of anthropological research (at least in some parts of the discipline, such as medical and applied anthropology). There is, however, also considerable agreement that there remains enormous room for improvement.

Despite a tendency to see a lack of full disciplinary approval of drug research in anthropology, study participants generally did not feel that specializing in this area has had a negative effect on their careers. Only four respondents answered in the affirmative to the question, "Do you feel you have suffered in your career as an anthropologist because of working on drug use and related topics?" One researcher who felt that his or her anthropology career had been hurt explained, "I feel that I've been pushed more into public health rather than pure anthropology; papers and conferences are more focused in this area than anthropology." Another indicated, "members of a search committee stated that they didn't want their department to be the 'place that studies drunks.'" Implying that anthropology has lost touch with the world beyond the ivory tower, a third respondent reported that pressing health issues such as drinking and drug use were "not taken seriously by academics, but that's OK, it's valued in the real world."

Overwhelmingly (96 percent), participants in the survey felt that their involvement in drug research helped their employment search. Similarly, the majority (87 percent) indicated that specializing in drug research was a benefit in seeking research funding. While most participants (73 percent) reported that they felt fully accepted and accorded equal status in the wider, multidisciplinary drug research and application field, a sizeable minority (27 percent) did not agree.

One question that has long burdened both medical and applied anthropologists is whether their subfield has much impact on anthropology generally. In the view of most study participants (62 percent), their work has had such impact. Participants identified a number of ways in which anthropological work on drug issues has influenced the field. As one participant noted, "Certain ethnographies, [such as] Bourgois' *In Search of Respect: Selling Crack in El Barrio* [2003b], to name just one, transcend the drug field and open others to our work." Others point to methodological contributions, such as refinement of ethnographic tools for studying private behaviors, inequality, identity, and urban environments. In addition, participants pointed to an expanded acceptance of involvement in multidisciplinary research teams, an increased relevance for anthropological work, an enhanced status for applied anthropology, a broadened scope for medical anthropology, and enhanced theoretical understanding of the link between political economy and on-the-ground observable behaviors as examples of the impact drug research has had on anthropology.

Similarly, there was general agreement (78 percent) that drug research by anthropologists has had identifiable impacts on the multidisciplinary drug research field generally. In particular, participants believed that anthropologists have made important methodological contributions to drug research. As one respondent indicated, "I think that ethnographic methods have become more acceptable and desirable as psychologists realize the limitations of surveys." Similarly, another stated that the "usefulness of ethnographic research in 'naturalistic' settings has challenged standard methods; our theory and findings have expanded others' understanding." In this regard, one respondent suggested that anthropologists have helped to redefine the role of the researcher in drug research (e.g., taking the researcher out of the office or laboratory and putting him or her in contexts in which drugs are actually acquired and consumed), as well as helping to reshape the boundaries of what constitutes scientific drug research. Further, respondents noted that anthropologists have called established epidemiological or other conceptions into question (e.g., syringe sharing) by assessing concepts in the bright light of ethnographic findings. Respondents also pointed out that anthropologists have "highlighted the importance of culture and diversity" in the study of drug use while influencing nonanthropological researchers to "attend to the sociocultural aspects and lived experience of drug use" as well as "symbolism, ritual, and meaning." The holistic nature of anthropological conceptions of research issues also has had an impact on nonanthropological drug researchers, according to study participants, broadening the issues of concern, including political economy. Another input has been in the area of funding, with several anthropological drug researchers seen by respondents as having played a role in influencing NIH funding priorities to include community-academic collaboration and "the value of intimate observation and insider vantage point and sensibility (emics)."

8

Gender and Drug Use

Drug Ethnography by Women about Women

Among anthropologists and sociologists, gender has become an increasingly important topic as gender roles in Western societies have undergone transformation. Androcentric interpretations of early twentieth-century anthropologists' ethnographic data, in which women's roles were either underreported or ignored altogether (e.g., Lamphere 2006) gave way in the 1970s and beyond to feminist interpretations that weighted women's roles more equitably in the same societies studied during the emergent era of ethnographic fieldwork by Bronislaw Malinowski and E. E. Evans-Pritchard. Beginning in the late 1960s, anthropologists' studies of subsistence and other activities in highly varied cultural contexts contributed fine-grained analyses of gender roles in terms of how tasks are assigned and what that system of assignments means to the group as a whole (e.g., Lee 1968). These analyses led to the conclusion that, across wide varieties of cultural traditions, women and men contributed to the subsistence of the group at least equally, if not unequally in favor of women, a finding that questioned the Western notion that men were responsible for subsistence and women were responsible for child-rearing and food preparation.

In contemporary Western societies, division of labor can be based almost entirely on the individual's preference for a given type of work or set of tasks, rather than on limited choices based on sex-linked characteristics involving physical bulk, strength, stature, or suppleness of hand (as in the early industrial era's preference for women and children to operate machines). The transitions that took place in the twentieth and early twenty-first centuries, resulting in fully transformed gender roles, continue to affect human relations, including the contexts in which people use drugs. As the nature of gender relations changes, formal scientific approaches to characterizing gender-related aspects of drug use have to adhere to gender-neutral perspectives.

No woman in the times of Herodotus or Sir Richard Burton would have embarked on journeys to discover little-known peoples and their customs, but by the beginning of the twentieth century, Western women were engaging in anthropological fieldwork in remote places. Nevertheless, for reasons having to do more with personal preference than with risk or danger (with anthropological expeditions up the Sepik River, Margaret Mead took as many risks as any of her male ethnographer contemporaries), males conducted most of the early ethnography of drug use. Lowie became interested in tobacco societies, and Schultes became interested in plant-derived drugs, and they therefore pursued these interests in patterns of drug use. Mead, on the other hand, was interested in how children learn gender roles (Mead 1963). Because women were at the forefront of ethnography by the early twentieth century, their involvement in drug ethnography was not only inevitable, but necessary. In the cultural complexes where drug use takes place, gender has great importance in shaping behavior. Female ethnographers of drug use became prominent by the early 1980s, as shown in previous chapters, with Marlene Dobkin de Rios leading the way in her ethnography of *curanderos'* therapeutic uses of ayahuasca (Dobkin de Rios 1972a), and Melanie Dreher was not far behind with her work on *ganja* use in Jamaica (1982), as part of the research team headed by Rubin and Comitas (1975). These researchers' most important contributions to the overall understanding of the human condition of drug users lay in their analyses of female drug users' life circumstances and in their exposition of female drug users' perspectives and roles in the drug trade.

Women Studying Street Drugs

Not very long at all after Agar's *Ripping and Running* (1973) attracted attention to the ethnographic study of drug use, Patricia Cleckner (later, Morningstar)[1] began publishing articles about her ethnographic studies of street-based drug use patterns, using her observations and interviews conducted in Miami, Florida to describe variants of cocaine use (Cleckner 1976a), heavy polydrug use and trafficking (Cleckner 1976b), and interactions among young black males who were involved in various ways in the distribution and consumption of illegal drugs (Cleckner 1977). These papers demonstrated the useful perspectives that a skilled ethnographer can gain after achieving access to cultural contexts where people use illegal drugs. They taught the reader how to decipher the conversations of users and dealers in terms of "game," "player," and "hustle" as conceptual frameworks for actions related to the consumption and marketing of drugs (Cleckner 1977). Cleckner's work also differentiated among the people involved in cocaine use in terms of occasional versus everyday use, assessing each pattern's impact on the users. The maelstrom of heavy drug use and drug trafficking received attention in Cleckner's article that described how some

users can be sucked into a spiral of involvement in both consumption and trafficking, while others may not (1976b). For the first months she lived in Miami,
Cleckner made a point of full immersion into the way of life that she was studying, complete with residence in a neighborhood of high drug-related activity. It
is worth noting that most drug ethnographers never made this kind of commitment to the ethnographer's role in the community, although Adler did so by
accident (1993) and Bourgois did so on purpose (2003). After experiencing her
third or fourth burglary, however, Cleckner abandoned this kind of immersion.
Nevertheless, her ethnography continued to develop and edify for about a
decade, based on field research in Miami, elucidating the subcultural complexes
of cocaine use (Morningstar and Chitwood 1982), the differences between street
and treatment cocaine users (Chitwood and Morningstar 1985), and gender and
cocaine procurement (Morningstar and Chitwood 1987).

Women Studying Female Drug Users

Until the publication of her article on gender and cocaine procurement
(Morningstar and Chitwood 1987), most of Morningstar's other work had focused
on behavior among male drug users in drug using cultural contexts. This article,
however, compared strategies used by males and females in the procurement
of their primary drug of choice—cocaine. It concluded that women and men
generally obtained cocaine by similar means—trade or purchase—but that
women tended to be dependent on men for access to the drug. By the time the
article was published, several other female ethnographers, including Jennifer
James (James 1977; James, Gosho, and Wohl 1979) and Marsha Rosenbaum (1981)
had published works on female participation in illegal drug using cultural
contexts. These works were the products of ethnographic inquiry, but to varying
degrees.

Unlike Patricia Morningstar, Jennifer James began her ethnographic studies by investigating the contexts in which women engaged in sex work and analyzing lexical features of sex workers' behavior in a sociolinguistic mode (James
1972). Later, she published on the linkage between sex work and drug use, delineating the relationship in which prostitution (the term she used throughout)
and drug use formed an interactive behavioral complex in which one could be
driven by the other (James 1976). In these and her later articles, James focused
on questions of etiology and the pathways that led to involvement in sex work
and drug use (James 1977; James, Gosho, and Wohl 1979). Her approach began by
finding women engaged in the sex trade, and it eventually led to characterizing
their use of drugs. Rather than spending observational time in the places where
her study participants plied their trade, James visited them in their domiciles
and conducted open-ended interviews. These activities provided the bulk
of data reported in her publications. After 1980, she embarked on a different

career as a motivational speaker and self-help advisor, eventually publishing a
book partially based on her research (James 1988).

James and Morningstar were clearly pioneers in the ethnographic study of
drug use by women and about women, but other accomplished female ethnographers soon followed their lead and provided their ethnographic perspectives
on the plight of women attempting to live in cultural contexts where drug use
was prevalent. The anthropology of drug use, however, also drew some women
who did not focus on illegal drug use, but rather on the impact of legal drugs,
particularly alcohol, in institutional contexts such as the family, workplaces,
and intervention environments. Genevieve Ames, Linda Bennett, and Miriam
Rodin noticed the growing subfield of anthropological drug and alcohol use
studies and, in 1979, convened an interest group in the recently formed Society
for Medical Anthropology, calling it the Alcohol and Drug Study Group. Each of
these women had conducted significant research on alcohol use—Ames in the
workplace (Janes and Ames 1989; Klee and Ames 1987), Bennett in church contexts and within families (Bennett 1985), and Rodin in twelve-step interventions
(Rodin 1985)—but they appreciated the commonalities among ethnographic
researchers who studied drugs of all kinds, and they acted to strengthen the
linkage among drug and alcohol researchers through the Alcohol and Drug
Study Group (A&DSG), which had its first meeting at the 1979 meetings of
the American Anthropological Association in Cincinnati, Ohio. Although the
A&DSG has modified its manner of networking and information sharing, given
the advent of the Internet, it still provides a forum for anthropologists and other
interested scientists to exchange research experience and support each other in
their research endeavors. In 2006, the group agreed to add tobacco to its name,
becoming the Alcohol, Tobacco and Other Drugs Study Group (AT&ODSG). It
maintains a Web page at http://www2.aptron.com/~adtsg/. Although not all of
the "founding mothers" continued to study drug or alcohol use (e.g., Rodin
became a psychiatrist), their initiative to form the A&DSG provided an important vehicle for the furtherance of the anthropological study of drug use of
all kinds.

Among sociologists and criminologists, a parallel development process for
female drug ethnographers progressed in the late 1970s and early 1980s. Marsha
Rosenbaum's *Women on Heroin* (1981) was the first book-length treatment of
drug use among women, and its merits as a book on what had previously been
material for journal articles were considerable. Given the space allowed by a
book, the breadth and texture of Rosenbaum's analysis could make the reader
understand the etiological factors, the ongoing barriers to "normal" life, the
gender role dynamics, and the childbearing rigors experienced by heroin
using women. Rosenbaum's association with Dan Waldorf in the Institute for
Scientific Analysis (ISA) in San Francisco led to the establishment of an ongoing
program in the ethnographic study of drug use. This work consistently included

consideration of women's roles in drug using social contexts (Feldman, Agar, and Beschner 1980; Waldorf and Murphy 1995).

The collaboration between Rosenbaum and Sheigla Murphy in the working environment of ISA advanced the ethnography of drug use among women on several different fronts. In some of their early publications, they presented studies of how addiction and treatment of addiction, including methadone maintenance, affected women, questioning whether the kinds of programs offered to heroin users improved the health outcomes among women, and pointing out that, whatever their outcomes, the methadone treatment system presented formidable barriers to their enrollment (Murphy and Rosenbaum 1988; Rosenbaum, Irwin, and Murphy 1988; Rosenbaum and Murphy 1981, 1984, 1987; Rosenbaum, Murphy, and Beck 1987). Murphy wrote some of the first statements on the double-edged threat of AIDS to women who use drugs (Murphy 1987). She later collaborated with Waldorf and Reinarman in one of the earliest publications to assess the risk that IDUs incurred in shooting galleries (Waldorf, Reinarman, and Murphy 1989). She also collaborated with these same colleagues during the height of the crack epidemic to delineate the nature of sexual risk among women who used cocaine (Macdonald, Reinarman, Waldorf, and Murphy 1988; Murphy, Reinarman, and Waldorf 1989). Murphy and Rosenbaum contributed to this research, comparing patterns of cocaine misuse—in both crack and powdered form—and delineating the class- and race-related dynamics of how these two forms of cocaine use are perceived (Kearney, Murphy, and Rosenbaum 1994a, 1994b; Murphy and Rosenbaum 1992). Their voice on the issue of cocaine use and pregnancy (Kearney, Murphy, Irwin, and Rosenbaum 1995) and drug use and pregnancy (Murphy and Rosenbaum 1995; Sales and Murphy 2000) asserted that the punitive approach embraced by the press and medical professions regarding drug using mothers is far from the best way to advocate for public health. They published a book that emphasized the ways in which women who were pregnant and used street drugs did not correspond to the stereotypes held by people in the larger society—stereotypes that represented women on heroin as dope-obsessed and negligent of all other concerns, including their children (Murphy and Rosenbaum 1999). They found pregnant women on heroin to express and enact great concern about the well-being of their babies. They also pointed out the daunting barriers faced by these women in pursuit of optimizing their babies' chances of thriving.

Among other topics, Murphy and Rosenbaum, in collaboration with their ISA colleagues, addressed general questions about the nature of addiction among women (Rosenbaum and Murphy 1998), the process of becoming a drug dealer (Jacinto et al. 2008; Murphy, Waldorf, and Reinarman 1990; Sales and Murphy 2007), and networks of social relations among cocaine users (Murphy, Reinarman, and Waldorf 1989). Although Waldorf is now deceased and Rosenbaum has left ISA, this independent research center continues to generate ethnographic studies of high quality with good attention to the human condition of drug using women. The next generation of ethnographers at ISA has learned the lessons of their predecessors well, as their output reflects collaboration with the pioneering ethnographic researchers working at that ongoing institution. In Hunt's work with gangs in the San Francisco Bay Area (Hunt, Joe-Laidler, and MacKenzie 2000, 2005), for example, the research gave special attention to the status of women affiliated with youth gangs.

Rather than practice the ethnographic study of drug use among women for its own sake, as James, Morningstar, and Rosenbaum had done, Barbara Lex placed her ethnographic findings into the context of studies that involved questions requiring expertise in physiology and psychopharmacology. Her collaborations with Jack Mendelson, Thomas Babor, and Nancy Mello, among others, produced several publications that investigated questions of how women respond to doses of Cannabis regarding changes in affect (Babor et al. 1983) as well as changes in pulse rate and mood (Lex et al. 1984) and the possibility of withdrawal syndrome (Mendelson et al. 1984). Lex and her colleagues directed their attention at various issues of particular relevance to female drug users, including the impact of marihuana smoking on the menstrual cycle (Griffin et al. 1986), alcohol and marihuana use and its influence on sexual behavior among women (Lex et al. 1988), and alcohol and marihuana's influence on mood states among women (Lex et al. 1989). In most of these publications, the authors tended to dwell on statistical analysis rather than on their ethnographic findings. Nevertheless, Lex's ethnographic perspective shaped the arguments to some extent. During the 1990s, Lex's research was marked by increased concentration on heroin use among women and their male partners, while she also ventured into the study of addiction treatment and the particular problems faced by women who try to get treatment for their addictions and how relationships with male heroin users affected these efforts (Lex 1990b, 1994; Mendelson et al. 1991). Lex used these experiences to draw general conclusions about alcohol and drug use among women (Lex 1994), and she continues to address questions regarding the barriers female drug users face in obtaining treatment for their addictions.

Female Ethnographers and the Nexus between HIV and Drug Use

Several female ethnographers recognized during the first decade of the AIDS epidemic that women's risks of exposure to HIV were qualitatively different from those affecting males. Murphy and colleagues delineated some of these differences (Murphy 1987; Waldorf, Reinarman, and Murphy 1989).

Claire Sterk took an investigative role early in the AIDS epidemic, pointing out that sexual exposure among female drug users constituted an especially important risk, regardless of whether they injected the drugs or not (Sterk 1988).

She also collaborated with investigators at NDRI to assess the additional risks incurred by injecting cocaine in shooting galleries, with attention paid to women's risks in these environments (Friedman et al. 1989). These relatively brief communications, which took the form of letters to the editor, nonetheless helped to underline the value of ethnographic approaches to understanding HIV and its spread. Eventually, Sterk conducted studies both in Europe (Netherlands) and the northeastern and southeastern United States.

Her focus on HIV/AIDS extended to concerns about the community environments in which women are particularly at risk. In publications on women in community environments, Sterk and her colleagues assessed the nature of risk in contexts of heavy drug use (Sterk 1998), the specifics of risk among female cocaine users (Sterk, Dolan, and Hatch 1999; Sterk, Elifson, and German 2000), and the influence of drug markets on the risks incurred by women (Sterk and Elifson 2000). By 1998, Sterk was collaborating in studies of how to prevent the spread of HIV through strategies such as needle/syringe exchange (MacGowan et al. 1998; Springer et al. 1999). This activity led her to conduct her own studies, with attention paid to the environments in which women are exposed to HIV and the unique pressures that they encounter in these environments. In these studies, Sterk and colleagues attempted to demonstrate the effectiveness of their interventions in reducing the risky behavior self-reported by African American women in depressed neighborhoods (Sterk 2002; Sterk, Theall, and Elifson 2003; Sterk et al. 2003). These efforts represented Sterk's growth from a predominantly descriptive reporter and analyst of women's risks of HIV infection to an interventionist, attempting to introduce harm-reducing change to the behaviors of women who may be at risk of that infection. The kinds of changes that she and her colleagues reported in these latter publications indicated that, when properly engaged in their community context, at-risk women are amenable to enacting risk-reducing changes in how they take drugs and have sex. Because all of the interventions attempted by Sterk's research team were thoroughly informed by community-based ethnographic research in which the existing community social structures had roles in the introduction of change, receptivity to these interventions was strong. Therein lay the contribution of Sterk to the field of ethnographic research on drug use: she went beyond suggesting preventive strategies and chose to implement them herself with assiduous attention to the community settings involved in the intervention.

In addition to conducting significant studies of preventive intervention, Sterk contributed methodological works (e.g., Rothenberg et al. 1998; Sterk 2003), works on community engagement (Sterk 1998; Sterk, Elifson, and Theall 2007), and assessments of emergent MDMA use (Sterk, Theall, and Elifson 2006, 2007). Throughout the process of producing significant studies based largely on her ethnographic acumen, Sterk built an accumulated body of knowledge on the cultural contexts in which drug using women operate.

By the late 1980s, a growing group of female ethnographers were engaged in studies of HIV, including Dooley Worth, Margaret Weeks, Nancy Romero-Daza, Jean Schensul, Michelle Shedlin, and Nina Glick-Schiller. All used ethnographic points of view to characterize the nuances of women's HIV risk in distinctive sociocultural settings—particularly minority cultural contexts. They each contributed, at minimum, a perspective on the local variants of risky behavior in the cities where they studied these behaviors. Weeks focused on the configuration of risks among minority women in Hartford, Connecticut (Weeks et al. 1993; Weeks, Grier, et al. 1998; Weeks, Himmelgreen, et al. 1998; Weeks et al. 2001). In Hartford, in collaboration with Schensul, Weeks designed and tested a network-based intervention among active drug users (Weeks et al. 2002). Nancy Romero-Daza benefited from the guidance of Weeks and Singer in the same group of Hartford-based researchers, collaborating on a study of the nexus between drug use and violence as related to HIV infection (Romero-Daza, Weeks, and Singer 1998; Romero-Daza 2003, 2005), and the conceptual model of how the violence occurs and is perpetuated has shown potential as a generalizable framework for prevention of partner violence and concomitant HIV infection. Their work played a role in the eventual enactment of needle/syringe exchange programs in the state of Connecticut.

Working in New York City in collaboration with Sherry Deren and, eventually, Eloise Dunlap, Michelle Shedlin conducted street ethnographic studies among sex workers, defining their risk of HIV infection in terms of both drug use and sexual exposure (Shedlin 1990). Her fluency in Spanish uniquely equipped Shedlin to study risk behaviors among Hispanic women in New York, which led to the publication of papers on the sexual behavior patterns of Hispanic women, both Puerto Rican and Dominican (Deren, Shedlin, and Beardsley 1996; Deren et al. 1996). This work suggested the need to modify preventive approaches used among Hispanic women in order to provide culturally appropriate and potentially successful preventive interventions. The work environment in which these studies took place had particular significance because much research on drug use and HIV/AIDS was in progress there, and much of it was dependent on the input of field ethnographers. This environment, formerly known as the National Drug Research Institute (NDRI), and more recently as the National Development and Research Institute, has a long record of devising, proposing, and implementing sophisticated research on various aspects of drug use. Its staff have conducted both "pure" ethnographies and mixed-methods research in which both qualitative and quantitative research techniques are utilized. NDRI has trained several of the female ethnographers who continue to have influence in ethnographic studies of drug use through its ongoing fellowship program funded by the National Institutes of Health.

As mentioned in chapter 1, some of the most fine-grained descriptions and analyses of needle/syringe use and disposition have been conducted by researchers working in projects run by the University of Puerto Rico's Rafaela Robles. Ann Finlinson demonstrated a high standard of contextual framing and definition of human motivations among injecting drug users in Puerto Rico (Finlinson et al. 1999), in which she described the procurement and dispensation of needles/syringes from the perspectives of both the provider and the consumer. This was done in a context where both legal and extralegal sources of needles/syringes were present, leaving the consumer with a hierarchy of choices depending on time of day, urgency of need, familiarity with the dispensation systems, and distances to be covered. Although these studies did not specifically focus on females' behaviors, they are some of the best of their kind.

Women and Prescription Drugs

Legal drug use among women has attracted the attention of journalists since the great patent medicine panic of the late nineteenth century (Morgan 1981, 40) when thousands of women in North America and Western Europe reportedly became addicted to elixirs containing cocaine hydrochloride. Self-disclosure books (e.g. Barbara Gordon's *I'm Dancing as Fast as I Can* [1979]) and songs such as the Rolling Stones' "Mother's Little Helper" (ca. 1967) chronicled the consequences of minor tranquilizer use among women who need help coping with daily stresses. Ethnographically, however, the illicit use and misuse of legal drugs remains underinvestigated. Gonzalez and Page reported on the coping strategies involving minor tranquilizers used by Cuban women when faced with the stressors of exile (1981). Specifically, they found Cuban exile women to be in need of strategies for mitigating stress from a double burden: they were required by financial exigencies to work outside of the home while they tried to fulfill their husbands' expectations of household maintenance. Cuban husbands in these circumstances did not expect to have to carry out domestic tasks; they instead left that burden for their wives. Some of these women resorted to home remedies and herbal teas (e.g., linden tea, *te de tilo*). Page conducted a NIDA-funded study of women's use of prescription anxiolytic medications in three different cultural settings (Page et al. 1983; Page and Rio 1987). Results from that study indicated intercultural differences in the approach to using prescription medications: African American women generally avoided them, Hispanic women used them for coping purposes but did not become addicted or impaired, and white non-Hispanic women used them to have fun (Page et al. 1983).

Women and the Study of Street Drugs Since 1990

As we have already seen, Sterk's analysis of women's lives as related to the use of crack cocaine built a more compassionate and comprehensive perspective on this population than had been previously done (Sterk 1999), although Murphy and Rosenbaum attempted something similar for pregnant heroin users (1999). These female ethnographic researchers' activities span three decades, but other highly productive researchers emerged after 1990 to make important contributions to the literature on drug use by women.

Jean Schensul, an already seasoned anthropological researcher, was drawn into the study of drugs as an outgrowth of responding to the local AIDS epidemic. Her extensive experience and initiative in the AIDS epidemic contributed to the development of drug ethnographers such as Margaret Weeks and Nancy Romero-Daza, first sharing in their publications on HIV risk among African American and Puerto Rican women (Weeks et al. 2001), and later writing on topics of ongoing vulnerability (Schensul and Burkholder 2005) and diffusion of Ecstasy (Schensul et al. 2005). The environment for applied anthropological research provided by Singer's ongoing presence at the Hispanic Health Council and Schensul's directorship of the Institute for Community Studies nurtured several female drug ethnographers, including Janie Simmons, Kim Koester, Susan Shaw, Claudia Santelices, Delia Easton, Kim Radda, Julie Eiserman, and April Gorry de Puga.

Patricia Adler initiated an atypical example of post-1990s drug ethnography. She studied her neighbors in the late 1980s and early 1990s to produce an unusual ethnography of marihuana trafficking among upper-middle-class residents of the neighborhood surrounding her own house (1993). The vast majority of "cultural others" studied by drug ethnographers are in working-class populations or populations in the margins of mainstream society, but Adler wrote about people who owned houses and had bank accounts but also happened to traffic in marihuana. The insights of her book, delineating the extent to which solid citizens of the community disobey drug laws, pointed out the folly of the War on Drugs in that it is tantamount to declaring war on yourself.

Lisa Maher—for a more typical example than Adler—began her creditable trajectory of publication with work in a drug-intensive Brooklyn neighborhood, with the support and tutelage of NDRI's capable staff. An early publication of this work examined the public perception of the female crack user and, as Sterk and colleagues had done before, it questioned the construction of this criminal identity (Maher 1992). In collaboration with Rick Curtis, an accomplished ethnographer from New Jersey, Maher cowrote a book chapter about the "urban female gangsta" woman—not necessarily a gang affiliate—involved in criminal activities, including drug traffic, gun violence, and crimes against property (Maher and Curtis 1995). Maher addressed the question of couple dynamics and the etiology of drug use among women in an article that delineated the influence of men over women in the initiation of drug use among young women (1995). A year later, she published an article on occupational norms among sex workers who smoke crack (1996a). At this point in her career, Maher shifted her local area of focus to Sydney, Australia, but she continued to publish on data collected in Brooklyn, as reflected especially in her book on the sex trade and drug use, in which she places these behaviors in the social contexts of race, gender, and class (Maher 1997). As these studies and publications progressed, a central tendency emerged in which Maher paid particular attention to the formulation of behavioral norms in situations perceived as normless by the wider society. This redefinition of cultural contexts usually defined as criminal constitutes a notable contribution to the literature on women who use illegal drugs. In Sydney, Maher embarked on new inquiries that focused on the spread of HIV and hepatitis C (HCV) in culturally distinctive populations, both in Australia and elsewhere in Asia (Higgs et al. 2001; Maher 2004; Maher and Sargent 2002). As this work progressed, it contributed to the wider policy discourse on the success and failure of needle/syringe availability and harm reduction (Maher 2004; Maher, Li, Jalaludin, Wand, et al. 2007).

Avril Taylor's studies of drug using women in Glasgow, Scotland focused on HIV infection risk, as might be expected given the era and context in which the studies took place (1993). She worked in collaboration with a highly productive team of researchers that focused relentlessly on HIV, and later on HCV, and the local population's responses to efforts at harm reduction. Taylor's first published works with this team presented descriptive studies of risk (e.g., Frischer et al. 1993; Green et al. 1993; Taylor 1993; Taylor et al. 1993; Taylor et al. 1994). As the team's ethnographic familiarity with the populations under study deepened, however, the research began to address questions of the long-term impact of harm-reduction policy, with follow-up studies, trajectories of efforts to prevent HIV, and HCV infection (e.g., Taylor et al. 2000; Hutchinson et al. 2000; Taylor et al. 2001; Gilchrist et al. 2001). This sequence highlights a notable feature of ongoing ethnographic study: the ability to develop longitudinal perspectives on the success or failure of interventions. The group in which Taylor was a key ethnographic researcher found themselves in a position to question the efficacy of the interventions they witnessed in Glasgow, and they collected the data necessary to answer their questions. The 10-year follow-up published by Gilchrist and colleagues (2001) exemplifies this advantage of long-term ethnographic perspectives on a given local area. Their findings suggested the need for sustained efforts in preventing harm in vulnerable populations such as the street sex workers who frequented the clinic they studied.

Alisse Waterston's *Street Addicts in the Political Economy* (1993) is not, strictly speaking, a full-on ethnography of heroin users. Rather, she relied on a corpus of textual data collected by a research team headed by Paul Goldstein of NDRI. The texts she analyzed consisted of ninety-eight open-ended interviews elicited from fifty-five individuals recruited by snowball sampling. Despite her lack of direct observational experience with the study participants, she succeeded in producing a book-length treatment of the texts through her use of qualitative analysis and assiduous inclusion of the participants' own words. This book constructed a cultural context in which the drug users who operated within it could demonstrably take part in very large political and economic processes. Far from being some kind of marginalized cultural "other," the study participants in Waterston's treatment were integral to the fabric of political and economic life in New York City. On the strength of their vitality and humanity, she suggested inclusion in political and activist processes and alluded to the illegality of street drugs as a primary barrier to this kind of inclusion (Waterston 1993, 248).

Another female researcher of note is Eloise Dunlap, who used her considerable talents to conduct ethnographic studies of drug users in New York City and define the career of the female crack dealer (Dunlap, Johnson, and Manwar 1994), delineate the role of family resources in the formation of a crack-selling career (Dunlap and Johnson 1996), and explain the process by which adults in a crack using household nurture the involvement of the next generation in crack use and traffic (Dunlap et al. 2001; Johnson, Dunlap, and Maher 1998). Her intimate inquiries into drug-intensive households as environments of inculcation in inner-city environments have no equal in the ethnography of drug use. Dunlap's research on the emergent phenomenon of "blunts" (street name for small cigars that substitute the tobacco with marihuana and/or crack cocaine) was made possible due to her strategic ethnographic position in the inner city (Dunlap et al. 2006). She also extended her inquiries to interpret societal processes by contributing her ethnographic insight to collaborative articles emanating from NDRI (e.g. Golub, Johnson, and Dunlap 2005).

Alice Cepeda, Claudia Santelices, and Janie Simmons exemplify the most recent (as of this writing) cohort of female drug ethnographers. In the tradition of James, Cepeda has conducted field research among sex workers, and in the tradition of Cleckner, she has spent time hanging out with drug users in their natural habitats. Her publications, however, do not dwell on the detailed description of risky behavior, but rather explore new theoretical constructs, such as paradoxical autonomy and survival among Mexican American women (Valdez, Kaplan, and Cepeda 2000), or party ethos among young Chicana women (Cepeda and Valdez 2003). Her work is clearly grounded in solid ethnographic practice, but it also has an eye for the meaning of findings in the context of large-scale social and economic processes. Santelices has collaborated with Singer as part of the research team at the Hispanic Health Council in delineating the risky dependencies observed among Puerto Rican women in Hartford (Santelices, Singer, and Nicolaysen 2003), also relating these studies to a larger discourse on health intervention (Stopka et al. 2003). More recently, she has collaborated with Hortensia Amaro on drug-related studies in Boston. Simmons also writes primarily about minority women and couples, addressing questions of the nexus between drug use, HIV, and partner violence (Duke et al. 2003; Simmons and Singer 2006). This work uses a constant perspective of the relationship between structural violence and behavior as seen in couple relationships, linking street perspective to large social and economic processes. These new ethnographic works, including the incipient work of Catrin Smith (2008) are indications of the established and enduring contribution of women researchers to our understanding of various aspects of drug production, distribution, and consumption.

Conclusion

Female ethnographers who study drug use have contributed greatly to this research field. While male ethnographers have certainly contributed to this arena of research, as well as research-based intervention (e.g., Singer and Snipes 1992), feminist sensibilities, as exercised in works by James, Rosenbaum, Dunlap, Murphy, Lex, Cleckner/Morningstar, and Ames opened up areas of inquiry that had received little attention from most male ethnographers. Reproduction and pregnancy, intrafamilial dynamics, interactions within drug using couples, and gender inequities came under the gaze of these ethnographers in their efforts to understand the particular dilemmas of female drug users. HIV/AIDS, for example, held acute risks for female drug users, and the work of Sterk, Shedlin, Maher, Murphy, Finlinson, Schensul, Romero-Daza, and Weeks defined those risks in gender-specific terms. As their studies increased in scope and sophistication, female drug ethnographers joined forces with proponents of other disciplines in order to solve specific problems of information and inference, and these studies advanced the field of drug research on several important fronts. Lex worked in the context of a transdisciplinary team that incorporated ethnographic perspectives into studying gender-specific responses to doses of certain drugs (Babor et al. 1983). Dunlap's collaborations with Johnson and Golub led to new insights into the development of drug-intensive cultural contexts in the inner city (Golub, Johnson, and Dunlap 2005). Taylor's team of researchers developed the wherewithal to evaluate the impact and efficacy of interventions among IDUs in Glasgow (Frischer et al. 1993; Gilchrist et al. 2001), eventually using the ethnographic perspective to develop a longitudinal perspective in their evaluation of interventions. These successes not only further demonstrate the utility of an ethnographic perspective in drug research, but they also show the desirable results to be had when ethnographers collaborate with other interested scientists. We perceive this application of drug ethnography as the field's most promising potential for future research, an issue addressed more fully in the next chapter.

9

The Future of Drug Ethnography as Reflected in Recent Developments

The use of drugs by human beings is a quintessentially anthropological topic of study because it directly connects diverse aspects of the human condition, from internal emotional states to the global political economy, and from intense religious experience to adventurist pleasure-seeking. Given its complexity, and its concurrent expression on multiple levels (individual, familial, communal, national, global), drug use requires a perspective that is committed to holistic understanding—one that tries to see the forest (macro-level) and the trees (micro-level) simultaneously and in interaction. Certainly, aspects of drug use among humans are most productively explored by focused approaches, such as disciplines that seek to address questions such as how the human brain performs under the influence of a particular drug or what impact the use of a certain drug has on personal nutrition. Nevertheless, these approaches can capture only part of the complexity presented by humans using drugs and can only produce partial accounts of the role of drugs in human life. They cannot, for example, explain, at the level of individual experience or in terms of human social processes, why particular groups use particular drugs in particular ways and in particular places with particular effects. Anthropology, however, seeks to learn from diverse approaches that address a diverse array of directly and indirectly related questions and carefully weave these seemingly disparate pieces into a flowing whole—ultimately rooted in an ethnographic account of actual behaviors and social contexts of human action—which is informed by the insider perspective of drug users.

As drug using populations adapt their behavior to changing conditions, it will be increasingly important to have ethnographers study those adaptations and translate them for other scientists who concern themselves with the health and behavior of the relevant populations. Regardless of the future legal status of drugs, ethnographers who study drug use will have much to do. If, for example, decriminalization eventually carries the political day, the process of adapting to conditions in which possession no longer makes users vulnerable to arrest will require renewed scientific examination by ethnographers. This final chapter seeks to summarize the position currently occupied by drug ethnography in the study of the human condition and comment on its future.

The Scientific Context of Ethnography

Ethnography as a method for understanding human behavior in natural habitats has become integral to the social science landscape. Without it, survey research is often at a loss to interpret its findings, or even to formulate the most important and accurately framed questions. The fields of social and medical research on drug use began to recognize the value of ethnography, initiating the first public health ethnographies in the 1970s (e.g., Rubin and Comitas 1975; Weidman 1978) and consistently supporting the research of ethnographers over the last 40 years. The National Institute on Drug Abuse and the National Institute of Mental Health took the lead in this kind of scientific activity, developing promising researchers and recognizing the importance of the understanding of human behavior that ethnographers could contribute to the advancement of science. In two of the early public health ethnographies, Rubin and Comitas (1975) and Carter (1980) encountered some resistance in the NIH to making an anthropologist the principal investigator of large, ethnographically driven projects. In both cases, the institute administrators indicated that they would be more comfortable with having a physician as principal investigator of projects of that size. The physicians in those projects declared that the anthropologists were necessary for navigating the problems presented to the projects by their foreign locations. The projects needed the anthropologists to represent the research team to the local officials and regime operatives in order to obtain the permissions and collaborations necessary to conduct the proposed studies. Both of these projects had multiple disciplinary components, ranging from drug ethnography to electroencephalography, and therefore, contact management between in-country physicians and technicians and North American scientists demanded much diplomacy and attention to local politics and interpersonal dynamics.

Not all projects that combine ethnography with other methods were as complex as the early public health projects funded by NIDA. In the study of street-recruited populations of illegal drug users, it became clear by the 1980s that ethnography combined with availability surveys—an approach that came to be known as ethnoepidemiology—represented a means of formulating questions that would succeed in eliciting the desired information from the population under study, and it would also provide a contextual perspective for interpreting survey responses. These dual method strategies took form in collaborations between survey investigators and street ethnographers such as Booth and Koester, Chitwood and Morningstar, and McCoy and Page.

Dual method collaborations usually take one of three forms: *front-loaded ethnography plus survey, survey plus back-loaded ethnography*, and *diachronic ethnography*. Front-loaded ethnography entails conducting ethnographic field-work before final formulation of the survey instrument. This process allows the survey instrument to benefit from the ethnographic findings, adding better phrased and more accurate elicitation items and sometimes using an ethno-graphically informed strategy for recruiting study participants. To formulate questions for a large-scale survey in which the investigators expect to interview hundreds of people, it is useful to have a lexicon of terms that easily draw a response from the interviewees without having to go into additional explana-tions. For example, terms for places where people go to inject drugs may vary from city to city, so the investigator will need the correct term to put into the survey instrument. In Miami, the term for these places is "get-off," which has the dual meaning of "getting your rocks off" (sexual release) and "getting the monkey off your back" (alleviating drug craving). In questions intended to find out how people in the sample choose venues for injecting drugs, use of the term "get-off" signifies to the respondent that the questioner understands something of the context in which he or she operates. It also limits the variety of different venues in which the respondent might inject.

Sequencing questions about patterns of activity according to patterns already observed by the ethnography team can help to engage the respondent because the order of business is familiar. For example, different drugs are con-sumed in different places in a consumption sequence. An ethnographer who witnesses a "pregame" dose of MDMA (Ecstasy) taken prior to a rave or other social event and then follows the partiers through the rest of the night will instruct the surveyor to ask next about pacifier lollipops, face masks, glow sticks, water bottles, and eventually minor tranquilizers to "come down" after the party. These considerations reinforce the utility of front-loaded ethnography, as demonstrated in Kelly's ethnographic construction of risk mediation and harm reduction among MDMA users in the club scene (2005, 2009), which eventually fed into Grov, Kelly, and Parsons's survey on risk perception among club-goers (2009). We expect more of this front-loaded approach in future studies of emer-gent drug use patterns.

Back-loaded ethnography involves the *a posteriori* initiation of ethnographic study to help investigators interpret survey data already gathered. This kind of dual-method design is actually only advisable if prior unrelated ethnographic studies have taken place in the same places where the investigation will pro-ceed and if the survey questions have been informed by the prior ethnographic studies. In drug research, there is hardly anything more tedious (for researchers and participants alike) than trying to administer an instrument that does not follow the logic of contemporary drug use behaviors and uses terms that the respondents do not understand. A back-loaded ethnography commonly emerges after the survey investigators find anomalies in their data and wish to initiate an additional qualitative component to be able to interpret their data. This situation can arise in a research environment where ongoing ethnographic studies have been conducted by members of a research group, and the survey instrument uses the findings of these prior ethnographies, but unanticipated response patterns occur in the survey data set. When that happens, the investigators may mount a new ethnographic study focused on the specific areas of information in which they have found anomalous results.

Diachronic ethnography represents a third alternative for combining ethnography with survey research in which ethnographers front-load some information into the survey (culturally accurate content items and astute recruitment strategies) and then continue to engage the study population to monitor cultural shifts over time. This approach has advantages over both front-loaded and back-loaded ethnography, as it establishes an interaction between the findings of the different approaches. For example, a study begins by having its ethnographic team focus on forms of cocaine use in a population of street users, and its results indicate that the forms of cocaine used include cocaine hydrochloride in powder form, either injected or snorted, sold in "dime bags" that contain about one-fifth of a gram (200 mg) each. The survey gathers information on street-recruited cocaine users, includes "girl" as the alternative word for cocaine, and has an elaborate plan for determining how much cocaine each respondent uses based on the "dime bag" unit and observed "partying" behavior among users. The survey begins administration, and a new form of cocaine, such as "ready rock," appears on the street scene. The ethnographers, who have been continuing to observe and interact with the population of cocaine users, notice this new form quickly and begin to record its particulars— it is neither snorted nor injected, but smoked, and the unit price is $3 per small rock which is much cheaper than the $10 bag. They also notice that the duration of the "high" is only a fraction of the duration of the typical effects of powder. This emergent pattern may have to be added to the survey, and the research team reviews the ethnographic findings carefully to determine whether and how to do so. Subsequent survey respondents often self-report use of the newly identified "ready rock," and the ethnographers observe its rapid diffusion into the target population. Crack presented this kind of emergent pattern faced by several studies in the mid-1980s, just as researchers were attempting to characterize HIV infection risk in terms of injecting drug use. Most, unfortunately, did not have the advantage of diachronic ethnography, but those who had an ongoing ethnographic presence were able to document this important shift in the street drug landscape.

Ethnography Combined with Multiple Disciplines

In attempts to address highly complex research questions regarding health status and risk behavior, anthropologists have engaged in a number of studies in which ethnography informs not only other social and behavioral scientists, but laboratory and medical scientists as well. These studies fall into two categories: *health consequences of drug use* and *prevention/intervention studies in transdisciplinary research.*

Health Consequences of Drug Use in Transdisciplinary Research

Ongoing concern about the health consequences of drug use led to the initiation of large-scale studies for the purpose of determining those consequences. In each case, prior literature on health effects of drugs suggested problem areas worthy of further study. In the case of Cannabis consumption, the areas of concern included cognitive function, based on the short-term memory problems observed in acute intoxication; vision, based on red conjunctiva observed in intoxication; testosterone reduction, based on a finding by Kolodny and colleagues (1974); and lung function, based on the fact that Cannabis is usually consumed by smoking. These identified problem areas led the investigators to assemble a team of specialists to apply the state of science at the time to characterize these problems in long-term users of Cannabis. Their combined efforts were reported in a book entitled *Cannabis in Costa Rica* (Carter 1980).

To study the relationship between injecting drug use and HIV required the formation of a research team at the University of Miami to characterize the kinds of risks incurred by the injecting drug users (IDUs), the prevalence of HIV infection among street-active IDUs, the immune status of street-recruited IDUs, and the health statuses of both the HIV positive and HIV negative IDUs. That team based its choice of tests and measurements on the state of the science regarding HIV at that time: HIV serostatus using ELISA with a confirmatory Western Blot, CD4 and CD8 cell counts/mm^3, immunoglobulins G, A, and M, and CD56 cell cytotoxicity. Each of these tests and measurements had precedent in the literature at the time the study began. Completion of the study depended heavily on laboratories, technicians, and scientists steeped in the study of immunology and a growing understanding of the relationship between immune dysfunction and illness in people with AIDS. Emergent knowledge about viral coinfections and progression of HIV-related disease led to the addition of tests for an additional virus (HTLV-II) and survival analysis of a cohort of HIV positive IDUs over time. Page and colleagues (Page, Lai, et al. 1990, 1996) published results of these kinds of analyses, which depended on ethnographic characterization of risk, assessment of viral infection, immune status, and health status. These studies later fomented further research in which assessments of nutrients, supplementation, and viral load became part of a growing repertoire of tests to characterize the health impact of HIV in drug using populations (e.g., Baum et al. 1997; Campa et al. 2005, 2007; Shor-Posner et al. 2000). Virological assessment of contaminated paraphernalia via real-time RNA-PCR (Page et al. 2006) added another transdisciplinary variant to the ongoing ethnographic study of injecting drug use and HIV risk.

The University of Miami's location, in a globalized city with people from many different cultural traditions, played an important part in the formation of transdisciplinary research teams that included anthropologists. Most of the clinicians and research scientists in the university's School of Medicine, by virtue of their location in this quintessentially transcultural place, had experienced their own personal and professional encounters with the importance of cultural context. The internist saw young Haitian men who appeared to be dying of tuberculosis but not responding to medication. The psychiatrist conducted psychotherapy sessions with Hispanic women who had been referred as schizophrenic but who showed almost no symptoms other than expressions of belief in a highly populated world of omnipresent spirit beings. The immunologist saw as many as 10 percent of positive ELISA come back negative after Western Blot confirmatory tests failed to find evidence of HIV. As scientists, their curiosity was piqued to discover what was behind these phenomena that appeared to be expressions of some form of interethnic variation. These experiences made them very receptive to the inclusion, on the research team, of scientists who specialized in studying questions of cultural context and interethnic variation.

Other drug ethnographers have participated in this way with scientists from the bench and the clinic. Singer, Koester, Weeks, and Clatts have collaborated with Robert Heimer to study the contamination of injection paraphernalia as related to HIV and HCV infection among IDUs (Koester et al. 2003; Singer et al. 2000). Bourgois also conducted health studies among injecting drug users, focusing on hepatitis C (Bourgois, Prince, and Moss 2004; Hahn et al. 2002) and other health consequences (Ciccarone et al. 2001). His collaborations with Dan Ciccarone gave new dimensions and impact to Bourgois's high-intensity ethnography showing the danger of HCV infections for young IDUs and soft tissue infections for all IDUs. The collaboration also moved Ciccarone, a physician, to venture into the world of behavior analysis, offering an explanation of geographic variations in IDUs' injection behavior (Ciccarone and Bourgois 2003). The key attribute of these collaborations is that they resulted in a gestalt, where the finished product was greater than the sum of its parts. This process also educated the disciplinary counterparts in one another's knowledge base, so all involved researchers learned key terms, appropriate syntax, and key concepts. In presentations where all investigators participate, it is not uncommon for people who do not know the team members in a transdisciplinary project to mistake the virologist for the anthropologist, or vice versa. This cross-education has the potential added benefit of leading to related projects that incorporate analogous models and theories imparted across disciplines.

Prevention/Intervention in Transdisciplinary Research

When health scientists discuss prevention, they speak of it in three different modes: primary, secondary, and tertiary. Primary prevention refers to the effort to keep undesired events from happening for the first time. In secondary prevention, efforts are aimed at keeping the undesired events from repeating, although they have already taken place at least once. Tertiary prevention involves keeping negative consequences of repeated undesired events from happening.

Scientists who attempt to accomplish prevention of any of these three types face the fundamental difficulty that cause and effect may not be easily attributable in preventive interventions. The first part of this difficulty involves the prediction that the undesired event will occur at all in the population chosen for study. The investigator has the burden of identifying participants for whom the study can expect a rate of incidence for the undesired behavior (e.g., initiation into tobacco smoking). Assessing individuals' potential for engaging in an undesirable behavior may be impossible, but researchers can expect populations of a certain size to have a percentage of individuals initiate the undesired behavior. This principle of population incidence, albeit presumptuous (there are still no guarantees that a secular factor of some kind was not affecting the outcome), allows prevention researchers to conduct assessments before and after administering a preventive intervention and to infer the impact of the intervention on the chosen population. The mere existence of secular factors capable of having an effect on the population under study (for example, the release of a new "stoner movie" encouraging Cannabis use or the promotion of a new ethnically targeted alcoholic beverage), has been a cautionary fact for would-be prevention researchers. Another difficulty in this kind of scientific activity lies in the utter lack of controls on the experiment. The people whom the intervention aims to change scatter in all directions, experiencing all kinds of things when they are no longer interacting with the prevention researchers. The researchers' hedge against that factor is an assumption of orthogonality— that is, the assumption that, if the study follows an experimental and a control group, that both groups will be affected equally by variable outside influences. Perhaps the most daunting problem in prevention research involves the use of self-report by participants to measure both baseline and follow-up behaviors. Some research, however, has indicated that self-report can be valid as long as the respondent does not connect the research with any institution that affects his or her well-being (Amsel et al. 1976). Otherwise, the phenomenon of social desirability, in which the respondent answers according to what he or she thinks the questioner wants to hear, causes distortions or untruths to be collected by interviewers (e.g., minimizing self-reported tobacco use because of awareness that the interviewer is working to prevent cancer). These three difficulties—inferential disconnect, secular factors, and flaws in self-reporting—have shaped the science of prevention since its inception.

The science of preventing health-threatening behavior made major strides in the 1990s and at the beginning of the twenty-first century. Largely driven by drug researchers' quest for strategies to prevent drug use among youth in the United States, Prevention Science formalized an organization for the empirical study of prevention in 1991 with the support of two NIDA staff members, Zili Sloboda and William Bukowski. Other institutes at the National Institutes of Health joined, and the organizational structure was further formalized into the Society for Prevention Research, including the establishment of a flagship journal, *Prevention Science*. Ethnographic study has yet to have a major impact on this important scientific area, but it has the potential to help prevention science by characterizing networks of informal social relations, delineating innovator influence in social relationships, and characterizing specific risky behaviors. To date, the journal has been dominated by articles on strategies to manipulate the behavior of large-scale populations, such as schools or school districts. Some articles, however, (e.g. Castro, Barrera, and Martinez 2004) allude to the utility of ethnography in the evaluation of intervention fidelity. Furthermore, most of the key participants in the Society for Prevention Research have some familiarity with the utility of ethnographic research, based on their experience with NIDA. Given the continued relevance of the cultural contexts in which preventive interventions operate, it would appear to be in the investigators' mutual interest to incorporate ethnographic components into their research.

Most of the studies presented in *Prevention Science* deal with problems in primary and/or secondary prevention; tertiary prevention is left to the category of addiction treatment or drug impairment. This part of prevention has occasionally enlisted ethnographers in its studies (e.g. Rosenbaum and Murphy 1981, 1984, 1987), and their perspective has contributed primarily by pointing out how ill-suited treatment programs, including methadone, are to meeting the needs of specific groups. Since those studies, not much ethnography has focused on the treatment of addiction or drug impairment, although some ethnographers (e.g., Brown 2006; Sexton et al. 2008) have obtained information on the treatment experience of drug users recruited while active in street drug use. Singer and colleagues also studied posttreatment drinking by drug users as it affected relapse into illegal drug use (Singer, Saleheen, et al. 2006). The delivery of treatment for drug use problems and the aftercare of patients' posttreatment remains an open field for ethnographers, whose perspective on the human condition of recovering addicts could help to generate improved strategies for mitigating this source of human misery.

Application: The Contributions of Drug Use Ethnography

Throughout the previous chapters, we have presented instances of how ethnographic studies of drug use can be useful in solving or reducing the problems posed by this highly variable and often destructive array of behaviors. Here, we present a summary of the topical areas in which drug ethnographers apply their work.

Surveillance

If a new pattern of drug use is present in a given location, ethnographers who have worked in that place are likely to be the first to know. Their in-depth familiarity with the cultural contexts in which people use drugs give ethnographers a head start on recognizing and characterizing emerging drug use. In San Francisco in the 1980s, for example, the ISA's group of ethnographers recognized the early manifestations of the "rave" subcultural activity, and the link between raves and the use of MDMA (Ecstasy). The group later proposed research on the drug's further spread into other cities. In 1983, as the availability of methaqualone was declining in Miami, Page noticed that some of the pills marketed as methaqualone contained 300 mg of diazepam, thirty times the standard dose of this minor tranquilizer. Singer and his group observed and characterized the use of "wets" or "illies"—marihuana joints soaked in embalming fluid—in Hartford, Connecticut and its environs. Not all of these emergent phenomena had lasting impact on the drug use scenes where they first appeared. Ecstasy first developed in a limited number of cities, but by the mid-1990s it had become widely distributed in the United States, Europe, and Asia (Gamella and Roldán 1997; Lyttleton 2006). Its popularity has reduced since then. Methaqualone and its imitators disappeared from the U.S. drug scene by 1985. Illies and wets continue to be observed in Hartford. This kind of on-the-ground surveillance has some support from the National Institute on Drug Abuse through its Community Epidemiology Work Group (CEWG) that has epidemiologists and some ethnographers reporting from key cities in the United States on the nature of drug consumption and availability, with an eye toward emergence of new trends. In the CEWG's reports, each city presents information, if data are available, on the standard parameters of drug use, such as emergency room overdose presentations, presence or absence of the most common varieties of mind-altering drugs, and any emergent phenomena observed or elicited from key informants. Ethnographers have reported regularly to the CEWG at times serving as standing members of the group. In two localities, Dayton (Siegal et al. 2000) and Hartford (Singer, Erickson, et al. 2006), state funding has made possible the kind of ethnographic field station surveillance systems envisioned by NIDA.

Prevention

We covered this aspect of applying ethnographic methods in the context of transdisciplinary research because prevention science has an established presence that includes clinicians and experts in school-level interventions and large-scale quantitative research activities. Nevertheless, ethnographic findings can contribute importantly to the framing of preventive interventions, especially through ethnographers' unique positions to observe the events that explain the etiology of drug use. In natural settings (e.g., city street corners, shopping malls, parks, alleys, schoolyards), ethnographers can watch young people take their first steps toward becoming drug users. (We hasten to add that all research of this nature must comply with the guidelines for studying children. Compliance is possible in part because, if the behavior takes place in public, the observed individual has no presumption of privacy and therefore need not go through an informed consent procedure. Ethnographers may not, however, record identifying information about youth observed under these circumstances.) It is possible for ethnographers to conduct interviews with study participants who are not of majority age as long as they obtain either parental consent or court clearance for studying emancipated minors. Hunt, Joe-Laidler, and MacKenzie successfully used the latter strategy in several studies (2000, 2005).

Ethnographic studies that did not set out to discover etiologic processes have done so by virtue of their observational presence and the holistic nature of their approach. In the study of Cannabis in Costa Rica (Carter 1980), for example, the field team spent time on street corners with study participants and also elicited open-ended interviews covering the participants' life histories. Qualitative analysis of these data produced a perspective in which the users' childhoods contrasted markedly with those of the nonuser controls. The users experienced significantly more deprivation of material needs during their childhood than the nonusers did, and they also tended to have households with either absent or weak fathers (True et al. 1980). These comparisons led the research team to formulate a theory of etiologic process, wherein young, working-class males avoided the household setting in search of male guidance. In the street environment, they found older peers willing to include them in their activities, one of which was marihuana smoking. Interestingly, a subset of these home-avoiding boys learned to smoke marihuana, not on street corners, but on the job (Page, Fletcher, and True 1988). In Little Havana during the 1960s and 1970s, Page found similar processes in place among young Cuban males in households where either both parents worked or only one parent was present (Page 1990). Activities on the street in that environment were intense and varied, including the use of illegal drugs, particularly marihuana and cocaine, and gangs (inevitable in U.S. immigrant populations) (Page 1997). Young men whose households did not offer much supervision or guidance sought what the street had to offer, and they discovered drugs, gangs, and the constant arousal of the street environment in a teeming neighborhood where most residents were trying to figure out how to get along in the English-speaking Miami community. Page and colleagues' findings on how middle-school–aged young people take up tobacco provided a perspective on peer pressure that deserved further study and application (2001). Rather than reporting direct, face-to-face pressure of one child by another to try tobacco for the first time, in-depth interviewees from two different urban areas reported that they had already made the decision to use tobacco if offered because they saw smoking as a normative behavior among the peer group that they wished to join. One interviewee practiced rolling notebook paper and lighting so that he would not choke on his first inhalation of smoke. He eventually took up consumption of a product called Black & Mild that contains pipe tobacco and has become iconic in the hip-hop subcultural complex (Page and Evans 2003).

These kinds of findings have a crucial element that is often missing from large-scale longitudinal studies of drug use (e.g., Kandel, Simchafagen, and Davies 1986; Brook, Whiteman, and Gordon 1984). That element is a characterization of the etiologic process. Longitudinal studies that collect short-answer data at periodic time points develop population-level theories about process, but their methods do not give these studies the opportunity to document the process as it takes place. This advantage is one of the reasons why studies that focus on health-related behaviors very often incorporate some qualitative strategy, often ethnography, to achieve a characterization of the etiologic process. Prevention projects to date have not taken advantage of this capability to frame the projects accurately, but as approaches to prevention become more sophisticated and tailored to local features of drug use, we can expect them to do so.

Treatment

Programs that treat drug problems proliferated during the 1970s under federal funding support and during the 1980s under private, nonprofit, and for-profit funding arrangements, all the while increasing the level of professionalism among program staff. In the early 1970s, the majority of drug treatment workers were ex-addicts whose energy and enthusiasm were high, but whose approaches were wildly variable, yielding uneven results and sometimes devising cures worse than the disease. All varieties of treatment—residential, maintenance, outpatient, group therapy, 12-step, and family structural intervention—have come under the scrutiny of ethnographers, and the conclusions derived from these studies are highly variable (e.g., Bourgois 2000; Hunt and Barker 1999; Rodin 1985; Rosenbaum and Murphy 1981, 1984, 1987; Skoll 1992; Stahler 2003; Stahler and Cohen 2000). In general, practically all program varieties succeed in helping patients stop using drugs, but not all of the effects of treatment are desirable. Highly intense residential treatment can replace drug dependence with dependence on the therapeutic community. In its worst examples, such as Synanon during the 1970s (Skoll 1992), the residential therapeutic community can become a recruitment center for other varieties of criminality. Youth outpatient group therapy can lead to the establishment of new connections among participants for obtaining and using drugs. Methadone can be diverted and sold or used as a strategy for getting high again.[1]

Long-term successful impact of treatment depends heavily on the kind of environment to which the patients are released after treatment. Recidivism is highly likely in most forms of drug impairment, so the patient's experience after completing detoxification, residential treatment, methadone maintenance, or drug-free outpatient regimens plays a crucial role in the length of time that he or she remains unimpaired by drugs. This particular area of drug treatment studies has not received adequate attention, given its importance. The follow-up studies that are required to verify the treatment programs' claims of long-term efficacy seldom exceed eighteen months in length, yet the authors' experiences in longitudinal studies of five years' duration shows that individuals may go through two or three complete or partial treatment experiences in that period. During that time, we have seen individuals go into treatment, emerge transformed with every intention of avoiding drugs, collide with the realities of life in depressed neighborhoods that swarm with former drug partners, and take up use of the same drug again. We can see that treatment "works" in the short term, transforming the patient's outlook and arming him or her with the tools necessary to resist going back to the same patterns of behavior. Treatment regimens fail, not with what they are able to do while the patients are in their sphere of influence, but when the patients have to confront their own impoverished, depressing, temptation-laden world for the long term. Twelve-step programs, with their heavy reliance on interpersonal support, represent the most successful strategy for counteracting the crushing effects of everyday life because they provide aftercare of a peer-support nature that never ends. Nevertheless, they also depend on the quality of the support afforded by recovering members, and that is far from uniform.

The treatment landscape for drug use problems is replete with opportunities for ethnographers to help refine and improve what providers are doing. Treatment strategies that have been shown empirically to have the desired impact must eventually be implemented in community settings, a process that is currently called *translation* (Singer and Snipes 1992). Ethnographers can help treatment developers gain entry into community settings and devise strategies to assure fidelity to treatment design in the real-world settings where innovative treatment should be implemented. They are the ones who take the time to develop detailed familiarity with the cultural contexts in which drug users operate and with the surrounding community that responds to their presence.

Similarly, they are the ones that pay attention to indigenous treatment systems and patterns that might hold important clues for the implementation of culturally competent treatment (Singer and Borrero 1984). Ethnographic techniques of focused observation and in-depth reviews of what just happened are apt tools for determining how well an intervention has been implemented. Ethnographers can also help treatment providers reach their target populations more effectively. They can apply their understanding of the drug users' behaviors to help maximize outreach efficiency and engagement of street-based users in need of treatment (e.g., Singer 1992). Most importantly, ethnographers can develop strategies for collecting follow-up information on treatment patients after they reenter life after treatment. This kind of information will instruct treatment providers in how best to prepare their patients for life without drug impairment, and it will ultimately tell them whether or not their preparatory interventions are successful.

Policy

Drug ethnographers have tended not to comment on the governmental policy that determines how drug use, drug users, and drug traffic are addressed by officers of the courts. Nevertheless, their research findings have often brought this policy under question, both in terms of severity of the offense to public health and in terms of the detriment to the health and safety of users caused by the drugs' illegality. On the latter question, ethnographers have weighed in heavily regarding HIV prevention among IDUs. As we saw in chapter 4, most ethnographers with experience in HIV studies have concluded that availability of clean disposable syringes would be desirable (although not a panacea) to prevent HIV infection among IDUs. With regard to incarceration of people in possession of small amounts of drugs, especially drugs of questionable health impact, few ethnographic studies have estimated the negative impact visited on the well-being of arrested individuals (Blankenship and Koester 2002; Shannon et al. 2008).

Cannabis users have borne the brunt of years of policy-driven patterns of arrest and incarceration since Harry Anslinger pushed through the Marihuana Tax Act of 1937. Localities chose to enforce laws against possession for personal consumption harshly in many cases, and because that particular drug is a staple for polydrug users, its illegality provided leverage for officers of the court seeking to justify more thorough investigation of an individual or case. This policy kept prison beds full, but it may not have had much effect at all on the rates of serious crime in the communities from which marihuana lawbreakers are drawn. Given the proportion of prison beds now maintained by private industry (about 40 percent) (Singer 2004), one might suspect that proprietors of this industry lobbied to keep drug possession penalties harsh, in order to keep prison beds occupied. Most of the ethnographic study of Cannabis concluded that, although not without consequences to health and well-being, Cannabis smoking has its most severe consequences because of its legal status and the fact that, in some societies, its users are subject to strong social disapproval (e.g. Costa Rica, Jamaica). Transdisciplinary studies of Cannabis's long-term effects on users indicated that gross health consequences of Cannabis smoking were elusive (e.g., Carter 1980; Rubin and Comitas 1975). Subsequent studies underlined both the elusiveness of long-term effects and the social opprobrium in which Cannabis users were held in Jamaica and Costa Rica (e.g. Dreher 1982; Page, Fletcher, and True 1988; Fletcher et al. 1996). Despite these results, the governmental organs that formulate policy continued to support punishments for possession and consumption of Cannabis, both in the United States and in the countries where the studies were conducted. This history of policy-relevant findings that made no impact on policy points out the difficulty of attempting to make policy statements based on science—policymakers can choose to ignore them based on unscientific aspects of their own operating agenda, especially attitudes of their constituencies and their own strong personal beliefs (Page 1997; Castro and Singer 2004).

Activist Ethnographers

As it is practiced in Hartford, Connecticut, drug ethnography has pursued the agenda of improving public health in that community with its findings. Singer, from his inner-city base at the Hispanic Health Council, worked constantly with an eye toward how his research activities would provide needed information for intervening in health problems among Hispanic residents. The prevalence of drug problems among Hispanics led Singer's group of researchers to focus on problems related to alcohol (Singer, Jia, et al. 1992), addiction (Singer and Snipes 1992), HIV risk (Singer et al. 1995), partner violence (Singer, Simmons, et al. 2001), drug distribution (Singer and Mirhej 2004), and needle exchange (Singer et al. 1995). This group, rather than setting out to gather information about the chosen research questions, had the objective of addressing identified problems with their ethnographic research. This activist approach to ethnographic research had several positive effects, not the least of which was a change in the Connecticut's official approach to the availability of needles/syringes. Regarding needles/syringes and their availability, the accumulated ethnographic experience of Singer and his research team could argue effectively that making these paraphernalia available in reliable, safe ways gave concerned health authorities subtle but crucial leverage in making IDUs aware of the other services, including drug treatment, medical care, education, and counseling, that were available to them. Regarding partner violence and HIV, the mere fact of participation in the study opened up possibilities to help women whose problems with abusive partners represented only a fraction of their total array of problems, from unemployment to child care.

Although she did not publish on her work advocating for access to clean needles/syringes until long after her first efforts on behalf of this cause, Moher Downing's career exemplified the linkage between ethnography and advocacy. Her eventual publications reflected efforts to accomplish safe access to needles/syringes in the context of a well-characterized community setting (Snead et al. 2003; Downing et al. 2005).

Ethnopharmacology

Indigenous peoples characterized by Schultes, Dobkin de Rios, Furst, and the like have extensive repertoires of drug use that may or may not offer new components to the international pharmacopeia. These possibilities have expression in two emergent phenomena: the rise of New Age use of psychotropics and Complementary and Alternative Medicine (CAM). The former development has its most avid constituency among the "seekers," or those people who wish to have the kinds of experiences in which they learn new insights into the meaning of human existence. The latter development has its constituency among the scientists who recognize that people in many parts of the world have interacted with their local biospheres for so long and with such intensity that they have discovered properties of plants and animals that may be useful to the pursuit of human health.

Carlos Castaneda's *Teachings of Don Juan* gave birth to a trend that continues among people who seek enlightenment, wisdom, secret knowledge, power, and/or ecstasy through the use of indigenous psychotropics such as psilocybin mushrooms and ayahuasca. Fascinating imagery produced under the influence of ayahuasca attracted the attention of anthropology with Gerardo Reichel-Dolmatoff's account (1990) of *yagé* (basically the same drink) in Colombia, Dobkin de Rios's account of the healing vine in eastern Peru (1971), and Norman Whitten's account of artworks produced under the influence of teas made from the bark of *Banisteriopsis caapi* (1985). The artists later published their own book of plates based on their paintings (Luna and Ameringo 1999). Those people in contemporary life who find their own life experience too mundane may be attracted to the idea of being able to have ecstatic experiences by merely quaffing an infusion concocted by a shaman; in fact, recently developed cults have attracted this kind of individual to various ritual activities, ranging from experimental communities and walk-in religious ceremonies (Dobkin de Rios 2005; Dobkin de Rios and Grob 2005) to paid "shaman-led journeys" (Winkelman 2003). This trend became so strong that the *Journal of Psychoactive Drugs* saw fit to dedicate a special issue (volume 37, number 2) to its implications. Again, Marlene Dobkin de Rios had a prominent role in describing and analyzing the ethnographic information available on this phenomenon, which includes spontaneous religious sects in Brazil, the United States, and Europe. These articles reflected the transdisciplinary nature of the interest in ayahuasca, ranging from a book on interviews with a shaman (Dobkin de Rios 2005) to analysis of the biochemical components of the potion (Callaway, Brito, and Neves 2005). The articles' content in general brings out the importance of using ethnographic techniques to determine the impact of emerging patterns of ritual hallucinogen consumption on the people who consume preparations such as ayahuasca (Barbosa, Giglio, and Dalgalarrondo 2005; Frenopoulo 2005). As institutions such as the União do Vegetal Church (Dobkin de Rios and Grob 2005) and other described patterns, including adolescent users (Doering-Silveira, Grob et al. 2005; Virtanen 2006), grow and establish themselves, and shamanistic practices like those of Guillermo Arrevalo (Dobkin de Rios 2005) become more widely disseminated, the question of their impact will increase in importance. Drug ethnographers will have an important role to play on the research teams that investigate these new phenomena.

As it happens, ayahuasca has become an apt case in point in the development of Complementary and Alternative Medicine. This traditional drink from the Amazon basin caught the attention of ethnobotanists as a possibly useful addition to the Western biomedical pharmacopoeia. Schultes continued to suggest its medicinal use (1993) and Callaway and colleagues reported the effect of ayahuasca on serotonin reuptake in platelets (1994). McKenna (1996) expounded on the potential of ayahuasca as a psychiatric drug. McKenna continued to hold forth on the potential of ayahuasca and its components as recently as 2005, and some assessments of its impact on the well-being of users have appeared in the literature (Halpern et al. 2008; Riba et al. 2001; Santos et al. 2007). These efforts have the agenda of "finding something useful" in the cultural practices of people who may have discovered plants with unique and pharmacologically active properties. As Hans Baer warned, however, when taken out of the cultural context in which it developed, the plant-derived preparation and practices that surround it may have an impact on health that is quite different from when it is applied in its native context (2004). Daniel Moerman emphasized that body and mind are in unity, and as a result each treatment must combat the biochemical nature of the disease and the patient's frame of mind (1978). A preparation seen to be effective within a specific cultural complex may not have the same effect when applied in a biomedical setting. Nevertheless, in order to develop a grasp of how a medicinal preparation affects people, biomedical researchers must devise the best possible strategies for detecting the impact of the preparations of interest. Ethnographers can contribute important information on how exotic plant preparations are used in their cultural contexts of origin, suggesting the most similar application in the biomedical setting. Ethnographers can also collect essential information about fidelity to recommended usage by the first biomedical patients to use an experimental form of the preparation. The *Journal of Ethnopharmacology* contains scores of articles on other pharmacologically active preparations used by indigenous groups throughout the world, and if only a fraction of them arrive at the stage of clinical testing, they will represent much potential work for drug ethnographers.

The Future of Drug Use Ethnography

Throughout drug ethnography's development into an increasingly coherent discipline, its practitioners identified sectors of discovery, where ethnography of drug use made valuable contributions to the advancement of knowledge. These sectors, expressed in general terms, include *surveillance of trends, contexts of use*, and *consequences of consumption*. They have been especially fertile in producing new knowledge about drug use behaviors. The following sections describe the development of these sectors and delineate the directions in which they point to future advances.

Trend Surveillance

As the twentieth century completed its final decades, patterns of drug use emerged that consistently took the National Institute on Drug Abuse and its predecessor by surprise. If the principal sensor points for trends in drug use are data on patients in treatment and their presentation in emergency rooms, as they had been during the 1970s and 1980s, the prospects of becoming apprised early about newly appearing patterns of drug use are practically nil. People who present for treatment of their drug use problems have usually been taking their drugs of choice for months, if not years. That is also usually the case with emergency room presentations, although there is a small chance of someone involved in emergent drug use behaviors (e.g., new drugs, new drug combinations, new routes of consumption, new consequences of consumption) seeking emergency room help. Nevertheless, most presentations of acute drug-related toxicity in ERs involve already familiar street drugs, especially heroin, cocaine, and alcohol. The epidemics that broke out during the 1980s and 1990s—crack, methamphetamine, Ecstasy, and oxycontin—continually surprised NIDA and the principal consumer of its information, the Office of National Drug Control Policy (ONDCP). The NIDA administrators during that period, however, became increasingly familiar with the capability of drug ethnographers to gain rapport and regular contact in drug using "scenes," and this capability led some administrators to contemplate setting up ethnographic field stations in key hot spots of drug activity. As originally conceived, these field stations would be located in inner-city areas and urban recreational zones in which the drug use activity and traffic was thought to be high. Experienced anthropologists who regularly visited places where drug activity occurred, and maintained a network of local people who would report new varieties of drug activity, would use the field stations as bases of operations, reporting their findings regularly to NIDA's chief of epidemiology. No such arrangement ever came into being, although the Community Epidemiology Work Group's regular meetings compiled as many ethnographically collected new trends as possible.

Nevertheless, NIDA succeeded in developing widespread networks by means of a different route. By recruiting and training new ethnographers during the 1980s and 1990s as part of the response to HIV, the agency may have gotten its wish, as ethnographers who were trained to study drug use and its relation to HIV joined the NADR and Cooperative Agreement local staffs. Eventually, some of these ethnographers became funded investigators in their own right, and they were widely distributed in Dayton, Denver, Atlanta, Miami, Hartford, New York City, Chicago, San Francisco, Houston, San Diego, Washington, D.C., Portland, and even Flagstaff, Arizona and Anchorage, Alaska. As these individuals continued to study their surrounding communities, the national agenda of ethnographic surveillance appeared to achieve its objective. Even more important was the establishment of collaborative networks among these independent investigators. Through technical reviews sponsored by NIDA, such as the ones cited in Chapter 4, professional meetings, listservs, and other routes of contact and communication, ethnographic investigators began to compare notes, circulate recent findings of interest, and determine whether or not a pattern found in one place represented a trend with potential for wider distribution. The study of Ultram, an extended-release pain killer (Cicero, Inciardi, and Surratt 2007; Inciardi et al. 2006), for example, benefited from the existence of an extensive network of drug researchers with a clear preference for on-the-scene accounts of drug activity to determine whether or not this particular prescription drug had seeped into the street pharmacopoeia. Researchers used quarterly accounts elicited from their networks of key informants to determine that no appreciable diversion of the drug in question had taken place in their local research sites. This study represented a creative and edifying way to take advantage of the fact that NIDA funds ethnographic researchers all over the United States. Another example of this process can be found in the report on multistate trials of making syringes available for purchase without a pharmacy prescription. Its list of authors indicates the extensive participation of people in the network of HIV researchers and drug ethnography (Compton et al. 2004).

Inevitably, broad conceptual categories have a tendency to overlap, and the sectors of discovery we have named for drug ethnography are no exception. Community studies, an important component of trend surveillance, also provide the background for the study of consequences. Regarding trends, practically all ethnographic studies of surveillance questions begin at the community level. The ethnographic investigator selects identifiable communities with some public reputation for having drug-related activity within their confines. After hanging out and asking around, the investigator can determine whether the reputation is correct and deserved.[2] The nature of drug use, both legal and illegal, is closely tied to local community environments, and these environments constantly shift as new events occur. Therefore, there is no such thing as a definitive drug ethnography of a given community, only a particular ethnography at a given point in time. For example, the use of mobile telephones reshaped the forms of seeking out and trafficking illegal drugs, moving transactions from the generic (and stationary) public telephone to the mobile cell phone. Indeed, one method used to control drug trafficking in the United States was to remove public phones from areas with active street drug markets. When law enforcement learned how to intercept cell phone signals, immediately tagging the cell phone's proprietor as a participant in drug trafficking, the traffickers went with untraceable disposable phones. In this age of designer drugs and highly remunerative rewards for success in illegal sales, distribution patterns have become a constantly moving target that has to be tracked by concerned ethnographers.

Ethnographic approaches that monitor trends in drug use will benefit in the future from analysis of a whole community. Rather than trace one or two networks of informal social relations, the ethnographic study will have to identify a community and then attempt to characterize the cultural context in such a way that most or all networks of drug users are contacted by members of the field team. In this way, studies of cultural context can produce a clear characterization of drug use as it takes place in that community. This approach has potential advantages for achieving a systemic perspective on the structure and process of drug consumption within a community: it can tap into economic and social processes, interethnic relations, health-related behavior, religion, and recreation patterns. In most street-based drug studies to date, this kind of holistic perspective has been, at best, subcultural in perspective—meaning that the research focused on drug users and their immediate social environments, rather than on the wider community environment and people not immediately connected by kin or commerce with drug users. Lost in narrowly conceived studies are the ways that drug users' lives are entwined with a wide array of people, from bankers involved in money laundering to restaurants that buy steaks from drug-addicted grocery store shoplifters, and from policemen who arrest and at times assist drug users to hospital emergency room staff who must deal with overdoses.

In the process of studying a community as a home for drug use, that community's opposition to or complicity with the drug use can be crucial to eventual efforts to intervene on behalf of harm reduction, mitigation, or prevention. A community-based approach to drug ethnography would provide an optimal platform for activist intervention because it fosters relations with and knowledge about the whole community, not just the drug users. Much of the work done through the Hispanic Health Council and the Institute for Community

Research in Hartford suggests a direction for community studies, because the cumulative effect of conducting studies in the same communities for many years provided the research group with a comprehensive understanding of risk, recidivism, cultural context, and community response to crisis (Singer and Weeks 2005). Although it did not necessarily set out to become a model for ethnographically based community studies, its body of work might serve planners of future community studies aimed at a comprehensive understanding of drug use in a full community context.

Unfortunately, funding limitations militate against the broadly conceived community study concept for two basic reasons: (1) the study of a whole community, even a relatively small one, requires a large commitment of funds—something that funding agencies are reluctant to dedicate to a single research grant; and (2) review committees are comprised of an assortment of experts who individually specialize in a single discipline. These individuals often have difficulty agreeing on the merit of a single project with aims derived from different disciplines. Again, the Hispanic Health Council / Institute for Community Research example can guide the construction of a community-based strategy to accomplish a comprehensive community study. The researchers at these two community-based institutes, often in collaboration but sometimes alone, identified specific issues (e.g., emergent drug use patterns, access to needles/syringes, diversion of drugs to the street, partner violence, and HIV) and proposed component studies under different applications, all aimed at understanding the local drug using population in Hartford and, in some cases, testing interventions to address specific issues. These component projects constituted a gestalt that can be interpreted as the prototype of the community study. For comparative purposes, studies were also carried out in nearby cities of similar size and community composition, allowing researchers to identify specific local context factors that shaped drug use and drug-related health risks.

With regard to both surveillance and health consequences of drug use, a key asset of future ethnographic studies will have to be agility. Rapid Assessment emerged at the end of the twentieth century as a methodological strategy for rapidly responding to emergent health-related problems. Originally presented as a way to obtain policy-useful information in highly varied cultural contexts in order to deal with new epidemics quickly (Scrimshaw and Hurtado 1987), by the 1990s investigators were applying the precepts of Rapid Assessment to aspects of the HIV epidemic related to injecting drug use. A Congressional Black Caucus initiative to investigate the ongoing acuteness of HIV spread in minority communities led to the Department of Health and Human Services supporting a nationwide rapid assessment project. The first of these studies took place in Miami between October and December 1999 (Needle et al. 2003).

The approach taken in this initiative, called Rapid Assessment Response and Evaluation (RARE), held that not all ethnographies need to be three-year immersions among a cultural "other." Rather, ethnography can serve the purpose of meeting immediate needs for intervening in a health emergency or exigency. The implementers of this approach did not have the luxury of entering a cultural setting "cold" and forming connections with key informants through a slow building of rapport. Rather, the investigators relied on a group of individuals recruited from the community of interest and used their lifelong familiarity with the local "scene" to identify and enlist (or serve themselves) as key informants. The rapid assessment process consisted of consulting with local community leaders; identifying, compiling, and summarizing all relevant data on local conditions; and conducting observational and interview studies of conditions relevant to the health question at hand (Bates, Singer, and Trotter 2007; Trotter and Singer 2005, 2007). In Miami, this question was, "Why in the late second decade of AIDS are minority communities still suffering a high incidence of new infections?" The study's findings were presented to the community advisory committee six weeks after beginning the RARE (Marcelin and Page 2007; Needle et al. 2003).

Rapid Assessment is proving to be an increasingly useful tool, especially in relation to the ethnographic study of drug use. Page was so taken with the concept after heading up the Miami effort in 1999 that he conducted several other projects in the same mode. One of these projects helped identify a pattern of tobacco use in middle school–aged youth (Page and Evans 2003) and another helped characterize drug use patterns in University of Miami students (Page et al. 2001). Another Rapid Assessment characterized patterns of primary care use in a depressed community (Brown et al. 2008). Rapid Assessment's ethnographic component benefits from the enlisting of indigenous field data collectors, allowing access that otherwise would not be possible in a short period of time (typically six weeks). This style of multimethod inquiry with ethnography at its center may be employed often in the years to come as we attempt to respond to new emergent trends in the use of mind-altering drugs. It is relevant both to the surveillance and consequences of drug use because of its agility and relevance to questions of health.

Networks of informal social relations are the pathways along which information, drugs, material goods, and sexual access move. Although the network paradigm has received considerable attention, especially in the era of AIDS, the rapidly expanding capabilities of computers to analyze highly complex data on social relations among drug users will likely make possible important new discoveries. The role of ethnography in this kind of study will continue to involve validation by observation in natural habitats and development of the kind of rapport necessary to elicit reliable and valid self-reports of network connections. Perhaps the most important contribution of ethnography to the study of networks among drug users will entail the meaning of varieties of network connections. As computers become capable of increasingly rapid analysis of increasingly complex data, we can reasonably expect them to handle aspects of linkage content—that is, the reasons people have for forming or maintaining network links that previous analysts had to set aside (e.g., Killworth and Bernard 1974). The findings of network studies can be expected to elucidate development and diffusion of drug use patterns, but they also have the potential to trace the consequences of drug use on both long-term and rapid trajectories.

Health Consequences

How patterns of drug use affect health can only be studied adequately through the inclusion of ethnographic components that characterize health-seeking and health-risking behavior. The model for this kind of study that seems to work best has anthropologists at the center and involves other disciplines as needed to provide specific bits of information. The model for this linking of ethnography with specialized disciplines is more than three decades old (e.g., Carter 1980; Rubin and Comitas 1975), but the understanding that it brings to highly complex questions of health and behavior continues to move fields of inquiry forward. As the epidemiologic details of drug-related health sequelae become more fully defined, ethnography of risky behaviors will play a bigger role in tracing relationships between behaviors and health consequences. For example, we already know that zinc and selenium deficiencies are related to the survival of HIV-infected drug users (Baum et al. 1997; Campa et al. 2005, 2007), but we do not know whether the deficiencies are related to dietary intake or absorption of what would be normal amounts of these micronutrients in food. Ethnographic perspective on dietary intake of drug users could help to answer that question by observing and recording dietary intake of study participants in natural habitats and eliciting interview materials on values related to nutrition among drug users (Himmelgreen et al. 1998; Romero-Daza et al. 1999). Ethnographic contributions to the improvement of risk avoidance and adherence can be easily imagined in ethnography's future.

Conclusion

Drug ethnography is both ancient and contemporary, providing information that is both arcane and highly relevant. Drug ethnography's past brought colorful and sometimes detailed descriptions of drug use in distant places as practiced by highly distinctive peoples. Its fundamental principles, however, promote holistic and relativistic appraisal of human behavior wherever we find descriptions of it. In the latter part of the twentieth century, it became increasingly clear that drug ethnography was not simply another exercise in learning

APPENDIX:
NUTS AND BOLTS OF
ETHNOGRAPHIC METHODS

Participant Observation

In chapter 1, we described the work of various drug ethnographers. Their success in characterizing drug using behaviors in difficult-to-reach populations can be attributed in large part to their ability to gain the trust necessary for opportunities to observe directly the behaviors of interest. We extensively discussed the issues of building rapport in chapter 1, but we did not discuss the details of doing field observations. Ethnographers have various systems for doing so, but each has a systematic way to collect and record observational data. We prefer field notes that consist of a sequential narrative of what happened during a period of observations. This narrative should attend to the contextual features of the observational setting(s) and provide pseudonyms for all observed actors. Often, the investigator will devise a checklist of site features to identify and describe, if present. After a period of observation, the ethnographer will record notes, either by audio recording (for later typing) or typing directly into a word processing file as soon as possible, while the sequence of events is fresh in mind and he or she has written notes in hand. This narrative represents the raw material from which analysis will yield ethnographic findings. In drug research, it is important to avoid giving the populace in an observational site a strong impression of gathering information through written notes or the use of recording devices on site. The occasional note jotted down unobtrusively may be acceptable in an observational context, but anything more can arouse suspicion.

As days and weeks of this kind of activity accumulate, the ethnographer builds a body of observational data that will be of great value, especially if it has been systematized through a process of content coding. A full set of field notes recorded over time represents the data from which the ethnographer eventually can draw inductive inferences about drug use, including illicit drugs, alcohol, tobacco, or some combination of these, in a cultural context. As the ethnographer gathers additional descriptive information about the topics of interest, he or she may form field hypotheses around which to organize and compare segments of the data or begin to form theories about cultural processes and relationships among actors and cultural concepts. Ethnographers who engage in drug use research employ microcomputer capabilities in order to make their observational data as useful and accessible as possible. Word processing software (e.g. Microsoft Word, WordPerfect) makes possible the recording of observations in text files which are amenable to edits, searches, and, with the use of text-based management software such as Atlas TI and QSR NVivo, analyses.

Regarding Page's experience in Costa Rica, most of his learning about Costa Rican men's patterns of marihuana use required months of observational sessions on street corners and in shanties, parks, and bars. After each observational session, he recorded field notes such as the ones shown at the beginning of chapter 1. He coded them for content retrievability and eventually analyzed them in aggregate to produce reports that summarized what he and his colleagues learned about marihuana use among Costa Rican working-class men. These processes constituted a major portion of the time spent doing ethnography.

Ethnographic Interviewing

What people say about what they do becomes especially useful if the ethnographer can establish a link between enacted behavior and reflective commentary on that behavior. Ethnographic interviewing has three components, each of which plays an important role in the ethnography of drug use.

Interviews in Context

During the course of rapport building and observation of drug using behavior, the ethnographer is expected to elicit, as much as is appropriate in a given setting, commentary from the actors being observed. As the ethnographer observes a behavior, he or she may formulate a field hypothesis which can then be posed to the actors in that setting to determine its viability. As Heath noted, based on his research on drinking among the Camba, "One of the simplest ways to check the reality of . . . [an] interpretation is to present it, in simple terms, to the principals, the actors themselves, and get their reactions" (2000, 161). When Heath did this with his initial ideas about Camba drinking patterns, he found his informants often responded, "You'd have to be an outsider to come with that." They then followed [with a] a smiling reassurance that "It really makes sense," or "You're right, that's how it worked, although we never knew it at the time." Once confirmed, partly confirmed, or rejected, the ethnographer can respond by reformulating a refined or an alternative hypothesis to be tested by further observation and further interviews in context. This entire process can transpire almost seamlessly in the course of a field observation. The passage at the beginning of chapter 1 does not exemplify that process, because the ethnographer, Page, in his first full-fledged field study, did not have the familiarity with the scene nor the conversational skill in the street argot spoken by the actors to carry on the kind of off-hand, smooth conversational style necessary to accomplish this feat. Bourgois, on the other hand, offered several passages that exemplify the on-site interview at its best (2003b, 83–85, 116–199). Inciardi and Page combined direct observation with informal conversation about self-injection practices to characterize the significant drug sharing strategies of front-loading and back-loading among injecting drug users (1991). Both of these behavioral variants practiced by injecting drug users in Miami had important implications for the spread of HIV. In their fieldwork with drug users in Hartford, Singer and coworkers used interviews within the context of field observations to encourage drug users to share patterned narratives (referred to by informants as "war stories") of street drug use (2001). The collection of these tales, built around themes such as street risk, unexpected opportunity, adventure, and learning the ropes of street survival, provided a base to identify tips for effective intervention approaches with street drug users. By carefully analyzing the narratives about their lives told to them by active street drug users, these researchers sought to identify deep-seated concerns and culturally constituted sentiments that should be taken into consideration when designing interventions that were deemed appropriate and friendly by the target audience.

Formal In-Depth Interviews

This variety of interview is a staple of qualitative research on drug use, because it represents a relatively efficient strategy for obtaining useful information about how drug use fits into individual people's lives. Because it typically uses a format wherein the interviewer asks an open-stimulus question and the respondent speaks until he or she runs out of things to say, this kind of ethnographic interviewing technique provides an opportunity to learn how the respondent structures his or her perspectives on the question at hand. Interviewers usually have some form of a guide sheet that lists the topics to be covered by the respondent. This sheet provides a means of checking whether or not the respondent covers all of the desired topics. In the in-depth format, additional questions often emerge from the free-flowing conversation. Therefore, the interviewer must remain alert throughout long responses by the interviewee, constantly ready to pursue the unusual comment or opinion when it occurs. If an individual comment suggests a pattern of behavior that may be widely distributed in the population of drug users, the research team may consider it as a potential content item for subsequent in-depth interviews.

Ethnographic Focus Groups

Many different research endeavors, from marketing to political science to psychology, use some variant of the focus group in their efforts to determine the reactions of people to specific questions, issues, or business products. The anthropological use of focus groups contrasts somewhat with those. Perhaps the most important area of contrast involves the anthropological expectation that the interactions in a focus group will help to establish areas of consensus regarding drug using practices and drug-related behaviors. Agar and MacDonald suggested a model of anthropological focus groups in drug use studies where the relationships among all participants were at least partially known to the facilitator at the time of the group interview (1995). With foreknowledge of interpersonal dynamics among the participants, the facilitator was able to avoid a discussion dominated by the strong personalities in the group. In a context that was perhaps more comfortable and accepting than their usual setting of interaction, the entire group could participate in the discussion in a frank style that allowed the anthropologists to derive a consensus understanding of the behaviors of interest. This approach to focus groups contrasts markedly with that of marketing focus groups, in which disparate individuals with no prior relationship gather to express disparate opinions about a product or idea. In our experience, carefully structured focus groups can yield edifying and helpful findings (Singer and Eiserman 2007). While focus groups commonly last about an hour or two, Singer and colleagues have successfully used five- and six-hour focus groups to fully explore cultural domains of keen interest.

Recording Devices

The three varieties of ethnographic interviewing named above may be collected, to varying degrees and with varying levels of risk, through the use of recording devices, including cameras, audio recorders, video recorders, and digital recording devices. The ease with which one can make and transmit recordings, with or without the subjects' knowledge, presents drug ethnographers with a singular challenge. If the key to rapport and successful data gathering is trust, then how, in the age of the candid video, can any ethnographer gain the trust of people whose behaviors may be prosecuted as crimes? Three principles must govern ethnographic data gathering in the study of drug use: (1) never bring a recording device near a venue of drug using activities or a prospective key informant until after the ethnographer has had sufficient contact to be able to gather frank, candid interview material; (2) when it is finally appropriate to use recording devices, obtain permission before doing so and always keep the device in plain sight, indicating when it is recording and when it is not; and (3) the use of recorded materials is especially sensitive in vulnerable populations, so voice recordings and images of people should only be presented to the public under conditions that maintain confidentiality and protect personal identity. When images of people appear in mass media—newspapers and television, but also blogs, Web pages, and other image-carrying media—the researcher cannot control who sees them or to what use the viewers will put them. In all cases, images must be carefully screened for even the subtlest of cues (e.g., a tattoo or unique scar) before use in these media, lest some enterprising police officer use the image as a clue to locate a fugitive or a dealer with a long memory decides to settle a remembered offense (Singer, Simmons et al. 2001).

These principles protect both the cultural object of study and the ethnographer (Singer et al. 1999). Arousing suspicion among drug using contacts can be dangerous (e.g., Bourgois in East Harlem or Jacobs in St. Louis), and carrying around a phone with which to snap pictures makes the fieldworker resemble a police officer—a potentially dangerous public image. Technology has made possible whole new areas of documentation, recording, and retrieval, and drug ethnographers must exercise extreme caution in their use. This discussion raises the far broader issue of the full range of ethical challenges encountered in drug ethnography, which we addressed in chapter 6.

NOTES

CHAPTER 1   THROUGH ETHNOGRAPHIC EYES

1. A small coffee plantation at the edge of the barrio.

2. This spelling (marihuana) of the common term for *Cannabis sativa* and *Cannabis indica* is pronounced the same in both English and Spanish, and it is therefore preferable to us.

3. According to Tylor, culture is "that complex whole which includes knowledge, belief, art, morals, law, custom, and any other capabilities and habits acquired by man as a member of society" (Tylor 1924: 1).

CHAPTER 3   SYSTEMATIC MODERNIST ETHNOGRAPHY
AND ETHNOPHARMACOLOGY

1. As the Department of Health, Education, and Welfare was breaking into separate departments, it formed a rubric called the Alcohol, Drug Abuse, and Mental Health Agency (ADAMHA), which was the agency that let the cannabis research contracts. In 1974, while the Costa Rica study was still in the field, the National Institute on Drug Abuse was formed, and its project officers oversaw the ongoing conduct of that project.

2. The study design, as specified in the contract, involved recruitment of 240 working-class male Costa Ricans, 80 of whom had histories of at least ten years of marihuana use. These individuals consented to a battery of screening tests, including haematologic and serologic assessments, a basic neurophysiological examination, and an ophthalmological examination. In addition, they responded to a comprehensive sociodemographic interview that included household composition, income, migration history, family mental health history, and self-reported drug and prescription medicine use. Of these 160 nonusers and 80 users, the research team was to select a minimum of 40 users, matched with 40 nonusers for six criteria: age, employment level, education, marital status, alcohol use, and tobacco use. The team selected a total of 42 matched pairs and conducted tests designed to detect differences between users and nonusers indicated by contemporary literature as potential problem areas, including psychomotor function, cognitive function, eye health, sleep electroencephalography, and lung function. This design reflected the limited power of 1973 computers which could not handle too many variables in analysis. A contemporary analytical design would have allowed these variables to be controlled statistically.

3. Participants in the Jamaican study smoked "spliffs" of mixed *ganja* and tobacco that dwarfed the size of the joints (marihuana cigarettes) smoked by North American

users. Costa Rican cannabis smokers' "motos" (joints) were somewhat smaller than the North American marihuana cigarettes, but the forty-two participants in the matched-pair study self reported consuming between 5 and 40 motos per day (a mean of 9.6 per day) for between 10 and 27 years (a mean of 16.7 years).

4. These individuals, most especially Eleanor Carroll, George Beschner, Barry Brown, and Richard Needle, recognized the ability of an ethnographic approach to gather critical data on actual behaviors and have, at times, held influential positions in these bureaucracies. Carroll strongly supported the early funding of ethnographic studies and the inclusion of ethnographers on NIDA grant review panels. Beschner participated directly in field research and helped to launch a number of efforts, such as the 1979 Chicago conference that led to the volume *Ethnography: a Research Tool for Policymakers in the Drug and Alcohol Fields* (Akins and Beschner 1980) and the National AIDS Demonstration Research Project (Brown and Beschner 1993), which incorporated ethnography in a nationwide multisited epidemiological study among drug injectors and their sex partners. Brown played a parallel role as the importance of drug use in the AIDS epidemic became clear. Needle, who (like Beschner and Brown) served as chief of the Community Research Branch at NIDA, continued and expanded the NIDA tradition of support for ethnography through major multisited studies of drug use and HIV studies such as the Cooperative Agreement for AIDS Community-based Outreach/Intervention Research (Inciardi and Needle 1998) and the Needle Hygiene Study (Koester 1995; Needle, Cesari, and Koester 1996), as well as through sponsoring technical reviews and conferences on the ethnography of HIV risk and prevention among drug users (e.g., Lambert, Ashery, and Needle 1995).

CHAPTER 8   GENDER AND DRUG USE: DRUG ETHNOGRAPHY BY WOMEN ABOUT WOMEN

1. Patricia Cleckner changed her surname to Morningstar in 1981, and subsequent publications reflect the change.

CHAPTER 9   THE FUTURE OF DRUG ETHNOGRAPHY AS REFLECTED IN RECENT DEVELOPMENTS

1. Methadone maintenance may be structured so that the dose is gradually titrated down until the patient is "clean." As opioids have the property of developing tolerance in the consumer, some heroin users develop habits that are both burdensome to maintain ($400 or more per day) and unsatisfying, because all that a single dose affords the highly tolerant user is relief from withdrawal sickness. A street heroin user may enroll in methadone maintenance in order to bring such a habit under control and be able to achieve the "rush" (quasi-orgasmic surge of pleasure upon injection) and the "nod" (dreamy state of well-being and pleasure) that follows.

2. "Hanging out" unfortunately has connotations of personal inertia that could not be further from the truth in the case of ethnographers, who in fact are noting contextual features such as buildings and thoroughfares, observing movement and interaction patterns, recording the garb of people on the street, establishing social contacts, looking for clues about the focal topic, and mapping spatial relations. Still, ethnographers in their participant-observer mode *appear* to be hanging out, and the expression is universally understood by nonethnographers.

REFERENCES

Abdala, N., J. C. Grund, Y. Tolstov, A. P. Kozlov, and R. Heimer. 2006. Can home-made injectable opiates contribute to the HIV epidemic among injection drug users in the countries of the former Soviet Union? *Addiction* 101(5): 731–737.

Adler, P. 1990. *Ethnographic research on hidden populations: Penetrating the drug world.* NIDA Research Monograph 98: 96–112.

Adler, P. 1993. *Wheeling and dealing: An ethnography of an upper-level drug dealing and smuggling community.* New York: Columbia University Press.

Adler, P., and P. Adler. 1987. *Membership roles in field research.* Newbury Park, CA: Sage Publications.

Agar, M. 1973. *Ripping and running: A formal ethnography of urban heroin addicts.* New York: Academic Press.

Agar, M. 1977. Ethnography on the Street and in the Joint. In *Street ethnography: Selected studies of crime and drug use in natural settings.* ed. R. S. Weppner 143–156. Beverly Hills, CA: Sage.

Agar, M. 1996. *The professional stranger.* San Diego: Academic Press.

Agar, M. 2003. The story of crack: Towards a theory of illicit drug trends. *Addiction Research and Theory* 11(1): 3–29.

Agar, M. 2007. *Dope double agent: The naked emperor on drugs.* Morrisville, NC: Lulu Books.

Agar, M., and J. MacDonald. 1995. Focus groups and ethnography. *Human Organization* 54: 78–86.

Agar, M., and H. S. Reisinger. 1999. Numbers and patterns: Heroin indicators and what they represent. *Human Organization* 58(4): 365–374.

Akins, C., and G. Beschner, eds. 1980. *Ethnography, a research tool for policymakers in the drug & alcohol fields.* Rockville, MD: National Institute on Drug Abuse.

Aldrich, M., and R. Barker. 1976. Historical aspects of cocaine use and abuse. In *Cocaine: Chemical biological, clinical, social, and treatment aspects.* Cleveland, OH: CRC.

Altschul, S. 1972. *The genus Anadenanthera in Amerindian cultures.* Cambridge, MA: Harvard University Botanical Museum.

Amsel Z., W. Mandel, L. Matthias, C. Mason, and I. Hocherman. 1976. Reliability and validity of self-reported illegal activities and drug-use collected from narcotic addicts. *International Journal of the Addictions* 11(2): 325–336.

Appelbaum, P., and A. Rosenbaum. 1989. Tarasoff and the researcher: Does the duty to protect apply in the research setting? *American Psychologist* 44: 885–894.

Arias, E. D. 2006. *Drugs and democracy in Rio de Janeiro.* Chapel Hill, NC: University of North Carolina Press.

Ashery, R. S. 1993. Nontraditional employees: Indigenous outreach workers employed as aids educators for street addicts. *Journal of Community Psychology* 21: 200–208.

Babor, T. F., B. W. Lex, J. H. Mendelson, and N. K. Mello. 1983. Marijuana, affect and tolerance: A study of subchronic self-administration in women. NIDA Research Monograph Series: 199–204.

Baer, H. 2004. U.S. health policy on alternative medicine: A case study on the co-optation of a popular movement. In *Unhealthy Health Policy,* ed. Arachu Castro and Merrill Singer, 317–327. New York: Altamira Press.

Baigent, H. 2007. The potential impact of PICTA on smaller forum island nations. In *Final Report for the Institute for International Trade and Pacific Consult.* Adelaide, Australia: University of Adelaide Press.

Bain, K. 2004. *What the best college teachers do.* Cambridge, MA: Harvard University Press.

Barbosa, P.C.R., J. S. Giglio, and P. Dalgalarrondo. 2005. Altered states of consciousness and short-term psychological after-effects induced by the first time ritual use of ayahuasca in an urban context in Brazil. *Journal of Psychoactive Drugs* 37(2): 193–201.

Barker, K. 2006. "Very bad" news on opium war. *Chicago Tribune,* September 3, p. 1.

Bates, C., M. Singer, and R. Trotter. 2007. The RARE model of rapid HIV risk assessment. *Journal of Health Care for the Poor and Underserved* 18 (suppl. 3): 16–34.

Baum, M. K., G. Shor-Posner, S. Lai, G. Zhang, H. Lai, M. A. Fletcher, H. Sauberlich, and J. B. Page. 1997. High risk of HIV-related mortality is associated with selenium deficiency. *Journal of AIDS* 15: 370–374.

Becker, H. 1953. Becoming a marihuana user. *American Journal of Sociology* 59: 235–242.

Becker, H. 1963. *Outsiders: Studies of the sociology of deviance.* New York: The Free Press.

Bell, R. 1971. *Social deviance: A substantive analysis.* Homewood, IL: Dorsey Press.

Bennett, L. 1985. Alcohol writ accountable: The Episcopal Diocese of Washington, D.C. In *Alcohol: The American experience,* ed. L. Bennett and G. Ames, 411–434. New York: Plenum Press.

Bennett, L., and P. Cook. 1996. Alcohol and drug studies. In *Medical Anthropology,* ed. C. Sargent and T. Johnson, 235–251. Westport, CT: Praeger.

Beschner, G., and E. Bovelle. 1985. Life with heroin: Voices of experience. In *Life with Heroin: Voices from the Inner City,* ed. B. Hanson, G. Beschner, J. Walters, and E. Bovelle, 75–108. Lexington, MA: Lexington Books.

Bezdek, M., and P. Spicer. 2006. Maintaining abstinence in a northern Plains tribe. *Medical Anthropology Quarterly* 20(2): 160–181.

Bibeau, G. 1989. For a biocultural approach to AIDS, dead ends and new leads. Paper presented at the International AIDS meetings, Montreal, Canada.

Black, P. 1984. The anthropology of tobacco use: Tobian data and theoretical issues. *Journal of Anthropological Research* 40: 475–503.

Blankenship, K. M., and S. Koester. 2002. Criminal law, policing policy, and HIV risk in female street sex workers and injection drug users. *Journal of Law Medicine and Ethics* 30(4): 548–559.

Bluthenthal, R., K. Heinzerling, R. Anderson, N. Flynn, and A. Kral. 2008. Approval of syringe exchange programs in California: Results from a local approach to HIV prevention. *American Journal of Public Health* 98(2): 278–283.

Bluthenthal, R. N., M. R. Malik, L. E. Grau, M. Singer, P. Marshall, and R. Heimer. 2004. Sterile syringe access conditions and variations in HIV risk among drug injectors in three cities. *Addiction* 99(9): 1136–1146.

Bluthenthal, R. N., and J. K. Watters. 1995. Multimethod research from targeted sampling to HIV risk environments. In *Qualitative Methods in Drug Abuse and HIV Research,* ed. E. Lambert, R. S. Ashery, and R. H. Needle. NIDA Research Monograph 157; NIH Pub. No. 95–4025. Washington, D.C.: U.S. Govt. Printing Office.

Boeri, M., D. Gibson, and L. Harbry. 2009. Cold cook methods: An ethnographic exploration on the myths of methamphetamine production and policy implications. *International Journal of Drug Policy* 20(5): 438–443.

Booth, R., S. Koester, J. T. Brewster, W. W. Weibel, and R. B. Fritz. 1991. Intravenous-drug-users and AIDS—risk behaviors. *American Journal of Drug and Alcohol Abuse* 17(3): 337–353.

Bourgois, P. 1998. Just another night in a shooting gallery. *Theory, Culture and Society* 15(2): 37–66.

Bourgois, P. 2000. Disciplining addictions: The bio-politics of methadone and heroin in the United States. *Culture, Medicine, and Psychiatry* 24(2): 165–195.

Bourgois, P. 2003. *In search of respect: Selling crack in el barrio.* 2nd ed. Cambridge: Cambridge University Press.

Bourgois, P. 2008. The mystery of marijuana: Science and the U.S. war on drugs. *Substance Use and Misuse* 43: 581–583.

Bourgois, P., and J. Bruneau 2000. Needle exchange, HIV infection, and the politics of science: Confronting Canada's cocaine injection epidemic with participant observation. *Medical Anthropology* 18: 325–350.

Bourgois P., B. Prince, and A. Moss. 2004. The everyday violence of hepatitis C among young women who inject drugs in San Francisco. *Human Organization* 63(3): 253–264.

Bourgois, P., and J. Schonberg. 2009. *Righteous dopefiend.* Berkeley, CA: University of California Press.

Bourguignon, E. 1968. World distribution and patterns of possession states. In *Trance and Possession States*, ed. R. Prince, 3–34. Montreal: R. M. Bucke Memorial Society.

Bourguignon, E. 1973. *Religion, altered states of consciousness and social change.* Columbus, Ohio: Ohio University Press.

Bovelle, E., and A. Taylor. 1985. Conclusions and implications. In *Life with Heroin: Voices from the Inner City,* ed. B. Hanson, G. Beschner, J. Walters, and E. Bovelle, 175–186. Lexington, MA: Lexington Books.

Brandes, S. 2002. *Staying sober in Mexico City.* Austin, TX: University of Texas Press.

Braunstein, M. 1993. Sampling a hidden population: Noninstitutionalized drug users. *AIDS Education and Prevention* 5: 131–139.

Broadhead, R. S. 1991. Social constructions of bleach in combating AIDS among injection-drug users. *Journal of Drug Issues* 21(4): 713–737.

Broadhead, R. S., and E. J. Fox. 1990. Takin' it to the streets—AIDS outreach as ethnography. *Journal of Contemporary Ethnography* 19(3): 322–348.

Broadhead, R. S., and E. Margolis. 1993. Drug policy in the time of AIDS: The development of outreach in San Francisco. *Sociological Quarterly* 34(3): 497–522.

Brody, J. L., J. P. Gluck, and A. S. Aragon. 1997. Participants' understanding of the process of psychological research. *Ethics and Behavior* 7: 285–298.

Brook, J., M. Whiteman, and A. Gordon. 1984. Onset of adolescent drinking: A longitudinal study of intrapersonal and interpersonal antecedents. *Alcoholism Clinical and Experimental Research* 8(1): 83.

Brown, B. S., and G. M. Beschner, eds. 1993. *Handbook on risk of AIDS: Injection drug users and sexual partners.* Westport, CT: Greenwood Press.

Brown, C. 1965. *Manchild in the promised land.* New York: Penguin Books.

Brown, E. J. 2006. The integral place of religion in the lives of rural African-American women who use cocaine. *Journal of Religion and Health* 45(1): 19–39.

Brown, D. R., A. Hernández, G. Saint-Jean, S. Evans, I. Tafari, L. G. Brewster, M. J. Celestin. 2008. Jefferson Reaves, Sr. Health Center (JRSHC) Community Rapid Assessment

Response and Evaluation (RARE): A participatory action research pilot study of urban health disparities. *American Journal of Public Health* 98: 28–38.

Buchanan, D., S. Shaw, W. Teng, P. Hiser, and M. Singer. 2003. Neighborhood differences in patterns of syringe access, use, and discard among injection drug users: Implications for HIV outreach and prevention education. *Journal of Urban Health* 80(3): 438–454.

Buchanan, D., J. A. Tooze, S. Shaw, M. Kinzly, R. Heimer, and M. Singer. 2006. Demographic, HIV risk behavior, and health status characteristics of 'crack' cocaine injectors compared to other injection drug users in three New England cities. *Drug and Alcohol Dependence* 81(3): 221–229.

Burawoy, M., J. J. Blum, S. George, Z. Gille, M. Thayer, T. Gowan, L. Haney, M. Klawiter, S. Lopez, and S. Riain. 2000. *Global Ethnography: Forces, Connections, and Imaginations in a Postmodern World.* Berkeley, CA: University of California Press.

Burroughs, W. S. 1977. *Junkie.* New York: Penguin Books.

Burton, R. 1885. *The Arabian nights: The book of the thousand nights and a night. Plain and literal translation of the Arabian nights entertainments.* Available (including footnotes) online at: http://www.wollamshram.ca/1001/index.htm. Accessed June 20, 2008.

Butler, B. Y. 2006. *Holy intoxication to drunken dissipation: Alcohol among Quichua speakers in Otovalo, Ecuador.* Albuquerque, NM: University of New Mexico Press.

Calabrese, J. 2001. The Supreme Court versus peyote: Consciousness alteration, cultural psychiatry, and the dilemma of contemporary subcultures. *Anthropology of Consciousness* 12(2): 4–18.

Callaway, J. C., M. M. Airaksinen, D. McKenna, G. S. Brito, and C. Grob. 1994. Platelet serotonin uptake sites increased in drinkers of ayahuasca. *Psychopharmacology* 116(3): 385–387.

Callaway, J. C., G. S. Brito, and E. S. Neves. 2005. Phytochemical analyses of *Banisteriopsis caapi* and *Psychotria viridis. Journal of Psychoactive Drugs* 37(2): 145–150.

Campa, A., D. T. Jayaweera, C. Rafie, S. Sales, J. B. Page, and M. K. Baum. 2007. When access to antiretroviral for all is not enough. *Journal of Public Administration and Management* 12(3): 147–159.

Campa, A., Z. Yang, S. Lai, L. Xue, J. C. Phillips, S. Sales, J. B. Page, and M. K. Baum. 2005. HIV-related wasting in HIV-infected drug users in the era of highly active antiretroviral therapy. *Clinical Infectious Diseases* 41(8): 1179–1185.

Campbell, H. 2008. Female drug smugglers on the U.S.-Mexico border: Gender, crime, and empowerment. *Anthropological Quarterly* 81(1): 233–268.

Campbell, N. 2005a. Oral history interviews with substance abuse researchers: Interview with Howard Becker. Available online at: http://sitemaker.umich.edu/substance.abuse .history/oral_history_interviews. Accessed June 18, 2008.

Campbell, N. 2005b. Oral history interviews with substance abuse researchers: Interview with Bruce Johnson. Available online at: http://sitemaker.umich.edu/substance.abuse .history/oral_history_interviews. Accessed June 20, 2008.

Carlson, R. G. 1996. The political economy of AIDS among drug users in the United States: Beyond blaming the victim or powerful others. *American Anthropologist* 98(2): 266–278.

Carlson, R. G., J. McCaughan, R. Falck, J. Wang, H. A. Siegal, and R. Daniulaityte. 2003. Perceived adverse consequences associated with MDMA/Ecstasy use among young polydrug users in Ohio: Implications for intervention. *International Journal of Drug Policy* 15(4): 265–274.

Carlson, R. G., and H. A. Siegal. 1988. The crack life: An ethnographic overview of crack use and sexual behavior among African Americans in a Midwest metropolitan city. *Journal of Psychoactive Drugs* 23(1): 11–20.

Carlson, R. G., H. A. Siegal, and R. S. Falck. 1995. Qualitative research methods in drug and AIDS prevention research: An overview. In *Qualitative Methods in Drug Abuse and HIV Research,* ed. E. Lambert, R. S. Ashery, and R. H. Needle. NIDA Research Monograph 157; NIH Pub. No. 95–4025. Washington, D.C.: U.S. Govt. Printing Office.

Carlson, R. G., H. A. Siegel, R. S. Falck, and J. Guo. 1994. An ethnographic approach to targeted sampling: Problems and solutions in AIDS prevention research among injection drug and crack-cocaine users. *Human Organization* 53: 279–286.

Carter, W. E., ed. 1980. *Cannabis in Costa Rica.* Philadelphia: ISHI Press.

Castro, A., and M. Singer, eds. 2004. *Unhealthy health policy: A critical anthropological examination.* Walnut Creek, CA: Altamira Press.

Castro, F. G., M. Barrera, and C. R. Martinez. 2004. The cultural adaptation of prevention interventions: Resolving tensions between fidelity and fit. *Prevention Science* 5(1): 41–45.

Cavan, S. 1966. *Liquor license: An ethnography of bar behavior.* Chicago: Aldine Publishing Company.

Cepeda, A., and A. Valdez. 2003. Risk behaviors among young Mexican American gang-associated females: Sexual relations, partying, substance use, and crime. *Journal of Adolescent Research* 18(1): 90–106.

Chitwood, D., C. B. McCoy, J. A. Inciardi, D. C. McBride, M. Comerford, E. Trapido, V. McCoy, J. B. Page, J. Griffin, M. A. Fletcher, and M. A. Ashman. 1990. HIV seropositivity of needles from shooting galleries in South Florida. *American Journal of Public Health* 80(2): 150–152.

Chitwood, D. D., and P. C. Morningstar. 1985. Factors which differentiate cocaine users in treatment from nontreatment users. *International Journal of the Addictions* 20(3): 449–459.

Ciccarone, D., J. Bamberger, A. Kral, B. Edlin, C. Hobart, A. Moon, E. Murphy, P. Bourgois, and D. Young. 2001. Soft tissue infections among injection drug users: San Francisco, California, 1996–2000. *Morbidity and Mortality Weekly Report* 50(19): 381–384.

Ciccarone, D., and P. Bourgois. 2003. Explaining the geographical variation of HIV among injection drug users in the United States. *Substance Use and Misuse* 38(14): 2049–2063.

Cicero, T. J., J. A. Inciardi, and H. Surratt. 2007. Trends in the use and abuse of branded and generic extended release oxycodone and fentanyl products in the United States. *Drug and Alcohol Dependence* 91(2–3): 115–120.

Clair, S., M. Singer, F. Bastos, M. Malta, C. Santelices, and N. Ebertoni. 2009. The role of drug users in the Brazilian HIV/AIDS epidemic: Patterns, perceptions, and prevention. In *Globalization of HIV/AIDS: An Interdisciplinary Reader,* ed. C. Pope, R. White, and R. Malow, 50–58. New York: Routledge.

Clatts, M. C. 1994. All the king's horses and all the king's men: Some personal reflections on ten years of AIDS ethnography. *Human Organization* 53(1): 93–95.

Clatts, M. C., R. Heimer, N. Abdala, L. A. Goldsamt, J. L. Sotheran, K. T. Anderson, T. M. Gallo, L. D. Hoffer, P. A. Luciano, and T. Kyriakides. 1999. HIV-1 transmission in injection paraphernalia: Heating drug solutions may inactivate HIV-1. *Journal of Acquired Immune Deficiency Syndrome* 22(2): 2.

Cleckner, P. J. 1976a. Blowing some lines: Intracultural variations among Miami cocaine users. *Journal of Psychedelic Drugs* 8: 37–42.

Cleckner, P. J. 1976b. Dope is to get high: A preliminary analysis of intracultural variation in drug categories among heavy users and dealers. *Addict Diseases* 2: 537–552.

Cleckner, P. J. 1977. Cognitive and ritual aspects of drug use among young black urban males. In *Drugs, Rituals, and Altered States of Consciousness,* ed. B. M. DuToit, 149–168. Rotterdam, Netherlands: A. A. Balkema.

Cohen, E. N., and H. D. Metzger. 1994. High-risk behaviors for HIV: A comparison between crack-abusing and opioid-abusing African-American women. *Journal of Psychoactive Drugs* 26(3): 233–241.

Compton, W., J. Horton, L. Cottler, R. Booth, C. Leukefeld, and M. Singer, R. Cunningham-Williams, et al. 2004. A multistate trial of pharmacy syringe purchase. *Journal Urban Health* 81: 661–670.

Cooper, M. 2002. Alcohol use and risky sexual behavior among college students and youth: Evaluating the evidence. *Journal of Studies on Alcohol* 14: 101–117.

Copeland, L., J. Budd, R. Robertson, and R. Elton. 2004. Changing patterns in causes of death in a cohort of injecting drug users, 1980–2001. *Archives of Internal Medicine* 164(11): 1214–1220.

Cornelius, M. 2001. Tobacco control: The Fiji experience. *Development Bulletin* 54: 69–71.

Courtwright, D. 2001. *Forces of habit: Drugs and the making of the modern world.* Cambridge, MA: Harvard University Press.

Courtwright, D., H. Joseph, and D. Des Jarlais. 1989. *Addicts who survived: An oral history of narcotic use in the U.S. 1923–1965.* Knoxville, TN: University of Tennessee Press.

Craig, G., A. Corden, and P. Thorton. 2000. Safety in social research. *Social Research Update, Issue 20.* Available online at: http://sru.soc.surrey.ac.uk/SRU29.html. Accessed January 22, 2010.

Crewe, B. 2005. Prisoner society in the era of hard drugs. *Punishment and Society* 7(4): 457–481.

Curtis, R., and T. Wendel. 2000. Toward the development of a typology of illegal drug markets. In *Illegal Drug Markets: From Research to Policy,* ed. M. Hough and M. Natarajan, 121–152. Monsey, NJ: Criminal Justice Press.

Dai, B. 1937. *Opium Addiction in Chicago.* Montclair, NJ: Patterson Smith.

Da Silveira, D. X., C. S. Grob, M. Dobkin de Rios, E. Lopez, L. K. Alonso, C. Tacla, and E. Doering-Silveira. 2005. Ayahuasca in adolescence: A preliminary psychiatric assessment. *Journal of Psychoactive Drugs* 37(2): 129–133.

Department of Health, Education, and Welfare (DHEW). 1978. The Belmont report: Ethical principles and guidelines for the protection of human subjects research. Appendix I, DHEW Publication No. OS 78–0012. Washington, D.C.: U.S. Govt. Printing Office.

Department of Health and Human Services (DHHS). 2001. Title 45 Public Welfare, Part 46, Code of Federal Regulations, Protection of Human Subjects.

De Queiroz, M. 2007. Guinea-Bissau: African paradise for South American traffickers. *IPS News,* August 27. Online at: http://ipsnews.net/news.asp?idnews=38857. Accessed June 2, 2008.

de Quincey, T. 1822. *Confessions of an English opium eater.* New York: F. M. Lupton.

Deren, S., Sanchez, J., Shedlin, M., Davis, W. R., Beardsley, M., Jarlais, D. D., Miller, K. 1996. HIV risk behaviors among Dominican brothel and street prostitutes in New York City. *AIDS Education and Prevention* 8(5): 444–456.

Deren, S., Shedlin, M., Beardsley, M. 1996. HIV-related concerns and behaviors among Hispanic women. *AIDS Education and Prevention* 8(4): 335–342.

Des Jarlais, D. C. 1986. Social science and AIDS. *Medical Anthropology Quarterly* 17(2): 33–34.

Des Jarlais, D. C., and S. R. Friedman. 1988. Needle sharing among IVDUs at risk for AIDS. *American Journal of Public Health* 78(11): 1498.

Des Jarlais, D. C., S. R. Friedman, D. M. Novick, J. L. Sotheran, P. Thomas, S. R. Yankovitz, D. Mildvan, et al. 1989. HIV infection among intravenous drug users in Manhattan, New York City, 1977–1987. *Journal of the American Medical Association* 261: 1008–1011.

Des Jarlais, D. C., S. R. Friedman, and D. Strug. 1986. AIDS and needle sharing. In *The Social Dimensions of AIDS: Method and Theory,* ed. D. Feldman and T. M. Johnson, 111–125. New York: Praeger.

Desmarchelier, C., A. Gurni, G. Ciccia, and A. M. Giulietti. 1996. Ritual and medicinal plants of the Ese'ejas of the Amazonian rainforest (Madre de Dios, Peru). *Journal of Ethnopharmacology* 52(1): 45–51.

Dobkin de Rios, M. 1970. Banisteriopsis used in witchcraft and folk healing in Iquitos, Peru. *Economic Botany* 24(35): 296–300.

Dobkin de Rios, M. 1971. Ayahuasca, the healing vine. *International Journal of Social Psychiatry* 17(4): 256–269.

Dobkin de Rios, M. 1972a. Curing with ayahuasca in a Peruvian Amazon slum. In *Hallucinogens and Shamanism,* ed. M. J. Harner. New York: Oxford University Press.

Dobkin de Rios, M. 1972b. *Visionary Vine: Psychedelic Healing in the Peruvian Amazon.* San Francisco: Chandler Publishing Company.

Dobkin de Rios, M. 2005. Interview with Guillermo Arrevalo, a shipibo urban shaman by Roger Rumrrill. *Journal of Psychoactive Drugs* 37(2): 203–207.

Dobkin de Rios, M, and C. S. Grob. 2005. Interview with Jeffrey Bronfman, representative mestre for the Uniao do Vegetal Church in the United States. *Journal of Psychoactive Drugs* 37(2): 189–191.

Doering-Silveira E., C. S. Grob, M. Dobkin de Rios, E. Lopez, L. K. Alonso, C. Tacla, and D. X. Da Silveira. 2005. Report on psychoactive drug use among adolescents using ayahuasca within a religious context. *Journal of Psychoactive Drugs* 37(2): 141–144.

Doering-Silveira E., E. Lopez, C. S. Grob, M. Dobkin de Rios, L. K. Alonso, C. Tacla, I. Shirakawa, P. H. Bertolucci, and D. X. Da Silveira. 2005. Ayahuasca in adolescence: A neuropsychological assessment. *Journal of Psychoactive Drugs* 37(2): 123–128.

Dorn, N., K. Murji, and N. South. 1992. *Traffickers: Drug markets and law enforcement.* London: Routledge.

Douglas, O. 1955. *A Solomon Island society.* Boston: Beacon Press.

Downing, M., T. H. Riess, K. Vernon, N. Mulia, M. Hollinquest, C. McKnight, D. C. Des Jarlais, and B. R. Edlin. 2005. What's community got to do with it? Implementation models of syringe exchange programs. *AIDS Education and Prevention* 17(1): 68–78.

Drake, St. C., and Cayton, H. 1970. *Black metropolis: A study of negro life in a northern city,* Vol. 2. New York: Harcourt, Brace and World.

Dreher, M. C. 1982. *Working men and ganja: Marihuana use in rural Jamaica.* Philadelphia: ISHI Press.

Duke, M., W. Teng, J. Simmons, and M. Singer. 2003. Structural and interpersonal violence among Puerto Rican drug users. *Practicing Anthropology* 25(3): 28–31.

Dunlap, E., E. Benoit, S. J. Sifaneck, and B. D. Johnson. 2006. Social constructions of dependency by blunts smokers: Qualitative reports. *International Journal of Drug Policy* 17(3): 171–182.

Dunlap, E., A. Golub, B. D. Johnson, and D. Wesley. 2001. Intergenerational transmission of conduct norms for drugs, sexual exploitation, and violence: A case study. *British Journal of Criminology* 42(1): 1–20.

Dunlap, E., and B. D. Johnson. 1996. Family and human resources in the development of a female crack-seller career: Case study of a hidden population. *Journal of Drug Issues* 26(1): 175–198.

Dunlap, E., B. D. Johnson, and A. Manwar. 1994. A successful female crack dealer: Case-study of a deviant career. *Deviant Behavior* 15(1): 1–25.

Dushay, R., M. Singer, M. Weeks, L. Rohena, and R. Gruber. 2001. Lowering HIV risk among ethnic minority drug users: Comparing culturally targeted intervention to a standard intervention. *American Journal of Drug and Alcohol Abuse* 27(3): 504–524.

Eber, C. 1994. *Women and alcohol in a highland Maya town: Water of hope, water of sorrow.* Austin, TX: University of Texas Press.

Eckert, P. 1983. Beyond the statistics of adolescent smoking. *American Journal of Public Health* 73(4): 439–441.

Edlin, B., K. Irwin, S. Faruque, C. McCoy, C. Word, Y. Serrano, J. A. Inciardi, B. P. Bowser, R. F. Schilling, and S. D. Holmberg. 1994. Intersecting epidemics: Crack cocaine use and HIV-infection among inner-city young-adults. *New England Journal of Medicine* 331(21): 1422–1427.

Ellickson, P., R. Collins, L. Bogart, D. Klein, and S. Taylor. 2005. Scope of HIV risk and co-occurring psychosocial health problems among young adults: Violence, victimization, and substance use. *Journal of Adolescent Health* 36(5): 401–409.

Engels, F. 1969 [1845]. *The Condition of the Working Class in England.* London: Granata.

Eriksen, T. H., ed. 2003. Introduction. In *Globalization: Studies in Anthropology.* London: Pluto Press.

Ernster, V., N. Kaufman, M. Nichter, J. Samet, and S. Y. Yoon. 2000. Women and tobacco: Moving from policy to action. *Bulletin of the World Health Organization* 78(7): 891–901.

Farmer, P. 1999. Cruel and unusual: Drug resistant tuberculosis as punishment. In *Sentenced to Die?,* ed. V. Stern and R. Jones, 70–88. London: King's College.

Farmer, P. 2003. Pathologies of power: Health, human rights, and the new war on the poor. *North American Dialogue* 6(1): 1–4.

Feldman, H. 1973. Street status and drug users. Society 10(4): 32–38.

Feldman, H. 1979. *Angel dust: An ethnographic study of phencyclidine users.* Lexington, MA: Lexington Books.

Feldman, H., M. Agar, and G. Beschner. 1980. *Angel dust in four American cities.* Rockville, MD: U.S. Dept. of Health and Human Services, Public Health Service, Alcohol, Drug Abuse, and Mental Health Administration.

Feldman, H., and M. Aldrich. 1990. The role of ethnography in substance abuse and public policy: Historical precedent and future prospects. In *The Collection and Interpretation of Data from Hidden Populations,* ed. E. Lambert, 12–30. NIDS Research Monograph #98. Rockville, MD: National Institute on Drug Abuse.

Feldman, H., and P. Biernacki. 1988. The ethnography of needle sharing among intravenous drug users and implications for public policies and intervention strategies. In *Needle Sharing among Intravenous Drug Abusers: National and International Perspectives,* ed. R. J. Battjes and R. W. Pickens, 28–39. Washington, DC: National Institute on Drug Abuse.

Fichtner, C., and J. Cavanaugh. 2006. Malignant criminalization: From hypothesis to theory. *Psychiatric Services* 57: 1511–1512.

Finestone, H. 1957a. Cats, kicks, and color. *Social Problems* 5(1): 3–13.

Finestone, H. 1957b. *Victims of change: Juvenile delinquents in American society.* Westport, CT: Greenwood Press.

Finlinson, H. A., H. M. Colon, R. R. Robles, S. Deren, M. Soto López, and A. Muñoz. 1999. Access to sterile syringes by injecting drug users in Puerto Rico. *Human Organization* 58(2): 201–212.

Finlinson, A., D. Oliver-Vélez, H. Colón, S. Deren, R. Robles, M. Beardsley, J. Cant, J. Andía, and M. López. 2000. Syringe acquisition and use of syringe exchange programs by Puerto Rican drug injectors in New York and Puerto Rico: Comparisons based on quantitative and qualitative methods. *AIDS and Behavior* 4(4): 341–351.

Finlinson, A., R. Robles, H. Colon, and J. B. Page. 1993. Recruiting and retaining out-of-treatment intravenous drug users in the Puerto Rico AIDS prevention project. *Human Organization* 52(2): 169–175.

Fisher, C. 1999. Relational ethics and research with vulnerable populations. In *Reports on Research Involving Persons with Mental Disorders That May Affect Decision-Making*

Capacity, Vol. 2, 29–49. Commissioned Papers by the National Bioethics Advisory Commission (NBAC), Rockville, MD.

Fisher, C. 2004. Ethics in drug abuse and related HIV risk research. *Applied Developmental Science* 8: 90–102.

Fisher, C. B., M. Oransky, M. Mahadevan, M. Singer, G. Mirhej, and D. Hodge. 2008a. Experimental realism, experimental mistrust, and therapeutic misconception in marginalized populations' understanding of drug addiction research. *IRB Journal* (in press).

Fisher, C. B., M. Oransky, M. Mahadevan, M. Singer, G. Mirhej, and D. Hodge. 2008b. Do drug abuse researchers have a 'duty to protect' third parties from HIV transmission?: Moral perspectives of street drug users. In *Ethical and legal issues in research with high risk populations: Addressing threats of suicide, child abuse, and violence,* ed. D. Buchanan, C. Fisher, and L. Gable. New York (in press).

Fisher, C. B., and S. A. Wallace. 2000. Through the community looking glass: Re-evaluating the ethical and policy implications of research on adolescent risk and psychopathology. *Ethics and Behavior* 10: 99–118.

Fletcher, J. M., J. B. Page, D. J. Francis, K. Copeland, M. J. Naus, C. M. Davis, R. Morris, D. Krauskopf, and P. Satz. 1996. Cognitive correlates of chronic Cannabis use in Costa Rican Men. *Archives of General Psychiatry* 53:1051–1057.

Fort, J. 1969. A World View of Drugs. In *Society and Drugs,* ed. R. Blum. San Francisco: Jossey-Bass.

Frenopoulo, C. 2005. The ritual use of ayahuasca. *Journal of Psychoactive Drugs* 37(2): 237–239.

Friedman, S. R. 1986. Thoughts about social science and AIDS. *Medical Anthropology Quarterly* 17(2): 34–36.

Friedman, S. R., D. Des Jarlais, J. Sotheran. 1986. AIDS health education for intravenous drug users. *Health Education & Behavior* 13(4) 383–393.

Friedman, S. R., D. Des Jarlais, C. Sterk, J. Sotheran, S. Tross, J. Woods, M. Sufian, and A. Abdul-Quadar. 1990. AIDS and the social relations of intravenous drug users. *Milbank Quarterly* 68 (suppl. 1): 85–110.

Friedman, S. R., W. de Jong, D. Rossi, G. Touzé, R. Rockwell, D. Des Jarlais, and R. Elovich. 2007. Harm reduction theory: Users culture, micro-social indigenous harm reduction, and the self-organization and outside-organizing of users' groups. *International Journal of Drug Policy* 18(2): 107–117.

Friedman, S. R., C. Sterk, M. Sufian, and D. C. Des Jarlais. 1989. Will bleach decontaminate needles during cocaine binges in shooting galleries? *Journal of the American Medical Association* 262(11): 1467.

Frischer, M., L. Elliott, A. Taylor, D. Goldberg, S. Green, L. Gruer, J. Cameron, N. McKeganey, and M. Bloor. 1993. Do needle exchanges help to control the spread of HIV among injecting drug users? *AIDS* 7(12): 1677–1678.

Furst, P. T. 1972. *Flesh of the gods: The ritual use of hallucinogens.* New York: Praeger Publishers.

Furst, P. T. 1976. *Hallucinogens and Culture.* San Francisco: Chandler and Sharp.

Furst, P. T. 1990. To find our life: Peyote among the Huichol Indians of Mexico. In *Flesh of the gods: The ritual use of hallucinogens,* ed. P. T. Furst, 136–184. Prospect Heights, IL: Waveland Press.

Gamburd, M. 2008. *Breaking the ashes: The culture of illicit liquor in Sri Lanka.* Ithaca, NY: Cornell University Press.

Gamella, J. 1994. The spread of intravenous drug use and AIDS in a neighborhood in Spain. *Medical Anthropology Quarterly* 8(2): 131–160.

Gamella, J., and A. A. Roldán. 1997. *Las rutas del éxtasis: Drogas de síntesis y nuevas culturas juveniles*. Barcelona, Spain: Editorial Arial, S.A.

Garcia, A. 2007. The pastoral clinic: Addiction and absolution along the Rio Grande. Ph.D. dissertation, Harvard University.

Garcia, A. 2008. The elegiac addict: History, chronicity, and the melancholic subject. *Cultural Anthropology* 23(4): 718–746.

Garcia, V. 2007. Meeting a binational research challenge: Substance abuse among transnational Mexican farmworkers in the United States. *Journal of Rural Health* 23: 61–67.

Garrity, J. F. 2000. Jesus, peyote, and the holy people: Alcohol abuse and the ethos of power in Navajo healing. *Medical Anthropology Quarterly* 14(4): 521–542.

Gayton, A. H. 1928. The narcotic plant, Datura, in aboriginal America culture. Ph.D. dissertation, University of California, Berkeley.

German, D., and C. E. Sterk. 2002. Looking beyond stereotypes: Exploring variations among crack smokers. *Journal of Psychoactive Drugs* 34(4): 383–392.

Gilchrist, G., A. Taylor, D. Goldberg, C. Mackie, A. Denovan, and S. T. Green. 2001. Behavioural and lifestyle study of women using a drop-in centre for female street sex workers in Glasgow, Scotland: A 10-year comparative study. *Addiction Research and Theory* 9(1): 43–58.

Goldstein, P., B. Spunt, T. Miller, and P. Bellucci. 1990. Ethnographic Field Stations. In *The Collection and Interpretation of Data from Hidden Populations*, ed. E. Lambert, 80–95. NIDA Research Monograph 98. Rockville, MD: National Institute on Drug Abuse.

Golub, A., B. D. Johnson, and E. Dunlap. 2005. Subcultural evolution and illicit drug use. *Addiction Research and Theory* 13(3): 217–229.

Golub, A., B. D. Johnson, E. Dunlap, and S. Sifaneck. 2004. Projecting and monitoring the life course of the marijuana/blunts generation. *Journal of Drug Issues* 34(2): 361–388.

Gonzalez, D. H., and J. B. Page. 1981. Cuban women, sex role conflicts, and use of prescription drugs. *Journal of Psychoactive Drugs* 13(1): 47–51.

Goode, E. 1984. *Deviant behavior*. Englewood Cliffs, NJ: Prentice-Hall.

Gordon, B. 1979. *I'm dancing as fast as I can*. New York: Harper & Row.

Gorman, E. M., P. Morgan, and E. Y. Lambert. 1995. Qualitative research considerations and other issues in the study of methamphetamine use among men who have sex with other men. In *Qualitative Methods in Drug Abuse and HIV Research*, ed. E. Lambert, R. S. Ashery, R. H. Needle. NIDA Research Monograph 157; NIH Pub. No. 95–4025. Washington, DC: U.S. Govt. Printing Office.

Gray, D., and S. Saggers. 1997. Supplying and promoting 'grog': The political economy of alcohol in aboriginal Australia. *Australian Journal of Social Issues* 32(3): 215–237.

Green, S. T., A. Taylor, M. Frischer, and D. J. Goldberg. 1993. 'Frontloading' ('halfing') among Glasgow drug injectors as a continuing risk behaviour for HIV transmission. *Addiction* 88(11): 1581–1582.

Griffin, M. L., J. H. Mendelson, N. K. Mello, and B. W. Lex. 1986. Marihuana use across the menstrual cycle. *Drug and Alcohol Dependence* 18(2): 213–224.

Grov, C., B. Kelly, and J. Parsons. 2009. Polydrug use among club-drug-going young adults recruited through time-space sampling. *Substance Use and Misuse* 44(6): 848–864.

Grund, J. 2004. Harm reduction for poppy farmers in Myanmar? *Asian Harm Reduction Network Newsletter* 34: 1–3.

Haddon, A. C. 1947. Smoking and tobacco pipes in New Guinea. *Philosophical Transactions of the Royal Society of London,* Series B, 232: 1–278.

Hahn, J. A., K. Page-Shafer, P. J. Lum, P. Bourgois, E. Stein, J. L. Evans, M. P. Busch, L. H. Tobler, B. Phelps, A. R. Moss. 2002. Hepatitis C virus seroconversion among young injection drug users: Relationships and risks. *Journal of Infectious Diseases* 186(11): 1558–1564.

Halpern, J. H., A. R. Sherwood, T. Passie, K. C. Blackwell, and A. J. Ruttenber. 2008. Evidence of health and safety in American members of a religion who use a hallucinogenic sacrament. *Medical Science Monitor* 14(8): SR15–SR22.

Hanson, B., G. Beschner, J. Walters, and E. Bovelle. 1985. *Life with heroin.* Lexington, MA: Lexington Books.

Harvard University Herbaria 2002. Richard Evans Schultes papers. Available online at: http://www.huh.harvard.edu/Libraries/Nash/schultes.htm. Accessed June 25, 2008.

Hays, T. 1991. "No tobacco, no hallelujah": Missions and the early history of tobacco in Eastern Papua. *Pacific Studies* 14: 91–112.

Heath, D. 1958. Drinking patterns of the Bolivian Camba. *Quarterly Journal of Studies on Alcohol* 19: 491–508.

Heath, D. 1976. Anthropological perspectives on alcohol: An historical review. In *Crosscultural approaches to the study of alcohol: An interdisciplinary approach,* ed. M. Everett. The Hague, Netherlands: Mouton.

Heath, D. 1991. Continuity and change in drinking patterns of the Bolivian Camba. In *Society, culture, and drinking patterns reexamined,* ed. D. Pittman and H. White. New Brunswick, NJ: Rutgers Center of Alcohol Studies.

Heath, D. 2000. *Drinking occasions: Comparative perspectives on alcohol and culture.* New York: Routledge.

Heath, D. 2004. Camba (Bolivia) drinking patterns: Changes in alcohol use, anthropology, and research perspectives. In *Drug use and cultural contexts: Beyond the West,* ed. R. Coomber and N. South, 119–136. London: Free Association Books.

Heckathorn, D. 1997. Respondent-driven sampling: A new approach to the study of hidden populations. *Social Problems* 44(2): 174–199.

Heckathorn, D. 2002. Respondent-driven sampling II: Deriving valid population estimates from chain-referral samples of hidden populations. *Social Problems* 49(1): 11–34.

Heckathorn, D. 2007. Extensions of respondent-driven sampling: analyzing continuous variables and controlling for differential recruitment. *Sociological Methodology* 37(1): 151–207.

Heimer, R., E. H. Kaplan, K. Khoshnood, B. Jariwala, and E. C. Cadman. 1993. Needle exchange decreases the prevalence of HIV-1 proviral DNA in returned syringes in New Haven, Connecticut. *American Journal of Medicine* 95(2): 214–220.

Herdt, G. 1987. *Sambia: ritual and gender in New Guinea.* New York: Holt, Rinehart, and Winston.

Herodotus. 2007. *The histories of Herodotus.* trans. G. C. Macaulay. Adelaide, Australia: University of Adelaide. Online at: http://etext.library.adelaide.edu.au/h/herodotus/h4m/complete.html#632. Accessed June 21, 2008.

Higgs, P., L. Maher, J. Jordens, A. Dunlop, and P. Sargent. 2001. Harm reduction and drug users of Vietnamese ethnicity. *Drug and Alcohol Review* 20(2): 239–245.

Hills, S. 1980. *Demystifying social deviance.* New York: McGraw-Hill.

Himmelgreen, D., R. Perez-Escamilla, S. Segural-Millan, N. Romero-Daza, M. Tranasescu, and M. Singer. 1998. A comparison of the nutritional status and food security of drug-using and non-drug-using Hispanic women in Hartford, Connecticut. *American Journal of Physical Anthropology* 107: 351–361.

Hoffer, L. 2006. *Junkie business: The evolution and operation of a heroin dealing network.* Belmont, CA: Thomson/Wadsworth.

Holland, J. A., L. Nelson, P. R. Ravikumar, and W. N. Elwood. 1998. Embalming fluid-soaked marijuana: New high or new guise for PCP? *Journal of Psychoactive Drugs* 30: 215–219.

Hong, Y., S. G. Mitchell, J. A. Peterson, C. A. Latkin, K. Tobin, and D. Gann. 2005. Ethnographic process evaluation: Piloting an HIV prevention intervention program among injection drug users. *International Journal of Qualitative Methods* 4(1): 2–10.

Hunt, D. E., D. S. Lipton, D. S. Goldsmith, D. L. Strug, and B. Spunt. 1985. It takes your heart: The image of methadone maintenance in the addict world and its effect on recruitment into treatment. *International Journal of Addictions* 20(11–12): 1751–1771.

Hunt, G., and J. Barker. 1999. Drug treatment in contemporary anthropology and sociology. *European Addict Research* 5: 126–132.

Hunt, G., and J. C. Barker. 2001. Socio-cultural anthropology and alcohol and drug research: Towards a unified theory. *Social Science and Medicine* 53(2): 165–188.

Hunt, G., and K. Joe-Laidler. 2001. Alcohol and violence in the lives of gang members. *Alcohol Research and Health* 25(1): 66.

Hunt, G., K. Joe-Laidler, and K. MacKenzie. 2000. Chillin,' being dogged, and getting buzzed: Alcohol in the lives of female gang members. *Drugs-Education Prevention and Policy* 7(4): 331–353.

Hunt, G., K. Joe-Laidler, and K. MacKenzie. 2005. Moving into motherhood: Gang girls and controlled risk. *Youth and Society* 36(3): 333–373.

Hunt, G., K. Mackenzie, and K. Joe-Laidler. 2000. 'I'm calling my mom': The meaning of family and kinship among homegirls. *Justice Quarterly* 17(1): 1–31.

Hunt, G., and S. Satterlee. 1986a. Drinking in an English village. *Man, New Series* 21(3): 521–537.

Hunt, G., and S. Satterlee. 1986b. The pub, the village and the people. *Human Organization* 45(1): 62–74.

Hutchinson, S. J., A. Taylor, L. Gruer, C. Barr, C. Mills, L. Elliott, D. J. Goldberg, R. Scott, and G. Gilchrist. 2000. One-year follow-up of opiate injectors treated with oral methadone in a GP-centred programme. *Addiction* 95(7): 1055–1068.

Inciardi, J. A. 1986. *The war on drugs: Heroin, cocaine, crime, and public policy.* Mountain View, CA: Mayfield.

Inciardi, J. A. 1992. *The war on drugs II.* Mountain View, CA: Mayfield.

Inciardi, J. A. 1995. Crack, crack house sex, and HIV risk. *Archives of Sexual Behavior* 24(3): 249–269.

Inciardi, J. A., T. J. Cicero, A. Muñoz, E. A.Geller, E. C. Senay, and G. E. Woody. 2006. The diversion of Ultram (R), Ultracet (R), and generic Tramadol HCl. *Journal of Addictive Diseases* 25(2): 53–58.

Inciardi, J. A., and R. Needle, eds. 1998. HIV/AIDS interventions for out-of-treatment drug users. *Journal of Psychoactive Drugs* 30(3): 225–315.

Inciardi, J. A., and J. B. Page. 1991. Drug sharing among intravenous drug users. *AIDS* 5(6): 772–773.

Institute for International Trade and Pacific Trade Consult. 2007. *The potential impact of PICTA on smaller forum island nations.* Adelaide, Australia: University of Adelaide Press.

Jacinto, C., M. Duterte, P. Sales, and S. Murphy. 2008. "I'm not a real dealer": The identity process of Ecstasy sellers. *Journal of Drug Issues,* 38(2): 419–444.

Jacobs, B. 1998. Research crack dealers: Dilemmas and contradictions. In *Ethnography at the edge: Crime, deviance, and field research,* ed. J. Ferrell and M. Hamm, 160–177. Boston: Northeastern University Press.

Jacobs, B. 1999. *Dealing crack: The social world of streetcorner selling.* Boston: Northeastern University Press.

James, J. 1972. Two domains of streetwalker argot. *Anthropological Linguistics* 14: 174–175.

James, J. 1976. Prostitution and addiction: An interdisciplinary approach. *Addictive Diseases: An International Journal* 2(4): 601–618.

James, J. 1977. Ethnography and social problems. In *Street ethnography: Selected studies of crime and drug use in natural settings,* ed. R. S. Weppner, 179–200. Beverly Hills, CA: Sage.

James, J. 1988. *Women and the blues: Passions that hurt, passions that heal.* San Francisco: Harper and Row.

James, J., C. Gosho, and R. W. Wohl. 1979. The relationship between female criminality and drug use. *Substance Use and Misuse* 14(2): 215–229.

James, W., and S. Johnson. 1996. *Doin' drugs: Patterns of African American addiction.* Austin, TX: University of Texas Press.

Janes, C. R., and G. Ames. 1989. Men, blue collar work, and drinking: Alcohol use in an industrial subculture. *Culture Medicine and Psychiatry* 13(3): 245–274.

Jöhncke, S. 2008. Treatmentality: A new approach to the policy and practice of drug use treatment. Presented at the European Association of Social Anthropologists' Conference Experiencing Diversity and Mutuality, Ljubljana, Slovenia.

Johnson, B. 1973. *Marihuana users and drug subcultures.* New York: John Wiley and Sons.

Johnson, B. 1980. *Toward a theory of drug subcultures.* National Institute on Drug Abuse Monograph 30: Theories on drug abuse: Selected contemporary perspectives, 110–119. Rockville, MD: National Institute on Drug Abuse.

Johnson B. 1985. *Taking care of business: The economics of crime by heroin abusers.* Lexington, MA: Lexington Books.

Johnson, B. D., E. E. Dunlap, and L. Maher. 1998. Nurturing for careers in drug use and crime: Conduct norms for children and juveniles in crack-using households. *Substance Use and Misuse* 33(7): 1511–1546.

Johnston, L., P. O'Malley, and J. Bachman. 1997. *National survey results on drug use from the Monitoring the Future study.* Rockville, MD: National Institute on Drug Abuse.

Kandell, J. 2001. Richard E. Schultes, 86, dies; trailblazing authority on hallucinogenic plants. *New York Times.* Online at: http://query.nytimes.com/gst/fullpage.html?res=9E04EEDF1231F930A25757C0A9679C8B63. Accessed June 25, 2008.

Kandel, D., O. Simchafagan, and M. Davies. 1986. Risk-factors for delinquency and illicit drug-use from adolescence to young adulthood. *Journal of Drug Issues* 16(1): 67–90.

Kane, S., and T. Mason. 2001. AIDS and criminal justice. *Annual Review of Anthropology* 30: 457–479.

Kearney, M. H., S. Murphy, K. Irwin, and M. Rosenbaum. 1995. Salvaging self: A grounded theory of pregnancy on crack cocaine. *Nursing Research* 44(4): 208–213.

Kearney, M. H., S. Murphy, and M. Rosenbaum. 1994a. Leading by losing: Sex and fertility on crack cocaine. *Quality Health Research* 4: 142.

Kearney, M. H., S. Murphy, and M. Rosenbaum. 1994b. Mothering on crack cocaine: A grounded theory analysis. *Social Science and Medicine* 38(2): 351–361.

Keesing, R. 1983. *Elota's story: The life and times of a Solomon Islands big man.* New York: Holt, Rinehart and Winston.

Kelly, B. C. 2005. Conception of risk in the lives of club drug using youth. *Substance Use and Misuse* 40(9–10): 1443–1459.

Kelly, B. C. 2006. Bongs and blunts: Notes on a suburban marijuana subculture. *Journal of Ethnicity and Substance Abuse* 4(3–4): 79–95.

Kelly, B. C. 2009. Mediating MDMA-related harm: Preloading and post-loading among Ecstasy-using youth. *Journal of Psychoactive Drugs* 41(1): 19–26.

Killworth, P., and H. R. Bernard. 1974. Catij: A new sociometric and its application to a prison living unit. *Human Organization* 33(4): 335–350.

Klee, L., and G. Ames. 1987. Re-evaluating risk factors for women's drinking: A study of blue-collar wives. *American Journal of Preventive Medicine* 3(1): 31–41.

Knipe, E. 1995. *Culture, society, and drugs: The social science approach to drug use.* Prospect Heights, IL: Waveland Press.

Koester, S. 1994a. Copping, running, and paraphernalia laws: Contextual variables and needle risk behavior among injection drug users. *Human Organization* 53(3): 287–295.

Koester, S. 1994b. The context of risk: Ethnographic contributions to the study of drug use and HIV. NIDA Research Monograph 143: 202–217.

Koester, S. 1995. The daily life of heroin-addicted persons: The biography of specific methodology. In *Qualitative methods in drug abuse and HIV research,* ed. E. Lambert, R. S. Ashery, and R. H. Needle, 84–99. NIDA Research Monograph 157; NIH Pub. No. 95–4025. Washington, D.C.: U.S. Govt. Printing Office.

Koester, S. 1998. Following the blood: Syringe reuse leads to blood-borne virus transmission among injection drug users. *Journal of Acquired Immune Deficiency Syndromes* 18: S139–S140.

Koester S., J. Glanz, and A. Baron. 2005. Drug sharing among heroin networks: Implications for HIV and hepatitis B and C prevention. *Aids and Behavior* 9(1): 27–39.

Koester S., R. Heimer, A. E. Baron, J. Glanz, and W. Teng. 2003. Risk of hepatitis C virus among young adult injection drug users who share injection equipment. *American Journal of Epidemiology* 157(4): 376–378.

Koester, S., and L. Hoffer. 1994. Indirect sharing: Additional HIV risks associated with drug injection. *AIDS and Public Policy Journal* 9(2): 100–105.

Kolodny, R. C., W. H. Masters, R. M. Kilodner, and G. Toro. 1974. Depression of plasma testosterone levels after chronic intensive marihuana use. *New England Journal of Medicine* 290: 872–874.

Kritikos, P. G., and S. P. Papadaki. 1967a. History of poppy and of opium and their expansion in antiquity in eastern Mediterranean area 2. *Bulletin on Narcotics* 19(3): 17–38.

Kritikos, P. G., and S. P. Papadaki. 1967b. History of poppy and of opium and their expansion in antiquity in eastern Mediterranean area 2. *Bulletin on Narcotics* 19(4): 5–10.

Kroeber, A. 1941. Salt, dogs, tobacco. *Anthropological Records* 6(1): i–ii, 1–20.

Kunitz, S. J. 2006. Life-course observations of alcohol use among Navajo Indians: Natural history or careers? *Medical Anthropology Quarterly* 20(3): 279–296.

La Barre, W. 1975 [original 1938]. *The peyote cult.* Hamden, CT: Archon Books.

La Barre, W., D. McAllester, J. S. Slotkin, O. Stewart, and S. Tax. 1951. Statement on peyote. *Science* 114: 582–583.

Lal, B. 2001. *Fiji before the storm: Elections and the politics of development.* Canberra, Australia: Asia Pacific Press.

Lambert, E., R. S. Ashery, and R. H. Needle. 1995. *Qualitative methods in drug abuse and HIV research.* NIDA Research Monograph 157; NIH Pub. No. 95–4025. Washington, DC: U.S. Govt. Printing Office.

Lamphere, L. 2006. Foreword: Taking stock—the transformation of feminist theorizing in anthropology. In *Feminist anthropology: Past, present, and future,* ed. P. L. Geller and M. K. Stockett, ix–xvi. Philadelphia: University of Pennsylvania Press.

Lang, G. C. 1979. Survival strategies of Chippewa drinkers in Minneapolis. *Central Issues in Anthropology* 1(2): 19–40.

Lee, R. B. 1968. What hunters do for a living, or, how to make out on scarce resources. In *Man the hunter,* ed. R. B. Lee and I. Devore, 30–48. Chicago: Aldine.

LeMasters, E. E. 1973. Social life in a working-class tavern. *Journal of Contemporary Ethnography* 2: 27–52.

León-Portilla, M. 2002. *Bernardino de Sahagún: First anthropologist.* Norman, OK: University of Oklahoma Press.

Levine, R. 1986. *Ethics and regulation of clinical research,* 2nd ed. Baltimore, MD: Urban and Schwarzenberg.

Lex, B. W. 1990a. Narcotic addicts' hustling strategies: Creation and manipulation of ambiguity. *Journal of Contemporary Ethnography* 18(4): 388–415.

Lex, B. W. 1990b. Male heroin addicts and their female mates: Impact on disorder and recovery. *Journal of Substance Abuse* 2(2): 147–175.

Lex, B. W. 1991. Some gender differences in alcohol and polysubstance users. *Health Psychology* 10(2): 121–132.

Lex, B. W. 1994. Alcohol and other drug abuse among women. *Alcohol Health and Research World* 8(3): 212–219.

Lex, B. W., M. L. Griffin, N. K. Mello, and J. H. Mendelson. 1989. Alcohol, marijuana, and mood states in young women. *Substance Use and Misuse* 24(5): 405–424.

Lex, B. W., J. H. Mendelson, S. Bavli, K. Harvey, and N. K. Mello. 1984. Effects of acute marijuana smoking on pulse rate and mood states in women. *Psychopharmacology* 84(2): 178–187.

Lex, B. W., S. L. Palmieri, N. K. Mello, and J. H. Mendelson. 1988. Alcohol use, marihuana smoking, and sexual activity in women. *Alcohol* 5(1): 21–25.

Liebling, A., and B. Stanko. 2001. Allegiance and ambivalence: Some dilemmas in researching disorder and violence. *British Journal of Criminology* 41: 421–430.

Lindesmith, A. R. 1947. *Opiate addiction.* Bloomington, IN: Principia.

Lindesmith, A. R. 1968. *Addiction and opiates.* Chicago: Aldine.

Lindesmith, A. R., A. Strauss, and N. Denzin. 1975. *Social psychology.* Hinsdale, IL: Dryden Press.

Lowie, R. 1983. *The Crow Indians.* Lincoln, NE: University of Nebraska Press.

Luna, E., and P. Ameringo. 1999. *Ayahuasca visions: The religious iconography of a Peruvian shaman.* Berkeley, CA: North Atlantic Books.

Lyttleton, C. 2006. Opiates to amphetamines: Development and change in the golden triangle. *Development Bulletin* 69: 22–26.

Macdonald, D. 2008. Afghanistan's hidden drug problem: The misuse of psychotropics. *Afghanistan research and evaluation unit briefing paper series.* Kabul, Afghanistan.

Macdonald, P. T., D. Waldorf, C. Reinarman, and S. Murphy. 1988. Heavy cocaine use and sexual behavior. *Journal of Drug Issues* 18(3): 437–455.

MacGowan, R. J., C. E. Sterk, A. Long, R. Cheney, R. M. Seeman, and J. E. Anderson. 1998. New needle and syringe use, and use of needle exchange programmes by street-recruited injection drug users in 1993. *International Journal of Epidemiology* 27(2): 302–308.

Mahadevan, M., C. Fisher, L. Bonet, M. Oransky, M. Singer, D. G. Hodge, and G. Mirhej, G. n.d. Willingness to participate in drug abuse research involving HIV testing: Participant perspectives. Manuscript under review.

Maher, L. 1992. Reconstructing the female criminal: Women and crack cocaine. *University of Southern California Review of Law and Women's Studies* 2(1): 131–154.

Maher, L. 1995. In the name of love: Women and initiation into illicit drugs. In *Gender and crime,* 132–166. Cardiff: University of Wales Press.

Maher, L. 1996a. Hidden in the light: Occupational norms among crack-using street-level sex workers. *Journal of Drug Issues* 26(1): 143–173.

Maher, L. 1996b. The illicit drugs reporting system trial: Ethnographic monitoring component. Sydney, Australia: National Drug and Alcohol Research Centre Technical Report.

Maher, L. 1997. *Sexed work: Gender, race, and resistance in a Brooklyn drug market.* 1997. New York: Oxford University Press.

Maher, L. 2002. Don't leave us this way: Ethnography and injecting drug use in the age of AIDS. *International Journal of Drug Policy* 13(4): 311–325.

Maher, L. 2004. Drugs, public health, and policing in indigenous communities. *Drug and Alcohol Review* 23(3): 249–251.

Maher, L., and R. Curtis. 1995. In search of the female urban 'gangsta': Change, culture, and crack cocaine. In *The criminal justice system and women: Offenders, victims, and workers,* ed. B. R. Price and N. J. Sokoloff, 147–166. 2nd ed. New York: McGraw-Hill.

Maher, L., J. Li, B. Jalaludin, K. G. Chant, and J. M. Kaldor. 2007. High Hepatitis C incidence in new injecting drug users: A policy failure? *Australian and New Zealand Journal of Public Health* 31(1): 30–35.

Maher, L., J. Li, B. Jalaludin, H. Wand, R. Jayasuriya, D. Dixon, and J. M. Kaldor. 2007. Impact of a reduction in heroin availability on patterns of drug use, risk behaviour, and incidence of hepatitis C virus infection in injecting drug users in New South Wales, Australia. *Drug and Alcohol Dependence* 89(2–3): 244–250.

Maher, L., and A. Salmon. 2007. Supervised injecting facilities: How much evidence is enough? *Drug and Alcohol Review* 26(4): 351–353.

Maher, L., and P. L. Sargent. 2002. Risk behaviours and hepatitis C infection among Indo-Chinese initiates to injecting drug use in Sydney, Australia. *Addiction Research and Theory* 10(6): 535–544.

Malow, R., J. Dévieux, T. Jennings, B. Lucenko, and S. Kalichman. 2001. Substance-abusing adolescents at varying levels of HIV risk: Psychosocial characteristics, drug use, and sexual behavior. *Journal of Substance Abuse* 13(1–2): 103–117.

Malcolm X. 1965. *The autobiography of Malcolm X.* New York: Grove Press.

Marcelin, L. H., and J. B. Page. 2007. The RARE experience in Miami. In *When Communities Assess Their AIDS Epidemics,* eds. B. P. Browser, E. Quimby, and M. Singer, 177–191. Lanham, MD: Lexington Books.

Marcus, G. 1995. *Ethnography through thick and thin.* Princeton, NJ: Princeton University Press.

Marshall, M. 1979. *Weekend warriors: Alcohol in a Micronesian culture.* Palo Alto, CA: Mayfield Publishing.

Marshall, M. 1983. *Through a glass darkly: Beer and modernization in Papua New Guinea.* Boroko, Papua New Guinea: Institute of Applied Social and Economic Research.

Marshall, M. 1990. *Silent voices speak: Women and prohibition in Truk.* Belmont, CA: Wadsworth Modern Anthropology Library.

Marshall, P. 1992a. Anthropology and bioethics. *Medical Anthropology Quarterly* 6(1): 49–73.

Marshall, P. 1992b. Research ethics in applied anthropology. *IRB: A Review of Human Subjects Research* 14(6): 1–5.

May, T., M. Duffy, B. Few, and M. Hough. 2005. *Understanding drug selling in communities: Insider or outsider trading?* York, U.K.: Joseph Rowntree.

May, T., and M. Hough. 2004. Drug markets and distribution systems. *Addiction Research and Theory* 12(6): 549–563.

McCoy, C. B., D. D. Chitwood, E. L. Khoury, and C. L. Miles. 1990. The implementation of an experimental research design in the evaluation of intervention to prevent AIDS among IV drug users. *Journal of Drug Issues* 20(2): 215–223.

McCoy, H. V., D. D. Chitwood, J. B. Page, and C. B. McCoy. 1997. Skills for HIV risk reduction: Evaluation of recall and performance in injecting drug users. *Substance Use and Misuse* 32(3): 229–247.

McGee, L., and M. Newcomb. 1992. General deviance syndrome: Expanded hierarchical evaluations at four stages from adolescence to adulthood. *Journal of Consulting and Clinical Psychology* 60(5): 766–776.

McGlothlin, W. H., and L. J. West. 1968. The marihuana problem: An overview. *American Journal of Psychiatry* 125(3): 120–134.

McGraw, S. 1989. Smoking behavior among Puerto Rican adolescents: Approaches to its study. Doctoral Dissertation, Department of Anthropology, University of Connecticut.

McKenna, D. J. 1996. Plant hallucinogens: Springboards for psychotherapeutic drug discovery. *Behavioural Brain Research* 73(1–2): 109–116.

McKenna, D. J. 2005. Ayahuasca and human destiny. *Journal of Psychoactive Drugs* 37(2): 231–234.

McKenzie, N. 2008. How police checkmate alleged drug chiefs. *The Age* 9: 17.

McKenzie, N., C. Houston, and T. Arup. 2008. Police swoop on drug ring. *The Age* 9: 1.

Mead, M. 1963. *Sex and temperament in three primitive societies.* New York: Morrow.

Mendelson, J. H., N. K. Mello, and B. W. Lex. 1986. Alcohol and marijuana: Concordance of use by men and women. Rockville, MD: NIDA Research Monograph Series 68, 117–141.

Mendelson, J. H., N. K. Mello, B. W. Lex, and S. Bavli. 1984. Marijuana withdrawal syndrome in a woman. *American Journal of Psychiatry* 141(10): 1289–1290.

Mendelson, J. H., R. Weiss, M. Griffin, S. M. Mirin, S. K. Teoh, N. K. Mello, and B. W. Lex. 1991. Some special considerations for treatment of drug abuse and dependence in women. Rockville, MD: NIDA Research Monograph Series, 313–327.

Mitchell, J. C., ed. 1969. *Social networks in urban situations: Analyses of personal relationships in Central African towns.* Manchester, U.K.: Manchester University Press.

Moerman, D. 1978. Surgeons and shamans: Implications of the effectiveness of medical metaphor. Paper presented at the annual meetings of the American Anthropological Association, Los Angeles, CA.

Mohan, S., A. S. Pradeepkumar, C. U. Thresia, K. R. Thankappan, W.S.C. Poston, C. K. Haddock, M. M. Pinkston et al. 2006. Tobacco use among medical professionals in Kerala, India: The need for enhanced tobacco cessation and control efforts. *Addictive Behaviors* 31(12): 2313–2318.

Moore, J. W. 1978. *Homeboys: Gangs, drugs, and prison in the barrios of Los Angeles.* Philadelphia: Temple University Press.

Morgan, H. W. 1981. *Drugs in America: A social history, 1800–1980.* Syracuse, NY: Syracuse University Press.

Morningstar, P. J., and D. D. Chitwood. 1982. Cocaine user subculture. *Proceedings of the Symposium on Cocaine.* New York: Narcotic and Drug Research, Inc. and New York State Division of Substance Abuse Services.

Morningstar, P. J., and D. D. Chitwood. 1987. How women and men get cocaine: Sex-role stereotypes and acquisition patterns. *Journal of Psychoactive Drugs* 19(2): 135–142.

Murphy, S. 1987. Intravenous drug use and AIDS: Notes on the social economy of needle sharing. *Contemporary Drug Problems* 14: 373.

Murphy, S., C. Reinarman, and D. Waldorf. 1989. An 11-year follow-up of a network of cocaine users. *British Journal of Addiction* 84: 427–436.

Murphy, S., and M. Rosenbaum. 1988. Money for methadone II: Unintended consequences of limited-duration methadone maintenance. *Journal of Psychoactive Drugs* 20(4): 397–402.

Murphy, S., and M. Rosenbaum. 1992. Women who use cocaine too much: Smoking crack vs. snorting cocaine. *Journal of Psychoactive Drugs* 24(4): 381–388.

Murphy, S., and M. Rosenbaum. 1995. The rhetoric of reproduction: Pregnancy and drug use. *Contemporary Drug Problems* 22: 581.

Murphy, S., and M. Rosenbaum. 1999. *Pregnant women on drugs: Combating stereotypes and stigma.* New Brunswick, NJ: Rutgers University Press.

Murphy, S., S. D. Waldorf, and C. Reinarman. 1990. Drifting into dealing: Becoming a cocaine seller. *Qualitative Sociology* 13(4): 321–343.

Natarajan, M. 2006. Understanding the structure of a large heroin distribution network: A quantitative analysis of qualitative data. *Journal of Quantitative Criminology* 22(2): 171–192.

Natarajan, M., and M. Belanger. 1998. Varieties of upper-level drug dealing organizations: A typology of cases prosecuted in New York City. *Journal of Drug Issues* 28(4): 1005–1026.

National Institutes of Health (NIH). 1999. Interim-research involving individuals with questionable capacity to consent: Points to consider. Online document: http://www.nih .gov/grants/policy/questionablecapacity.htm. Accessed: August 18, 2008.

Needle, R. H., H. Cesari, and S. Koester. 1996. Multi-person use of drug injection equipment: HIV transmission risk associated with drug preparation and injection practices. Presented at the 10th International Conference on AIDS, Yokohama, Japan.

Needle, R. H., S. Coyle, H. Cesari, R. Trotter, M. Clatts, S. Koester, L. Price et al. 1998. HIV risk behaviors associated with the injection process: Multiperson use of drug injection equipment and paraphernalia in injection drug user networks. *Substance Use and Misuse* 33(12): 2403–2423.

Needle, R. H., S. Coyle, S. Genser, and R. Trotter. 1995. Social networks, drug abuse, and HIV transmission. NIDA Research Monograph 151. Rockville, MD: National Institute on Drug Abuse.

Needle, R. H., R. T. Trotter, M. Singer, C. Bates, J. B.Page, D. Metzger, and L. H. Marcelin. 2003. Rapid assessment of the HIV/AIDS crisis in racial and ethnic minority communities: An approach for timely community interventions. *American Journal of Public Health* 93(6): 970–979.

Nichter, M. 2003. Smoking: What does culture have to do with it? *Addiction* 98(suppl. 1): 139–145.

Nichter, M. 2006. Introducing tobacco cessation in developing countries: An overview of Project Quit Tobacco International. *Tobacco Control* 15(suppl. 1): i12–i17.

Nichter, M. 2008. *Global health: Why cultural perceptions, social representations, and biopolitics matter.* Tucson, AZ: University of Arizona Press.

Nichter, M., and E. Cartwright. 1991. Saving the children for the tobacco industry. *Medical Anthropology* 5: 236–256.

Nichter, M., and M. Nichter. 1994. Tobacco research in the US: A call for ethnography. Paper presented at the Annual Meeting of the American Anthropological Association, Atlanta, GA.

Nichter, M., M. Nichter, P. J. Thompson, S. Shiffman, and A. B. Moscicki. 2002. Using qualitative research to inform survey development on nicotine dependence among adolescents. *Drug and Alcohol Dependence* 68: S41–S56.

Nichter, M., M. Nichter, and D. V. Sickle. 2004. Popular perceptions of tobacco products and patterns of use among male college students in India. *Social Science and Medicine* 59(2): 415–431.

Nichter, M., and M. Nichter. 2006. Introducing tobacco cessation in developing countries: An overview of Project Quit Tobacco International. *Tobacco Control* 15(suppl. 1): i12–i17.

O'Day, P., and R. Venecia. 1999. Cazuelas: An ethnographic study of drug trafficking in a small Mexican border town. *Journal of Contemporary Criminal Justice* 15(4): 421–443.

Opler, M. E. 1938. *Dirty boy.* Menasha, WI: American Anthropological Association.

Ott, J. 1993. *Pharmacotheon: Ethnogenic drugs, their plant sources, and history.* Kennewick, WA: Natural Products Company.

Ouellet, L. J., W. W. Weibel, and A. D. Jimenez. 1995. Team research methods for studying intranasal heroin use and its HIV risks. In *Qualitative methods in drug abuse and HIV research,* ed. E. Lambert, R. S. Ashery, R. H. Needle. NIDA Research Monograph 157; NIH Pub. No. 95-4025. Washington, DC: U.S. Govt. Printing Office.

Pacheco de Oliveira, J. 1990. Frontier security and the new indigenism: Nature and origins of the Calha Norte project. In *The future of Amazonia: Destruction or sustainable development?* ed. D. Goodman and A. Hall. London: Macmillan.

Page, J. B. 1990. Streetside drug use among Cuban drug users in Miami, Florida. In *Drug use in Hispanic communities,* ed. R. Glick and J. Moore, 169–191. New Brunswick, NJ: Rutgers University Press.

Page, J. B. 1997. Vulcans and jutes: Cuban fraternities and their disappearance. *Free Inquiry in Creative Sociology* 25(1): 65–74.

Page, J. B. 1999. Historical overview of other abusable drugs. In *Prevention and societal impact of drug and alcohol abuse,* ed. R. T. Ammerman, P. J. Ott, and R. E. Tarter. Mahwah, NJ: Laurence Erlbaum.

Page, J. B. 2004. Drug use. In *Encyclopedia of medical anthropology,* ed. C. Ember and M. Ember, 372–384. New York: Kluwer Academic.

Page, J. B. 2009. Drug, substance, stupefacient, intoxicant, and the rest: How we talk about altered states and what that means for research. Paper presented at the annual meetings of the Society for Applied Anthropology, Santa Fe, NM, March 18–22.

Page, J. B., D. D. Chitwood, P. C. Smith, N. Kane, and D. C. McBride. 1990. Intravenous drug abuse and HIV infection in Miami. *Medical Anthropology Quarterly* 4(1): 56–71.

Page, J. B., and S. Evans. 2003. Cigars, cigarillos, and youth: Emergent patterns of subcultural complexes. *Journal of Ethnicity in Substance Abuse* 2(4): 63–76.

Page, J. B., S. Evans, A. Brittain, M. Pastore, K. Brelsford, R. Cardenal, M. R. Faraldo et al. 2001. *Tobacco use among youth in Florida: An ethnographic study.* Report Presented in Partial Completion of a Contract with the State of Florida, June 30.

Page, J. B., J. M. Fletcher, and W. R. True. 1988. Psychosociocultural perspectives in chronic Cannabis use: The Costa Rican follow-up. *Journal of Psychoactive Drugs* 20(1): 57–65.

Page, J. B., S. H. Lai, D. D. Chitwood, N. G. Klimas, P. C. Smith, and M. A. Fletcher. 1990. HTLV-I/II seropositivity and mortality among HIV-1 seropositive IV drug users. *Lancet* 335(8703): 1439–1441.

Page, J. B., S. Lai, M. A. Fletcher, R. Patarca, P. C. Smith, H. Lai, and N. G. Klimas. 1996. Predictors of survival in HIV-1 seropositive intravenous drug users. *Clinical and Diagnostic Laboratory Immunology* 3(1): 51–60.

Page, J. B., C. McKay, L. Rio, and J. Sweeney. 1983. *Ethnography of prescription drug use among women.* Report submitted to the National Institute on Drug Abuse in fulfillment of Grant No. 1-R01-DA-02675-01,02, 1983.

Page, J. B., and L. Rio. 1987. Use of psychotropic medication among elderly Hispanic women: Symptoms of poverty and social isolation. *Florida Journal of Anthropology* 10(1): 59–68.

Page, J. B., and J. Salazar. 1999. Use of needles and syringes in Miami and Valencia: Observations of high and low availability. *Medical Anthropology Quarterly* 4(4): 413–435.

Page, J. B., P. Shapshak, E. M. Duran, G. Even, I. Moleon-Borodowski, and R. Llanusa-Cestero. 2006. Detection of HIV-1 in injection paraphernalia: Risk in an era of heightened awareness. *AIDS Patient Care* 20(8): 576–585.

Page, J. B., and P. C. Smith. 1990. Venous envy: The importance of having usable veins. *Journal of Drug Issues* 20(2): 291–308.

Page, J. B., P. C. Smith, and N. Kane. 1990. Shooting galleries, their proprietors, and implications for prevention of AIDS. *Drugs and Society* 5(1–2): 69–85.

PakTribune. 2006. Heroin lab workers suffering from different diseases. *Pakistan News Service,* July 16.

Partridge, W. L. 1974. Exchange relationships in a community on the north coast of Colombia with special reference to Cannabis. Ph.D. dissertation. Ann Arbor, MI: University Microfilms.

Paulozzi, L. 2007. Unintentional poisoning deaths: United States 1999–2004. *Morbidity and Mortality Weekly Report* 56(05): 93–96.

Pepper, A., and L. Pepper. 1994. *Straight life*. New York: Da Capo Press.

Peyrot, M. 1985. Coerced volunteerism: The micropolitics of drug treatment. *Journal of Contemporary Ethnography* 13(4): 343–365.

Pine, A. 2008. *Working hard, drinking hard: On violence and survival in Honduras*. Berkeley, CA: University of California Press.

Preble, E., and J. J. Casey, Jr. 1969. Taking care of business: The heroin user's life on the street. *International Journal of the Addictions* 4(1): 1–24.

Quintero, G. 2002. Nostalgia and degeneration: The moral economy of drinking in Navajo society. *Medical Anthropology Quarterly* 16(1): 3–21.

Rapp, R. 2000. *Testing women, testing the fetus*. London: Routledge

Reichel-Dolmatoff, G. 1971. *Amazonian cosmos: The sexual and religious symbolism of the Tukano Indians*. Chicago: University of Chicago Press.

Reichel-Dolmatoff, G. 1990. The cultural context of an aboriginal hallucinogen: *Banisteriopsis caapi*. In *Flesh of the gods: The ritual use of hallucinogens*, ed. P. T. Furst, 84–113. Prospect Heights, IL: Waveland Press.

Rettig, R., M. Torres, and G. Garrett. 1977. *Manny: A criminal-addict's story*. Boston: Houghton Mifflin.

Rhodes, L. 2001. Toward an anthropology of prisons. *Annual Review of Anthropology* 30: 65–87.

Rhodes, N., D. Roskos-Ewoldsen, A. Edison, and M. Bradford. 2008. Attitude and norm accessibility affect processing of anti-smoking messages. *Health Psychology* 27(suppl. 3): S224–S232.

Rhodes, T., and D. Moore. 2001. On the qualitative in drugs research. *Addiction Research and Theory* 9(4): 279–297.

Ribaı, J., A. Rodríguez-Fornells, G. Urbano, A. Morte, R. Antonijoan, M. Montero, J. C. Callaway, and M. J. Barbanoj. 2001. Subjective effects and tolerability of the South American psychoactive beverage ayahuasca in healthy volunteers. *Psychopharmacology* 154(1): 85–95.

Ripoll, C. A., J. B. Page, and J. M. Salazar. 2003. Drug use in sex workers on the streets of Valencia. *Ethnicity in Drug Abuse* 1(4): 1–27.

Robb, J. 1986. Smoking as an anticipatory rite of passage: Some sociological hypotheses on health-related behaviour. *Social Science and Medicine* 23(6): 621–627.

Rodd, R. 2008. Reassessing the cultural and psychopharmacological significance of *Banisteriopsis caapi*: Preparation, classification, and use among the Piaroa of southern Venezuela. *Journal of Psychoactive Drugs* 40(3): 301–307.

Rodin, M. 1985. Getting on the program: A biocultural analysis of alcoholics anonymous. In *Alcohol: The American experience*, ed. L. Bennett and G. Ames, 41–60. New York: Plenum Press.

Romero-Daza, N. 2003. 'Nobody gives a damn if I live or die': Violence, drugs, and street-level prostitution in inner-city Hartford, Connecticut. *Medical Anthropology: Cross Cultural Studies in Health and Illness* 22(3): 233–259.

Romero-Daza, N. 2005. Conceptualizing the impact of indirect violence on HIV risk among women involved in street-level prostitution. *Aggression and Violent Behavior* 10(2): 153–170.

Romero-Daza, N., D. Himmelgreen, R. Pérez-Escamilla, S. Segura-Millán, and M. Singer. 1999. Food habits of drug-using Puerto Ricans in inner-city Hartford. *Medical Anthropology* 18(3): 281–298.

Romero-Daza, N., M. Weeks, and M. Singer. 1998. Much more than HIV! The reality of life on the streets for drug-using sex workers in inner city Hartford. *International Quarterly of Community Health Education* 18(1): 107–119.

Rosenbaum, M. 1981. *Women on heroin.* New Brunswick, NJ: Rutgers University Press.

Rosenbaum, M., J. Irwin, and S. Murphy. 1988. De facto destabilization as policy: The impact of short-term methadone maintenance. *Contemporary Drug Problems* 15: 491.

Rosenbaum, M., and S. Murphy. 1981. Getting the treatment: Recycling women addicts. *Journal of Psychoactive Drugs* 13(1): 1–13.

Rosenbaum, M, and S. Murphy. 1984. Always a junkie? The arduous task of getting off methadone maintenance. *Journal of Drug Issues* 14(3): 527–552.

Rosenbaum, M., and S. Murphy. 1987. Not the picture of health: Women on methadone. *Journal of Psychoactive Drugs* 19(2): 217–226.

Rosenbaum, M., and S. Murphy. 1998. *Women and addiction: Process, treatment, and outcome.* Rockville, MD: NIDA Research Monograph Series.

Rosenbaum, M., S. Murphy, and J. Beck. 1987. Money for methadone: Preliminary findings from a study of Alameda County's new maintenance policy. *Journal of Psychoactive Drugs* 19(1): 13–19.

Rothenberg, R. B., C. Sterk, K. E. Toomey, J. J. Potterat, D. Johnson, M. Schrader, and S. Hatch. 1998. Using social network and ethnographic tools to evaluate syphilis transmission. *Sexually Transmitted Diseases* 25(3): 154–160.

Rothenberg, R., D. Woodhouse, J. Potterat, S. Muth, W. Darrow, and A. Klovdahl. 1995. Social networks in disease transmission: The Colorado Springs study. In *Social networks, drug abuse and HIV transmission,* ed. R. Needle, S. Coyle, S. Genser, and R. Trotter II, 3–19. Rockville, MD: National Institute on Drug Abuse.

Rubin, V., and L. Comitas. 1975. *Ganja in Jamaica.* The Hague, Netherlands: Mouton.

Saggers, S., and D. Gray. 1998. *Dealing with alcohol: Indigenous usage in Australia, New Zealand, and Canada.* Cambridge, U.K.: Cambridge University Press

Sahagún, B. de.1956. *Historia general de las cosas de Nueva España,* Vol. 3, 292. Mexico City, Mexico: Editorial Porrua.

Sales, P., and S. Murphy. 2000. Surviving violence: Pregnancy and drug use. *Journal of Drug Issues* 30(4): 695–724.

Sales, P., and S. Murphy. 2007. San Francisco's freelancing ecstasy dealers: Towards a sociological understanding of drug markets. *Journal of Drug Issues* 37(4): 919–950.

Salganik, M., and D. Heckathorn. 2004. Sampling and estimation in hidden populations using respondent-driven sampling. *Sociological Methodology* 34: 193–239.

Salmon, E. 2008. Narco-trafficking in the Sierra Tarahumara. *Cultural Survival.* Online at: http://www.culturalsurvival.org/ourpublications/voices/article/narco-trafficking-sierra-tarahumara. Accessed December 6, 2008.

Santelices, C., M. Singer, and A. M. Nicolaysen. 2003. Risky and precarious dependencies of Puerto Rican IDUs in El Barrio: An ethnographic glimpse. *Practicing Anthropology* 25(3): 23–27.

Santos, R.G., J. Landeira-Fernandez, R. J. Strassman, V. Motta, and A.P.M. Cruz. 2007. Effects of ayahuasca on psychometric measures of anxiety, panic-like, and hopelessness in Santo Daime members. *Journal of Ethnopharmacology* 112(3): 507–513.

Schensul, J. J., and G. J. Burkholder. 2005. Vulnerability, social networks, sites, and selling as predictors of drug use among urban African American and Puerto Rican emerging adults. *Journal of Drug Issues* 35(2): 379–407.

Schensul, J. J., S. Diamond, W. Disch, R. Bermudez, and J. Eiserman. 2005. The diffusion of Ecstasy through urban youth networks. *Ethnicity in Substance Abuse* 4(2): 39–72.

Schensul, J., M. LeCompte, R. Trotter, and M. Singer. 1999. *Mapping social networks, spatial data and hidden populations. Book 4,* the ethnographer's toolkit. Walnut Creek, CA: Altamira Press.

Schultes, R. E. 1938. The appeal of peyote (*Lophophora williamsii*) as a medicine. *American Anthropologist* 40(4): 698–715.

Schultes, R. E. 1976. *Hallucinogenic plants.* New York: Golden Press.

Schultes, R. E. 1977. The botanical and chemical distribution of hallucinogens. In *Drugs, rituals, and altered states of consciousness,* ed. M. M. Du Toit, 25–55. Rotterdam, Netherlands: A. A. Balkema.

Schultes, R. E. 1993. Amazonian ethnobotany and the search for new drugs. *Ciba Foundation Symposium: Ethnobotany and the Search for New Drugs* 185: 106–112.

Schultes, R. E., and A. Hoffman. 1991. *The botany and chemistry of hallucinogens.* Springfield, IL: Charles C. Thomas.

Schultes, R. E., and S. Von Reis. 1995. *Ethnobotany: Evolution of a discipline.* Portland, OR: Dioscorides Press.

Schuster, C. R. 1992. Drug abuse research and HIV/AIDS: A national perspective from the U.S. *British Journal of Addiction* 87: 355–361.

Scrimshaw, S., and E. Hurtado. 1987. *Rapid assessment procedures for nutrition and primary health care: Anthropological approaches to improving programme effectiveness.* Los Angeles: UCLA Latin American Center for Publications.

Sexton, R. L., R. G. Carlson, C. G. Leukefeld, and B. M. Booth. 2008. Trajectories of methamphetamine use in the rural South: A longitudinal qualitative study. *Human Organization* 67(2): 181–193.

Shafer, R. P., D. Farnsworth, H. Brill, T. L. Carter, J. G. Cooney, C. O. Galvin, J. A. Howard, et al. 1972. *Marihuana: A signal of misunderstanding. The official report of the National Commission on Marihuana and Drug Abuse.* New York: New American Library.

Shah, S. M., P. Shapshak, J. E. Rivers, R. V. Stewart, N. L. Weatherby, K. Q. Xin, J. B. Page et al. 1996. Detection of HIV-1 DNA in needle/syringes, paraphernalia, and washes from shooting galleries in Miami: A preliminary laboratory report. *JAIDS* 11: 301–306.

Shannon, K., M. Rusch, J. Shoveller, D. Alexson, K. Gibson, and M. W.Tyndall. 2008. Mapping violence and policing as an environmental-structural barrier to health service and syringe availability among substance-using women in street-level sex work. *International Journal of Drug Policy* (2): 140–147.

Shapshak, P., R. K. Fujimura, J. B. Page, D. Segal, J. E. Rivers, J. Yang, S. Shah et al. 2000. HIV-1 RNA load in needles/syringes from shooting galleries in Miami: Preliminary laboratory report. *Drug and Alcohol Dependence* 58: 153–157.

Shapshak, P., C. B. McCoy, S. M. Shah, J. B. Page, J. E. Rivers, N. L. Weatherby, D. D. Chitwood, and D. C. Mash. 1994. Preliminary laboratory studies of inactivation of HIV-1 in needles and syringes containing infected blood using undiluted household bleach. *Journal of AIDS* 7: 754–759.

Shedlin, M. G. 1990. An ethnographic approach to understanding HIV high-risk behaviors: Prostitution and drug abuse. NIDA Research Monograph Series 93: 134–149.

Shor-Posner, G., A. Campa, G. Zhang, N. Persaud, M. J. Miguez-Burbano, J. Quesada, M. A. Fletcher, J. B. Page, and M. K. Baum. 2000. When obesity is desirable: A longitudinal study of the Miami HIV-1-infected drug abusers (MIDAS) cohort. *Journal of AIDS* 23: 81–88.

Siegal, H. A., R. S. Falck, J. Wang, and R. G. Carlson. 2000. Crack-cocaine users as victims of physical attack. *Journal of the National Medical Association* 92(2): 76–82.

Simmons, J., and K. Koester. 2003. Hidden injuries of research on social suffering among drug users. *Practicing Anthropology* 25: 53–57.

Simmons, J., and M. Singer. 2006. I love you . . . and heroin: Care and collusion among drug-using couples. *Substance Abuse Treatment, Prevention, and Policy* 1(1): 7.

Singer, M. 1986. Toward a political economy of alcoholism: The missing link in the anthropology of drinking behavior. *Social Science and Medicine* 23(2): 113–130.

Singer, M. 1992. Matching programs to populations in substance abuse treatment. *Addictions Nursing Network* 4(2): 33–43.

Singer, M. 1993. Knowledge for use: Anthropology and community-centered substance abuse research. *Social Science and Medicine* 37(1): 15–26.

Singer, M. 1996a. The evolution of AIDS work in a Puerto Rican community organization. *Human Organization* 55(1): 67–75.

Singer, M. 1996b. A dose of drugs, a touch of violence, a case of AIDS: Conceptualizing the SAVA syndemic. *Free Inquiry in Creative Sociology* 24(2): 99–110.

Singer, M. 1999. The ethnography of street drug use before AIDS: A historic review. In *Cultural, observational, and epidemiological approaches in the prevention of drug abuse and HIV/AIDS,* ed. P. Marshall, M. Singer, and M. Clatts, 228–264. Bethesda, MD: National Institute on Drug Abuse.

Singer, M. 2000. Updates on projects recovery and CONNECT. In *Careers in anthropology: Profiles of practitioner anthropologists,* ed. P. Sabloff , 64–66. NAPA Bulletin #20. Washington, DC: National Association for the Practice of Anthropology and American Anthropological Association.

Singer, M. 2001. Toward a bio-cultural and political economic integration of alcohol, tobacco, and drug studies. *Social Science and Medicine* 53(2): 199–213.

Singer, M. 2004. Why is it easier to get drugs than drug treatment? In *Unhealthy health policy: A critical anthropological examination,* ed. A. Castro and M. Singer, 287–303. Walnut Creek, CA: Altamira Press.

Singer, M. 2006a. *The face of social suffering: Life history of a street drug addict.* Prospect Heights, IL: Waveland Press.

Singer, M. 2006b. *Something dangerous: Emergent and changing illicit drug use and community health.* Prospect Heights, IL: Waveland Press.

Singer, M. 2006c. What is the 'drug user community'? Implications for public health. *Human Organization* 65(1): 71–79.

Singer, M. 2007. *Drugging the poor: Legal and illegal drug industries and the structuring of social inequality.* Prospect Heights, IL: Waveland Press.

Singer, M. 2008. *Drugs and development: Global impact on sustainable growth and human rights.* Prospect Heights, IL: Waveland Press.

Singer, M. 2009. *Introduction to syndemics: A systems approach to public health and community health.* San Francisco, CA: Jossey-Bass.

Singer, M., and B. Borrero. 1984. Indigenous treatment for alcoholism: The case for Puerto Rican spiritism. *Medical Anthropology* 8(4): 246–272.

Singer, M., S. Clair, J. Schensul, C. Huebner, J. Eiserman, R. Pino, and J. Garcia. 2005. Dust in the wind: The growing use of embalming fluid among youth in Hartford, CT. *Substance Use and Misuse* 40: 1035–1050.

Singer, M., and J. Eiserman. 2007. Twilight's last gleaning: Rapid assessment of late night HIV risk in Hartford, CT. In *Communities assessing their AIDS epidemics: Results of the Rapid Assessment of HIV/AIDS in eleven U.S. cities,* ed. B. Bowser, E. Quimby, and M. Singer, 193–208. Lanham, MD: Lexington Books.

Singer, M., P. Erickson, L. Badiane, D. D. Ortiz, T. Abraham, and A. M. Nicolaysen. 2006. Syndemics, sex, and the city: Understanding sexually transmitted disease in social and cultural context. *Social Science and Medicine* 63(8): 2010–2021.

Singer, M., C. B. Fisher, D. Hodge, H. Saleheen, and M. Mahadevan. 2008. Ethical issues in conducting research with Latino drug users. In *Handbook of US Latino psychology: Developmental and community based perspectives,* ed. F. A. Villarruel, G. Carlo, J. M. Grau, M. Azmita, N. Cabrera, and T. and J. Chahn. Thousand Oaks, CA: Sage Publications (in press).

Singer, M., C. Flores, L. Davison, G. Burke, and Z. Castillo. 1991. Puerto Rican community mobilizing in response to the AIDS crisis. *Human Organization* 50(1): 73–81.

Singer, M., E. Huertas, and G. Scott. 2000. Am I my brother's keeper?: A case study of the responsibilities of research. *Human Organization* 59(4): 389–400.

Singer, M., R. Irizarry, and J. J. Schensul. 1991. Needle access as an AIDS prevention strategy for IV drug users: A research perspective. *Human Organization* 50: 142–153.

Singer, M., Z. Jia, J. J. Schensul, M. Weeks, and J. B. Page. 1992. AIDS and the IV drug user: The local context in prevention efforts. *Medical Anthropology* 14: 285–306.

Singer, M., J. A. Juvalis, and M. Weeks. 2000. High on illy: Studying an emergent drug problem in Hartford, CT. *Medical Anthropology* 18: 365–388.

Singer, M., P. Marshall, R. Trotter, J. J. Schensul, M. Weeks, M., J. Simmons, and K. Radda. 1999. Ethics, ethnography, drug use, and AIDS: Dilemmas and standards in federally funded research. In *Cultural, observational, and epidemiological approaches in the prevention of drug abuse and HIV/AIDS,* ed. P. Marshall, M. Singer, and M. Clatts, 198–222. Bethesda, MD: National Institute on Drug Abuse.

Singer, M., and G. Mirhej. 2004. The understudied supply side: Public policy implications of the illicit drug trade in Hartford, CT. *Harvard Health Policy Review* 5(2): 36–47.

Singer, M., G. Mirhej, D. Hodge, H. Salaheen, C. Fisher, and M. Mahadevan. 2008. Ethical issues in research with Hispanic drug users: Participant perspectives on risks and benefits. *Journal of Drug Issues* (in press).

Singer, M., G. Mirhej, J. B. Page, E. Hastings, H. Salaheen, and G. Prado. 2007. Black 'N Mild and carcinogenic: Cigar smoking among inner city young adults in Harford, CT. *Journal of Ethnicity and Substance Abuse* 6(3): 81–94.

Singer, M., G. Mirhej, S. Shaw, C. Huebner, J. Eiserman, R. Pino, and J. Garcia. 2005. When the drug of choice is a drug of confusion: Embalming fluid use in inner city Hartford, CT. *Journal of Ethnicity and Substance Abuse* 4(2): 71–96.

Singer, M., N. Romero-Daza, M. Weeks, and P. Pelia. 1995. Ethnography and the evaluation of needle exchange in the prevention of HIV transmission. In *Qualitative methods in drug abuse and HIV research,* ed. E. Lambert, R. Ashery and R. Needle, 231–257. National Institute on Drug Abuse Research Monographs No. 157. Washington, DC: National Institute on Drug Abuse.

Singer, M., H. Saleheen, G. Mirhej, and C. Santelices. 2006. Research findings on drinking among street drug users. *American Anthropologist* 108(3): 502–506.

Singer, M., G. Scott, S. Wilson, D. Easton, and M. Weeks. 2001. War stories: AIDS prevention and the street narratives of drug users. *Qualitative Health Research* 11(5): 589–611.

Singer, M., C. Santelices, G. D. Hodge, Z. Medina, and M. Solomon. 2010 (in press). Assessing and responding to a community health risk: Second-hand smoking in Puerto Rican households. *Practicing Anthropology.*

Singer, M., J. Simmons, M. Duke, and L. Broomhall. 2001. The challenges of street research on drug use, violence, and AIDS risk. *Addiction Research and Theory* 9(4): 365–402.

Singer, M., and C. Snipes. 1992. Generations of suffering: Experiences of a pregnancy and substance abuse treatment program. *Journal of Health Care for the Poor and Underserved* 3(1): 325–339.

Singer, M., T. Stopka, S. Shaw, C. Santelices, D. Buchanan, W. Teng, K. Khooshnood, and R. Heimer. 2005. Lessons from the field: From research to application in the fight against AIDS among injection drug users in three New England cities. *Human Organization* 64(2): 179–191.

Singer, M., T. Stopka, C. Siano, K. Springer, G. Barton, K. Khoshnood, A. G. de Puga, and R. Heimer. 2000. The social geography of AIDS and hepatitis risk: Qualitative approaches for assessing local differences in sterile-syringe access among injection drug users. *American Journal of Public Health* 90(7): 1049–1056.

Singer, M., F. Valentín, H. Baer, and Z. Jia. 1992. Why does Juan Garcia have a drinking problem?: The perspective of critical medical anthropology. *Medical Anthropology* 14(1): 77–108.

Singer, M., and M. Weeks. 2005. The Hartford model of AIDS practice/research. In *Community interventions and AIDS,* ed. E. Trickett and W. Pequegnat, 153–175. Oxford, U.K.: Oxford University Press.

Skeer, M., M. L. Land, D. Cheng, and M. Siegel. 2004. Smoking in Boston bars before and after a 100% smoke-free regulation: An assessment of early compliance. *Journal of Public Health Management and Practice* 10(6): 501–507.

Skoll, G. 1992. *Walk the walk and talk the talk: An ethnography of a drug abuse treatment facility.* Philadelphia: Temple University Press.

Smith, C. 2008. An ethnographic study of female injecting drug users in rural North Wales. Paper presented at the annual meeting of the American Society of Criminology, Atlanta, GA.

Smith, D. E., ed. 1970. *The new social drug: Cultural, medical, and legal perspectives on marihuana.* Englewood Cliffs, NJ: Prentice-Hall.

Snead, J., M. Downing, J. Lorvick, B. Garcia, R. Thawley, S. Kegeles, and B. R. Edlin. 2003. Secondary syringe exchange among injection drug users. *Journal of Urban Health-Bulletin of the New York Academy of Medicine* 80(2): 330–348.

Spicer, P. 1997. Toward a (dys)functional anthropology of drinking: Ambivalence and the American Indian experience with alcohol. *Medical Anthropology Quarterly* 11(2): 306–323.

Spradley, J. 1970. *You owe yourself a drunk: An ethnography of urban nomads.* Prospect Heights, IL: Waveland Press.

Spradley J., and B. Mann. 2008 [1975]. *The cocktail waitress: Woman's work in a man's world.* Long Grove, IL: Waveland Press.

Springer, K. W., C. E. Sterk, T. S. Jones, and L. Friedman. 1999. Syringe disposal options for injection drug users: A community-based perspective. *Substance Use and Misuse* 34(13): 1917–1934.

Stahler, G. 2003. Using ethnographic methodology in substance abuse treatment outcome research. *Journal of Substance Abuse Treatment* 18(1): 1–8.

Stahler, G. J., and E. Cohen. 2000. Using ethnographic methodology in substance abuse treatment outcome research. *Journal of Substance Abuse Treatment* 18(1): 1–8.

Stebbins, K. 1990. Transnational tobacco companies and health in underdeveloped countries: Recommendations for advancing a smoking epidemic. *Social Science and Medicine* 30: 227–235.

Stebbins, K. 2001. Going like gangbusters: Transnational tobacco companies 'making a killing' in South America. *Medical Anthropology Quarterly* 15: 147–170.

Stefanis, C., R. L. Dornbush, and M. Fink. 1977. *Hashish: A study of long-term use.* New York: Raven Press.

Stephens, R. 1991. *The street addict role: A theory of heroin addiction.* Albany, NY: State University of New York Press.

Stephens, R. C., D. D. Simpson, S. L. Coyle, and C. B. McCoy. 1993. Comparative effectiveness of NADR interventions. In *Handbook on AIDS, IV drug users, and sexual behavior in the*

United States: Trends, issues, and intervention strategies, ed. B. S. Brown and G. M. Beschner. Westport, CT: Greenwood Publishing.

Sterk, C. 1988. Cocaine and HIV seropositivity. *Lancet* I(8593): 1052–1053.

Sterk, C. 1995. Determining drug use patterns among women: The value of qualitative research methods. In *Qualitative methods in drug abuse and HIV research,* ed. E. Lambert, R. S. Ashery, R.H. Needle. NIDA Research Monograph 157; NIH Pub. No. 95–4025. Washington, DC: U.S. Govt. Printing Office.

Sterk, C. 1998. Women and AIDS: A brief update. *International Journal of STD and AIDS* 9(suppl. 1): 16–18.

Sterk, C. 1999. *Fast lives: Women who use crack cocaine.* Philadelphia: Temple University Press.

Sterk, C. E. 2002. The health intervention project: HIV risk reduction among African American women drug users. *Public Health Reports* 117 (suppl. 1): S88–S95.

Sterk, C. E. 2003. Drug research: Ethnographies or qualitative works. *International Journal of Drug Policy* 14(1): 127–130.

Sterk, C. E., K. Dolan, and S. Hatch. 1999. Epidemiological indicators and ethnographic realities of female cocaine use. *Substance Use and Misuse* 34(14): 2057–2072.

Sterk, C., and K. Elifson. 2000. Fluctuating drug markets and HIV risk taking: Female drug users and their relationship with drug markets. *Medical Anthropology: Cross Cultural Studies in Health and Illness* 18(4): 439–455.

Sterk, C., and K. Elifson. 2005. Qualitative methods in the drug abuse field. In *Epidemiology of drug abuse,* ed. Z. Sloboda, 133–144. New York: Springer.

Sterk, C. E., K. W. Elifson, and D. German. 2000. Female crack users and their sexual relationships: The role of sex-for-crack exchanges. *Journal of Sex Research* 37(4): 354–360.

Sterk, C. E., K. W. Elifson, and K. P. Theall. 2007. Individual action and community context: The Health Intervention Project. *American Journal of Preventive Medicine* 32(suppl. 6): S177-S181.

Sterk, C. E., K. P. Theall, and K. W. Elifson. 2006. Young adult Ecstasy use patterns: Quantities and combinations. *Journal of Drug Issues* 36(1): 201–228.

Sterk, C. E., K. P. Theall, and K. W. Elifson. 2003. Effectiveness of a risk reduction intervention among African American women who use crack cocaine. *AIDS Education and Prevention* 15(1): 15–32.

Sterk, C. E., K. P. Theall, K. W. Elifson, and D. Kidder. 2003. HIV risk reduction among African-American women who inject drugs: A randomized controlled trial. *AIDS and Behavior* 7(1): 73–86.

Sterk, C. E., K. P. Theall, and K. W. Elifson. 2007. Getting into Ecstasy: Comparing moderate and heavy young adult users. *Journal of Psychoactive Drugs* 39(2): 103–113.

Stewart, O. 1987. *Peyote religion: A history.* Norman, OK: University of Oklahoma Press.

Stoller, P. 1997. Globalizing method: The problems of doing ethnography in transnational spaces. *Anthropology and Humanism* 22(1): 81–94.

Stopka, T., M. Singer, C. Santelices, and J. Eiserman. 2003. Public health interventionists, penny capitalists, or sources of risk? Assessing street syringe sellers in Hartford, Connecticut. *Substance Use and Misuse* 38(9): 1339–1370.

Stopka, T., M. Singer, W. Teng, J. Horton, and W. Compton. 2005. Pharmacy access to over-the-counter (OTC) syringes in Connecticut: Implications for HIV and hepatitis prevention among injection drug users. *AIDS and Public Policy Journal* 17(4): 115–126.

Sullivan, K. 2008. How a tiny West African nation became a key smuggling hub for Colombian cocaine, and the price it is paying. *Washington Post,* May 25, A01.

Sutter, A. 1966. The world of the righteous dope fiend. *Issues in Criminology* 2: 177–222.

Taylor, A. 1993. *Women drug users: An ethnography of a female injecting community.* London: Oxford University Press.

Taylor, A., M. Frischer, N. McKeganey, D. Goldberg, S. Green, and S. Platt. 1993. HIV risk behaviours among female prostitute drug injectors in Glasgow. *Addiction* 88(11): 1561–1564.

Taylor, A., M. Frischer, S. T. Green, D. Goldberg, N. McKeganey, and L. Gruer. 1994. Low and stable prevalence of HIV among drug injectors in Glasgow. *International Journal of STD and AIDS* 5(2): 105–107.

Taylor, A., D. Goldberg, S. Hutchinson, S. Cameron, S. M. Gore, J. McMenamin, S. Green, A. Pithie, and R. Fox. 2000. Prevalence of hepatitis C virus infection among injecting drug users in Glasgow 1990–1996: Are current harm reduction strategies working? *Journal of Infection* 40(2): 176–183.

Taylor, A., D. Goldberg, S. Hutchinson, S. Cameron, and R. Fox. 2001. High-risk injecting behaviour among injectors from Glasgow: Cross sectional community-wide surveys 1990–1999. *Journal of Epidemiology and Community Health* 55(10): 766–767.

Tessler, L. 2000. Locations of self in smoking discourses and practices: An ethnography of smoking among adolescents and young adults in the United States. Master's thesis, University of Arizona, Tucson.

Thomas, P. 1967. *Down these mean streets.* New York: Knopf.

Trotter, R. T. 1995. Drug use, AIDS, and ethnography: Advanced ethnographic research methods exploring the HIV epidemic. In *Qualitative methods in drug abuse and HIV research,* ed. E. Lambert, R. S. Ashery, R. H. Needle. NIDA Research Monograph 157; NIH Pub. No. 95–4025. Washington, DC: U.S. Govt. Printing Office.

Trotter, R. T., A. M. Bowen, and J. M. Potter. 1995. Network models for HIV outreach and prevention programs for drug users. In *Social networks, drug abuse, and HIV transmission,* ed. R. H. Needle, S. L. Coyle, S. G. Genser, and R. T. Trotter II, 144–180. NIDA Research Monograph 151. NIH Pub. No. 95–3889. Washington, DC: U.S. Govt. Printing Office.

Trotter, R., and S. Singer. 2005. Rapid assessment strategies for public health: Promise and problems. In *Community interventions and AIDS,* ed. E. Trickett and W. Pequegnat, 130–152. Oxford, U.K.: Oxford University Press.

Trotter, R., and S. Singer. 2007. Rapid assessment: A method in community-based research. In *Communities assessing their AIDS epidemics: Results of the Rapid Assessment of HIV/AIDS in eleven U.S. cities,* ed. B. Bowser, E. Quimby, and M. Singer, 9–28. Lanham, MD: Lexington Books.

True, W. R., M. A. Hovey, J. B. Page, and P. L. Doughty. 1980. Marihuana and user lifestyles. In *Cannabis in Costa Rica,* ed. W. Carter, W. Coggins, and P. Doughty, 98–115. Philadelphia: ISHI Press.

Tylor, E. B. 1924 [orig. 1871] *Primitive culture.* 2 vols. 7th ed. New York: Brentano's.

UCSF News Office. 2001. Press release: Heroin users released from methadone detox or jail may be at higher risk for overdose according to UCSF researchers. Online at: http://pub.ucsf.edu/newsservices/releases/2003123084. Accessed December 12, 2008.

Valdez, A., C. D. Kaplan, and A. Cepeda. 2000. The process of paradoxical autonomy and survival in the heroin careers of Mexican American women. *Contemporary Drug Problems* 27: 189.

Varga, L., D. D. Chitwood, and I. M. Fernandez. 2006. Factors associated with skin cleaning prior to injection among drug users. Paper presented at the Annual Meeting of the American Sociological Association, Montreal Convention Center, Montreal, Quebec, Canada.

Virtanen, P. K. 2006. The urban machinery: Youth and social capital in western Amazonian contemporary rituals. *Anthropos* 101(1): 159–167.

Wacquant, L. 2002. The curious eclipse of prison ethnography in the age of mass incarceration. *Ethnography* 3(4): 371–397.

Waldorf, D. 1973. *Careers in dope*. Englewood Cliffs, NJ: Prentice-Hall.

Waldorf, D., and P. Biernacki. 1981. The natural recovery from opiate addiction—some preliminary findings. *Journal of Drug Issues* 11(1): 61–74.

Waldorf, D., and S. Murphy. 1995. Perceived risks and criminal justice pressures on middle class cocaine sellers. *Journal of Drug Issues* 25(1): 11–32.

Waldorf, D., S. Murphy, D. Lauderback, C. Reinarman, and T. Marotta. 1990. Needle sharing among male prostitutes: Preliminary findings of the Prospero project. *Journal of Drug Issues* 20(2): 309–335.

Waldorf, D., S. Murphy, C. Reinarman, and B. Joyce. 1977. *Doing coke: An ethnography of cocaine users and sellers*. Washington, D.C.: Drug Abuse Council.

Waldorf, D., C. Reinarman, and S. Murphy. 1989. Needle sharing, shooting galleries, and AIDS risks among intravenous drug users in San Francisco: Criminal justice and public health policy. *Criminal Justice Policy Review* 3(4): 391–406.

Waldorf, D., C. Reinarman, and S. Murphy. 1991. *Cocaine changes: The experience of using and quitting*. Philadelphia: Temple University Press.

Waters, W. 2001. Globalization, socioeconomic restructuring, and community health. *Journal of Community Health* 26(2): 79–92.

Waterston, A. 1993. *Street addicts in the political economy*. Philadelphia: Temple University Press.

Watts, M. 1992. Space for everything (a commentary). *Cultural Anthropology* 7(1): 115–129.

Weeks, M., M. Singer, M. Grier, J. Hunte-Marrow, and C. Haughton. 1993. AIDS prevention and the African American injection drug user. *Transforming Anthropology* 4(1–2): 39–51.

Weeks, M., D. Himmelgreen, M. Singer, S. Woolley, N. Romero-Daza, and M. Grier. 1996. Community-based AIDS prevention: Preliminary outcomes of a program for African American and Latino injection drug users. *Journal of Drug Issues* 26(3): 561–590.

Weeks, M., M. Grier, N. Romero-Daza, M. Puglisi, and M. Singer. 1998. Streets, drugs, and the economy of sex in the age of AIDS. *Women and Health* 27(1/2): 205–228.

Weeks, M., D. Himmelgreen, M. Singer, P. Richmond, and N. Romero-Daza. 1998. Drug use patterns of substance abusing women: Implications for treatment providers. *Drugs and Society* 13(1/2): 35–61.

Weeks, M., S. Clair, M. Singer, K. Radda, J. Schensul, S. Wilson, M. Martinez, G. Scott, and G. Knight. 2001. High-risk drug-use sites, meaning, and practice. *Journal of Drug Issues* 31(1): 781–808.

Weeks, M., S. Clair, S. Borgatti, K. Radda, and J. Schensul. 2002. Social networks of drug users in high-risk sites: Finding the connections. *AIDS and Behavior* 6(2): 193–206.

Weidman, H. H. 1978. *The health ecology project*. Report submitted in partial fulfillment of a grant from the Commonwealth Fund (1971–1976).

Weiner, A. 1988. *The Trobrianders of Papua New Guinea*. New York: Holt, Rinehart and Winston.

Wejnert, C. 2009. An empirical test of respondent-driven sampling: Point estimates, variance, degree measures, and out-of-equilibrium data. *Sociological Methodology* 39(1): 73–116.

Weller, S., and A. K. Romney. 1988. *Systematic data collection*. Newbury Park, CA: Sage.

Whitten, N. E. 1985. *Sicuanga Runa: The other side of development in Amazonian Ecuador*. Urbana, IL and Chicago: University of Illinois Press.

Wilbert, J. 1990. Tobacco and shamanistic ecstasy among the Warao Indians of Venezuela. In *Flesh of the gods: The ritual use of hallucinogens*, ed. P. T. Furst, 5–83. Prospect Heights, IL: Waveland Press.

Winkelman, M. 2003. Drug tourism or spiritual healing? Ayahuasca seekers in Amazonia. *Journal of Psychoactive Drugs* 37(2): 209–218.

World Health Organization. 2000. *The global tobacco crisis: Tobacco—global agent of death.* Geneva, Switzerland: WHO.

World Health Organization. 2008. *Report on the global tobacco epidemic.* Geneva, Switzerland: WHO.

Worthington, C., and T. Myers. 2002. Desired elements of HIV testing services: Test recipient perspectives. *AIDS Patient Care and STDs* 16: 537–548.

INDEX

addict role, 50–52; lifestyle variants, 64
addiction, 3, 9, 10, 18, 37–39, 43, 44, 48
Adler, Patricia, 9, 16, 141, 158
Afghanistan, 92
African Americans, 8, 37–38, 45
Agar, Michael, 15, 22, 55–57, 133–134
AIDS, 4, 26, 36, 70–82; co-infection with
    HTLV-II, 81–82, 166, 167; epidemic in
    Puerto Rico, 79–80; natural history of
    progression in IDUs, 166–167; networks
    among IDUs and HIV risk, 80–81
alcohol, 13–14; drinking and solidarity, 17, 18;
    drinking places, drinking spaces, 13, 16–17,
    18, 20
Alcohol and Drug Study Group, 152
Alcohol, Tobacco and Other Drug Study
    Group, 152
altered states of consciousness, 28, 176–177
Ames, Genevieve, 152
anthropology: impacts of drug ethnography
    on, 3; view of drug use, 162
applied anthropology, 36
Arias, Enrique Desmond, 87

Becker, Howard, 53
Bennett, Linda, 152
Black, Peter, 11
Boeri, Myriam, 9
Bourgois, Philippe, 16, 19, 20, 84, 141
Bourguignon, Erika, 28
Brown, Claude, 46
Bukowsky, William, 169
Burton, Sir Richard, 31–32

Camba, 6, 14, 57
career: burnout, 144; choosing, 141;
    pathways, 67–68, 133; rewards of, 134.
    See also employment of ethnographers;
    survey on careers in drug ethnography
Carroll, Eleanor, 59–61
Cepeda, Alice, 160
Chicago School, 36–37
Ciccarone, Daniel, 167
Clatts, Michael, 167
Cleckner (Morningstar), Patricia, 150, 151
cognitive methods, 117–119; analytic
    technique, 118; free listing, 118; typology,
    117; uses for prevention, 119

Comitas, Lambros, 60–61
Community Epidemiology Work Group
    (CEWG), 170
community intervention, 155
community studies, 179–181
Complementary and Alternative Medicine
    (CAM), 176–177; biomedical assessment
    of, 177
Confidentiality, Certificate of, 131–132
context, 4, 5, 6, 7, 8, 9, 18, 20, 26, 29, 32, 33,
    34
Costa Rica, 2, 60–61, 135, 166, 171
couple dynamics, 158
criminal justice/legal issues, 3, 5, 35,
    106–107; drug overdose, 108; injection
    risks, 107–108; paraphernalia laws and
    arrest, 107; risk in prison, 108–109
culture, defined, 5–7
Curtis, Rick, 158

Dai, Bingham, 34–36
deviance theory of drug abuse, 38–39
deviance model, 34, 38–39
de Quincey, Thomas, 32–33
Dobkin de Rios, Marlene, 58, 150
Downing, Moher, 176
Dreher, Melanie, 150, 175
drugs: defined, 5; demand for, 91; coca, 30;
    cocaine, 10, 18, 63, 83; crack cocaine,
    83–84, 165; Ecstasy, 170; hallucinogens,
    40–41; heroin, 10, 18, 44, 45, 47, 62; history
    of, 83; "illies," 170; jimson weed, 30–31;
    legal, 100; marihuana, 1–2, 28, 31–32, 47;
    methaqualone, 170; mixing, 14;
    mushrooms, 30; opioids, 28; opium, 28,
    32, 33; peyote, 25, 35, 40, 42; peyote, in
    Native American Church, 35–36;
    phencyclidine (PCP), 65–67; snuff,
    hallucinogenic, 29; speedballs, 14, 18;
    tranquilizers, minor, 157; Ultram, 179;
    "wets," 170. See also alcohol; tobacco
Dunlap, Eloise, 156, 160

economy, global, 86
economy, street, 64–65; ancillary influence
    on local drug sellers, 97; ethnic
    differentiation of customers, 98; typology
    of local market strategies, 95–97

emic perspective, 5, 25, 33, 36, 43
employment of ethnographers, 84–85, 135–137. *See also* career
Engels, Frederick, 33–34
ethical challenges (field work), 3, 126–132; in study of minors, 171
ethnicity and drug research, 8–9
ethnographer role, 15, 19, 20, 104–105; activist, 175–176; marginality of drug ethnographers, 133–134; and risk, 99; safe practices, 99; and violence experienced, 99; and violence witnessed, 99
ethnography: advantages of, 23–27, 66, 67; blunders in, 19–20; bureaucratic advocacy for, 69; career trajectories in, 134 (*see also* career); checklists, 185; defined, 4–5, 27, 29; DHHS regulations for, 128; discovery in, 14; effects of globalization on, 103; ethics and, 3, 126–132, 171; ethnocentrism of biomedical protections, 131; future of, 178; global dimensions of, 90; importance of history in, 26; importance in study of AIDS, 70–71, 77; longitudinal, 82; multisited, 64, 80, 124–126; new methods in, 114; participant observation, 2, 3, 22, 23–24, 185; participant observation, of drug treatment, 109–110; in prisons, 109; protection of raw data, 132; protection of study participants, 129–130; and public health, 3–4, 12, 14, 18; respect for study participants, 130; risk exposure of participants, 126–127; risks taken by ethnographers, 113; scientific context of, 163; social disparity between researcher and participant, 130; standards of practice, 75–76; status relative to other methods, 69; thick description and, 18; training in, 139; in transdisciplinary context, 84–85; vulnerability of participants, 126, 128. *See also* field notes; field stations; multi-methods
ethnography of risk, 3, 4, 9, 10, 12, 19; and alcohol, 13; and drug sharing, 19
ethnopharmacology, 176
etiology of drug use, 171–172

Feldman, Harvey, 29, 31, 43
field notes, 1–2, 185; coding, 185; collecting, 186
field stations, 121–122; access to community, 122–123, 179–181; weaknesses, 122
Finestone, Harold, 50–51
Finlinson, Ann, 20–21, 157
Furst, Peter, 58–59

Gamburd, Michelle, 87
Garcia, Angela, 88
gender roles, 87, 149, 159
Glick-Schiller, Nina, 156
global imagination, 90
globalization: connections between sites, 90; defined, 89–90; external forces in, 90; as related to ethnography, 90; as related to social science, 90

Goldstein, Paul, 121–122
Gonzalez, Diana Haydee, 157
Guinea-Bissau, 94–95

"hanging out," 55–56
harm reduction, 21, 159
Heath, Dwight, 6, 13, 14, 42, 57
health consequences of drug use, 166–167, 175, 181–183. *See also* AIDS; hepatitis C virus
Heimer, Robert, 77, 79, 167
hepatitis C virus (HCV), 3, 77, 107, 159, 167
Herdt, Gilbert, 11
Herodotus, 28–29
Heroin Lifestyle Study, 125
hidden populations, 3, 105
Hoffer, Lee, 16, 104–105
holism, 7
Human Immunodeficiency Virus (HIV), 167. *See also* AIDS
Hunt, Geoffrey, 14, 17
"hustle," 50, 52, 62, 65

illegality issues. *See* criminal justice/legal issues
injection practices, 18; "front-loading," 18–19
Institute for Community Research, 158
Institute for Scientific Analysis, 152–154; Murphy-Rosenbaum collaboration, 153, 158
Institutional Review Boards (IRBs), 128–129
interviewing, 186; focus group, 187–188; formal by appointment, 187; informal on-site, 187

Jacobs, Bruce, 15–16, 17–18
James, Jennifer, 151
Johnson, Bruce, 64–65

Kelley, Brian, 9
Koester, Stephen, 78, 167
Kroeber, Alfred, 11

La Barre, Weston, 34–36
labeling theory, 54
LeMasters, E. E., 17
Lex, Barbara, 154
life histories of drug users, 50–51, 62
Lindesmith, Alfred, 43–45
longitudinal ethnography, 159
Lowie, Robert, 41–42

Maher, Lisa, 9, 158
Malcolm X, 45–46
Marshall, Mac, 11, 57–58
Mead, Margaret, 150
McGraw, Susan, 10, 11
minority drug researchers, 9
moral critique of drug use, 35, 48
Morningstar (Cleckner), Patricia, 150–151
multi-methods, 116–117; back-loaded ethnography, 164–165; diachronic ethnography, 165; dual methods (ethnography and survey), 163–164;

front-loaded ethnography, 164; triangulation, 123–124
Murphy, Sheigla, 21, 153

National AIDS Demonstration Research (NADR) project, 73–75, 80; cooperative agreement, 76; ethnographers' opinions, 74; Hartford project, 79; impact on the practice of ethnography, 76; results of intervention, 74–75; role of ethnography in, 73
National Drug Research Institute/National Development and Research Institute (NDRI), 156, 158
National Institutes of Health (NIH): National Institute on Alcohol Abuse and Alcoholism (NIAAA), 13, 14; National Institute on Drug Abuse (NIDA), 15, 60–62, 66, 68–69, 163, 179
Needle, Richard, 80
network analysis, 82, 114–116, 169, 180, 182–183; contagion and, 115; morphology of, 115; prevention potential, 116–117; seed method, 105–106, 115–116
networks of ethnographic researchers, 179
Nichter, Mark and Mimi, 10–12, 102–103

O'Donnell, Jack, 134

Page, J. Bryan, 1–2, 15, 18–19, 22, 135, 157
Pané, Friar Ramon, 29–30
patterns of drug use, emerging, 89, 170
PCP study, 124
Pine, Adrienne, 14
policy, 4, 14, 20, 48; harm reduction, 61, 111, 164, 180; regarding marihuana, 175; as related to scientific findings, 61, 174–175
politicians and drug traffic, 87–88
pregnancy and drug use, 153
prevention: defined, 168; research, 168–169; through etiologic studies, 171
professional stranger, 7–8
prostitution, 22, 39

Rapid Assessment, 66, 124, 181–182
rapport and research, 16, 17, 21, 188–189
recordings, 188
"recreational" drug use, 9–10
relativism in research, 7
ritual drug use, 10, 11, 14, 30–31, 35–36, 41–42
Robles, Rafaela, 157
Rodin, Miriam, 152
Romero-Daza, Nancy, 156
Rosenbaum, Marsha, 21, 151, 152, 153
rural drug use, 88

Sahagún, Bernardino de, 25, 30–31
sampling in drug-using populations, 105; respondent-driven, 105–106, 115–116
Santelices, Claudia, 160–161
Schensul, Jean, 156, 158
Schultes, Richard Evans, 35, 40–41, 43
Shedlin, Michelle, 156
Singer, Merrill, 15, 17, 23, 135–137, 167

Sloboda, Zili, 169
social mapping, 120–121
sociocultural model of drug use, 14, 43–44
socioeconomic status, 9; "studying up," 9
Spradley, James, 4, 16–17
Stebbins, Kenyon, 11–12, 100–102
Sterk, Clare, 15, 21–22, 154–155; community intervention, 155; methodology contribution, 155
Stoller, Paul, 88–89
structural exclusion and drug use, 88
subcultures among drug users paradigm, 50–53
surveillance, 170, 178–179
survey on careers in drug ethnography, 137; acceptance of drug ethnographers, 145–146; employment, 146; features of anthropological drug research, 144–145; grant funding, 146; impact on anthropology, 147; impact on drug research, 147; response rates, 138; responses to open-ended questions, 140–144; results, 138–144; sample sources, 138; trends, 139; types of careers, 141, 143
syndemics, 82
syringes, 9, 18, 20–21, 26, 111, 167

Tarahumara, 93
Taylor, Avril, 159
Thomas, Piri, 47
Tikuna, 94–95
tobacco, 10–12, 29, 30; Black & Mild, 172; differential tar content, 102; diffusion, 30; in Fiji, 101; industry, 11–12, 100; sales in the developing world, 100–101; semiotics of use, 103; U.S. support of in South America, 102
Torres, Manuel, 47
transdisciplinary research team, 4, 6, 76–77, 82, 163, 166
transnational drug flows, 91; bi-directional flows, 92; changeability, 98; colonial influence on, 91–92; corridors, 93–94; cross-border traffic, 97; diversion, 94; income source for poor, 92–93; regions of production, 92–93; regions of transshipment, 95; retail sale in local markets, 95; role of drug labs, 93; role of women, 97–98; smuggling success, 95
treatment for drug abuse, 110–111, 154, 172–174
Trotter, Robert T., II, 80–81
True, William Ray, 114
trust in ethnography, 188–189

University of Miami, 166–167

Waldorf, Dan, 62–63, 153
Waterston, Alisse, 23, 159
Weeks, Margaret, 156, 167
Wilbert, Johannes, 59
women, in drug-using contexts, 151; and cocaine use, 151; and sex work, 151
women, in ethnography, 150

ABOUT THE AUTHORS

J. BRYAN PAGE, Ph.D., is a professor and the chair of the Department of Anthropology at the University of Miami, with secondary appointments in Psychiatry and Behavioral Sciences and Sociology. He also has collaborative affiliations with the Department of Internal Medicine, the Department of Pediatrics, the Department of Family Medicine, the Department of Epidemiology and Public Health, and the School of Nursing. Dr. Page began his career as a researcher on patterns of drug use in 1973 as part of a transdisciplinary team charged with investigating the effects of long-term cannabis use in Costa Rica. He has conducted studies in Costa Rica, Spain, and Miami/Dade County, Florida, on topics such as polydrug use, the impact of HIV among injecting drug users, and the connection between youth gangs and drugs. Dr. Page has contributed articles on this research in journals ranging from *Medical Anthropology Quarterly* to *The Lancet*. His total published works, including book chapters and other materials, number more than 120. Dr. Page has participated in the National Institute of Health's extramural system of application review for twenty years, reviewing hundreds of grant applications for numerous programs. He is a newly appointed member of the Center for Scientific Review's application review committee for Community Influences on Health Behavior. He is also a member of the advisory committee for the University of Houston's project to train Hispanic scholars, contributing to the development of minority health scientists. His participation in the field of drug use anthropology for more than thirty-six years has given him opportunities to work and interact with many of the pioneers in drug use research, especially the ethnography of drug use.

MERRILL SINGER, Ph.D., is the past director of the Center for Community Health Research at the Hispanic Health Council in Hartford, Connecticut, and the director of the Community Connections Core of the Connecticut Center of Excellence for Eliminating Health Disparities among Latinos. Currently, he is a senior research scientist with the Center of Health, Intervention, and Prevention (CHIP) and a Professor in the Department of Anthropology, University of Connecticut. Additionally, he is a research affiliate of the Center for Interdisciplinary Research on AIDS (CIRA) at Yale University. Dr. Singer has been directly involved in drug research and program development since 1979, beginning as a National Institute of Mental Health postdoctoral fellow at George Washington University, and he has been a lead investigator on a long series of basic and applied federally funded drinking, drug use, and AIDS prevention studies dating to 1984. He currently is involved in environmental health research in addition to his work on drug-related health issues. Dr. Singer has published more than 200 articles and chapters in health and social science journals and books and has authored or edited more than 20, including *The Political Economy of AIDS* (edited), *Medical Anthropology and the World System* (with Hans Baer and Ida Susser), *Introducing Medical Anthropology* (with Hans Baer), *Unhealthy Health Policy: A Critical Anthropological Examination* (edited with Arachu Castro), *Something Dangerous: Emergent and Changing Illicit Drug Use and Community Health, New Drugs on the Street,* and *Drugging the Poor: Legal and Illegal Drug Industries and the Structuring of Social Inequality.*

Breinigsville, PA USA
29 June 2010
240848BV00001B/2/P